Contemporary Jewish Thought

The B'nai B'rith History of the Jewish People
was first published during the years 1959–1964
as the B'nai B'rith Great Book Series.
The present edition, in five volumes,
has been selected to be part of the B'nai B'rith Judaica Library.
The Library is sponsored by the
B'nai B'rith International Commission on Adult Jewish Education
in an effort to promote a greater popular understanding
of Judaism and the Jewish tradition.
The volumes in the series are:

Creators of the Jewish Experience in Ancient and Medieval Times
Creators of the Jewish Experience in the Modern World
Concepts that Distinguish Judaism
Great Jewish Thinkers of the Twentieth Century
Contemporary Jewish Thought

The B'nai B'rith History of the Jewish People

CONTEMPORARY JEWISH THOUGHT

Edited with introductory notes by
Simon Noveck

Annotated bibliographies by
Arthur Kurzweil

B'nai B'rith Books
Washington, D.C.

Jerusalem • London • Paris • Buenos Aires • East Sydney

Library of Congress Cataloging in Publication Data

Contemporary Jewish thought

Bibliography: p.   Includes index.
1. Judaism—20th century—Addresses, essays, lectures.
2. Judaism— Doctrines—Addresses, essays, lectures.
3. Zionism—Philosophy— Addresses, essays, lectures.
I. Noveck, Simon
BM195.C66 1985   296'.09'04   85-72301
ISBN 0-910250-08-1   ISBN 0-910250-9-x (pbk.)

Contents

ABRAHAM ISAAC KUK

GERMAN JEWISH THINKERS

HERMANN COHEN

AMERICAN JEWISH THINKERS

Introduction

The towering achievement in publishing by the B'nai B'rith International Commission on Adult Jewish Education has been, to this date, the B'nai B'rith Great Book Series edited for four volumes by Simon Noveck and for the fifth by Abraham Ezra Millgram. These books, as Rabbi Noveck described, presented "the inner-content of Jewish tradition, the great personalities and thinkers, the ideas, beliefs and religious movements of Judaism." In short, they are a *History of the Jewish People*. The nearly fifty scholars, teachers, and rabbis who contributed original essays to these volumes were a preponderant majority of the great interpreters of Jewish civilization at mid-century. Twenty-five years after they began to appear, the freshness and vigor of each essay is undiminished.

The continuing demand for each of the volumes by colleges and universities, synagogues and day schools, is being met by this revised edition. The essays are presented as they originally appeared, though for greater clarity the volumes themselves have been retitled and the series renamed. It was my belief that this new edition would enjoy a greater utility if each of the essays were supplemented by annotated bibliographies that reviewed the literature relevant to the subjects of the essays. Three distinguished scholars and teachers have joined me in the preparation of these bibliographies: Steven T. Katz of Cornell University, Reuven Kimelman of Brandeis University and Arthur Kurzweil, the noted author and lecturer. Each of us benefitted as students from this series, and the opportunity to enhance its value has brought us much satisfaction.

The American journalist George Will recently wrote of the growing rootlessness of our lives, our failure to connect to our past and our neglect of our legacy of a shared and valuable civilization. He was addressing himself to the inadequacies of the American educational system as it teaches the essence of Western civilization, but his point applies with a special urgency to the demands of a sound Jewish education. He chose, quite fortuitously, a Biblical example to illustrate his argument:

> In 1940, a British officer on Dunkirk beach flashed to London a three-word message, "But if not. . ." It was instantly recognized as a quotation from the Book of Daniel, where Nebuchadnezzar commands Shadrach, Meshach and Abednego to worship the golden image or be thrust into the fiery furnace. They reply defiantly; "If our God whom we serve is able to deliver us, he will deliver us from the fiery furnace, and out of thy hand, O king. But if not, be it known unto thee, O king, that we will not serve thy gods, nor worship the golden image which thou hast set up."

The message from Dunkirk is stirring evidence of a community deriving cohesion, inspiration and courage from a shared history. The question this story raises is how many of us today could either receive or transmit such a message from the rich legacy of Jewish civilization?

B'nai B'rith International through its Commission on Adult Jewish Education is sponsoring the republication of these volumes in the belief that they can play a large role in stimulating a desire to learn about Judaism, Jewish history and Jewish civilization, and that of themselves they are superb examples of the living Jewish tradition.

The joy of being a Jew is not derived from books. It is a product of a rich family life wherein Judaism radiates a happiness and contentment that passes beyond the ability of language to describe. It is the product of partaking of the company of other Jews. Yet for the connectedness of one Jew to his religion and peoplehood there is a need for the passion to be grounded in understanding and knowledge. These essays can play an important part in awakening and satisfying a desire to learn and comprehend.

There is nothing obscure in these volumes. They have been written with an enviable clarity, and they will inform the non-Jewish reader as fully as the Jewish reader. In presenting these volumes to the public, B'nai B'rith looks forward to a full engagement of the ideas presented therein with the wisdom and curiosity of men and women everywhere.

The B'nai B'rith Commission on Adult Jewish Education continues to enjoy the support, advice and commitment of its founder Maurice A. Weinstein, and the then B'nai B'rith International President who worked diligently to establish the Commission's work at the center of the B'nai B'rith—Philip M. Klutznick.

This new edition has benefitted from the encouragement of B'nai B'rith International President Gerald Kraft and key members of the Board of Governors. Mr. Abe Kaplan, the immediate past chairman of the Commission, and Dr. A.J. Kravtin, the current chairman have been effectively energetic in promoting this work. Executive Vice President Dr. Daniel Thursz and Associate Director Rabbi Joel H. Meyers provide the leadership and environment necessary for a Jewish educational program of quality to flourish, and within the Commission my patient secretary Mrs. Edith Levine does the same. My collaborator on this project has been Mr. Robert Teitler, a devoted B'nai B'rith member and a creative publisher.

> Michael Neiditch, Director
> B'nai B'rith International Commission
> on Adult Jewish Education

Washington, D.C.
July 24, 1985
5 Av 5785

Foreword

One of the encouraging developments in contemporary adult education in America has been the increased emphasis on the use of classical sources of western thought as material for adult study groups. Adult educators stress the importance of studying the original works of the great thinkers and philosophers from ancient times to the present as sources urgently needed in the modern world.

Experiments in the group reading of the classic books of mankind began at Columbia University soon after the First World War. The radio program "Invitation to Learning" in the 1930's, the "Great Books" groups conducted by Robert Hutchins and Mortimer Adler at the University of Chicago, and the launching of the Great Books Foundation in 1946 are all attempts to implement this idea. This use of great books in adult education is based on the conviction that through contact with the great minds of the past, we can find the knowledge and the wisdom to cope with the problems of our troubled world. These books, it is held, lead us to other books and give us a standard by which to judge them. They also furnish insights from other cultures into the art of living.

This approach has also found its advocates among Jewish educational theorists. Martin Buber in one of his essays stresses the idea that Jews are a "community based on memory" and that there is a great danger to Jewish survival in the loss of the "passion for handing down" the treasures of the past which once characterized the Jew. He urges a more thorough immersion in the literary sources of Judaism and the re-establishment of the "age old bond of memory" through a study of the language, Scriptures, and the great works of Jewish thought.

Franz Rosenzweig also stressed renewed contact with classical Jewish writings as the best way of restoring something genuinely

Jewish to the western intellectual, and as a pre-condition for a renaissance of Jewish life. At the Lehrhaus, the school for adults he established in Frankfurt in the early 1920's, the watchword was a "return to the great documents of classical Judaism." "Learning," to Franz Rosenzweig, entailed a "patient examination of sources and a patient consideration of what a book has to say."

American Jewish educators are also coming to recognize that the most meaningful learning experience consists in having contact with the original sources of Jewish religion. Such a study, it has been pointed out, can provide us with the basic terms for communication from our generation to the next and give us the perspective with which to judge Jewish life and literature. Such good judgment can only be acquired as a result of years of association with the authentic Jewish tradition in its original sources. More and more, therefore, texts are beginning to replace or supplement the lecture method in adult Jewish education.

The basic sources of the Jewish religion are the Bible, the Talmud, the prayerbook and the medieval philosophical classics. But several works written during the past six or seven decades also have a great value for the present day Jew. Wrestling with the problems that we face at the present time—the challenges of modern thought and the spiritual crisis of the contemporary situation—we find in them a particular relevance often missing in some of the older works. They speak directly to the contemporary Jew. Their universe of discourse is, for the most part, similar to our own. Several of these works, like the essays of Ahad Ha-am and Hermann Cohen, Leo Baeck's *Essence of Judaism,* many passages from Buber, and Kaplan's *Judaism as a Civilization,* have already become classics.

The purpose of this volume is to make available to the reader selections from these twentieth century thinkers. While anthologies exist of the writings of Ahad Ha-am and Martin Buber, and the works of Baeck and Kaplan are readily available, there is no book, to our knowledge, which contains the variety of passages and essays included here. These excerpts are taken from thirty different volumes, some of which are no longer in print. Most of the selections from Hermann Cohen's works are here made available in English for the first time.

In selecting the passages I have had a primary goal in mind—to provide material for a study of some of the fundamental ideas of Judaism as interpreted by the best minds of the twentieth century. With the exception of Ahad Ha-am, all of the men are concerned with the concept of God in Jewish tradition. They all reaffirm (aside from Mordecai Kaplan) the idea of the chosen people, and stress the

ethics of the prophets, the importance of the Sabbath and the reten-
tion of Hebrew as central to Judaism. Several thinkers attempt to
interpret the idea of immortality, though twentieth century Jewish
thought does not frequently deal with the subject of the hereafter.
Emphasis is also put on Jewish education and the role of community
in the Jewish way of life. Most of the thinkers are also concerned
with comparisons between Judaism and Christianity. We therefore
present a number of essays which examine essential differences between the two faiths.

In their interpretations of these ideas, the thinkers differ widely,
approaching Judaism from various philosophical standpoints. Ahad
Ha-am was a positivist, Gordon an intuitionist, Kuk a mystic, Hermann Cohen a rationalist, Rosenzweig and Buber existentialists and
Kaplan a pragmatist and religious naturalist. There is also a diversity of attitudes towards the role of Jewish theology and the place of
Jewish law. Five of the thinkers are Jewish nationalists, while four
are opposed to the Zionist movement and its political aspirations.
But in spite of these differences, in all of these writings there is the
conviction of the relevance of Judaism for the modern world and a
desire to understand its distinctive teachings. In contrast to the
negativism of the nineteenth century when men like Marx,
Nietzsche and Freud insisted that religion would soon disappear,
these pages reveal a great concern with the religious ideas of
Judaism. A comparison of the differing viewpoints in this book on
some of these religious ideas should therefore be valuable to the student of contemporary Jewish thought.

Finally, this anthology can have an inspirational value. Some of
the excerpts are deeply moving and directly relevant to the spiritual
perplexities of our time. Buber's passages on *The Word "God"* and
on *The Way of Man According to Hasidism,* Franz Rosenzweig's essay
On Being a Jewish Person, Baeck's description of *Mystery and Commandment,* Hermann Cohen's essay on the *Sabbath* and A.D. Gordon's
piece on *Death* are examples of inspirational writing that can be read
and reread with great benefit. It is hoped that rabbis will find here
resources for their preaching and cogent analyses of some of the basic
problems of present-day Judaism. Jewish groups whose practice it is
to open their meetings with a *Dvar Torah* (word of Torah or inspiration) or those who attend regular worship and want to read from the
Jewish tradition between *Minhah* and *Maariv* may find these selections suited for their purposes.

All anthologies, by cutting up or condensing an important work,
do an injustice to the author. The selections remain somewhat on the
surface and cannot offer what a reading of the entire original would.

The present volume undoubtedly suffers from some of these defects. Knowing this, we have tried, wherever possible, to give complete or representative passages so that the reader will sense the mode of presentation, style and approach of the thinker. It should be emphasized, however, that these selections do not include the views of each thinker on all aspects of Judaism. On some topics no appropriate material was available and in many instances limitations of space prevented our including additional passages. We have tried, rather, to offer an introduction to the comprehensive works of each thinker in the hope that the reader will want to read further wherever additional sources are available.

With these goals in mind and to make this anthology as useful a learning tool as possible, an editor's note precedes each group of selections. These notes include a brief statement on the significance of the thinker, a capsule biography, a word on his style and a few words of orientation to most of the individual selections. These notes also enable this book to stand on its own, for the benefit of those who may want to use it independently. Readers who prefer to dip into the original texts without any advance comments should skip over the introductory note and return to it after reading the excerpts.

Every effort has been made to maintain in form and style, punctuation and spelling, the excerpts as they originally appeared in English.

A word of reminder is in order to those who want to get the maximum benefit from these selections. All the thinkers in this book were serious men who recognized the importance of religion in human life, and were concerned with the meaning of Jewish existence. The reader should therefore be prepared, in many instances, for serious and difficult reading. In the words of A.D. Gordon: "And now even after all attempts at simplification, at concentration and at laying out of clear roads through the involved theme, the article still calls for the most serious thought as an aid to comprehension."

I am indebted to a number of colleagues and friends who have been helpful in making this anthology possible. A warm word of thanks goes to Professor Oscar I. Janowsky, chairman of the Publications Committee of the B'nai B'rith Department of Adult Jewish Education, and to Dr. Ira Eisenstein, a committee member, for reading the selections and the foreword, and for their personal interest in this project. I am grateful to Dr. Ephraim Fischoff for selecting and translating the passages from Hermann Cohen, and for stimulating conversations I had with him, to Professor Maurice Friedman for several very good suggestions in choosing the Buber passages, to Professor Nahum Glatzer for his cooperation in connection with the selections from Franz Rosenzweig, to the late Professor

Samuel Cohen for selecting the passages from Kaufmann Kohler, and to Dr. Ira Eisenstein for choosing the passages from Kaplan. Dr. Eisenstein's comments on several of the selections from Kaplan's writings were helpful in preparing the final editor's note.

Rabbis Ludwig Nadelmann, Steven Schwarzschild, and Arthur Zuckerman read the editor's notes and made a number of insightful suggestions. It is a pleasure to express my thanks to them for their warm and friendly spirit of cooperation. Dr. Walter Henry Brann, Rabbi Arthur Lelyveld, Dr. Emanuel Rackman, Rabbi Harold Schulweis, Isaac Toubin, and Harold Noveck were helpful in various personal ways. My wife read the foreword and all the editor's notes and made many valuable suggestions both as to content and style. Her devotion, help and encouragement were invaluable to me in completing this project. Vera Zabelle also read the editor's notes and made many very good suggestions. I am grateful to her for her fine spirit of cooperation. During the preparation of this volume I enjoyed the excellent cooperation of Abraham Berger and his staff at the Jewish Division of the New York Public Library.

SIMON NOVECK

EAST
EUROPEAN
JEWISH
THINKERS

AHAD HA-AM
(1856–1927)

EDITOR'S NOTE

Few thinkers of the twentieth century have had greater influence on the making of the modern Jewish mind than Asher Ginzberg, better known by his pen name of Ahad Ha-am (one of the people). His philosophy of cultural Zionism and his nationalistic interpretation of Judaism have shaped the thought of many Jewish leaders of our century. His penetrating essays analysing the challenges to Jewish survival, his insights into the problems of Jewish culture and education make him one of the most relevant thinkers for our time.

Ahad Ha-am, son of a wealthy *Hasidic* family, was born in 1856 in a small town in the Russian Ukraine where he spent the first thirty years of his life. After mastering the Talmud and other rabbinic sources, he acquired a knowledge of modern Hebrew literature as well as general culture, and became an adherent of *Haskalah* (enlightenment). He soon became disillusioned with *Haskalah* and gradually evolved his philosophy of cultural Zionism. In 1886 he settled in the cosmopolitan center of Odessa, where he began to write the famous essays on Judaism which brought him to the attention of the Jewish world.

Some of these essays dealt with issues important at the time—the aims of the *Hibbat Zion* movement, his reactions to the various Zionist Congresses and reports on his trips to Palestine; in others he attempted an interpretation of Judaism from the standpoint of a secular nationalist. These included such well known essays as *Priest and Prophet, Sacred and Profane* and *Moses.* Several of his best essays concerned themselves with the "plight of Judaism" as he saw it—the breakdown of the threefold basis of Jewish life—language, culture and religion. In all of them he advocated the revitalization of Jewish life by means of the establishment of a spiritual center in Palestine. These essays were published in the course of the years in four volumes under the title, *At the Crossroads.*

In 1896 Ahad Ha-am undertook the editorship of a new Hebrew periodical, *Ha-Shiloah*, which, under his guidance, became the most notable Hebrew magazine ever to have been published. The following year Theodor Herzl issued his call for the first Zionist Congress.

Because of its indifference to the moral and cultural aims of Zionism and its complete reliance on diplomacy, Ahad Ha-am became a critic of the new movement. To him the purpose of Palestine was not to resolve the economic plight of the Jew nor alleviate the problem of anti-Semitism. In his view, the land should serve as a spiritual center which would revivify Jewish life in the Diaspora.

In 1907, after turning down an invitation to become the head of Dropsie College for Hebrew and Cognate Learning in Philadelphia, he moved to London and became an executive of the Wissotsky Tea Firm. Ill health, however, kept him from creative work for most of this period. He finally settled in Palestine in 1921, where he lived greatly honored and revered until his death in 1927.

Ahad Ha-am's essays have a special quality which has made them classics of modern Jewish thought. Their logical construction, clear development of thought and their preciseness of language are evident even in translation. During his lifetime they were translated into several languages and were eagerly read both in Eastern Europe and in America. To this day they are included in the curriculum of Israeli schools and in the United States are a part of all courses dealing with modern Jewish literature and thought.

Our first selection introduces the reader to an aspect of Ahad Ha-am's concept of Judaism and indicates how close he was, though a secularist, to Jewish spiritual values. To Ahad Ha-am the essence of Judaism was to be found in its distinctive ethics which, unlike Christian ethics, are oriented to the salvation of the group rather than that of the individual and are based on an objective standard of justice rather than on sentiment or mercy. The original essay, *Between Two Opinions*, from which this selection was taken, was published in 1910 in England as a review of a two-volume study on the Gospels by the British liberal Jewish thinker Claude Montefiore.

The second selection is taken from his well-known essay *Transvaluation of Values* published in 1898 in reply to the Hebrew writers Berdichevsky and Brenner. These followers of Nietzsche called for a break with Jewish spiritual values, an "extension of the bounds," as they put it, and participation by Jews in all the fruits of human progress. Ahad Ha-am pointed out to them that while it was possible to accept Nietzsche's general concept of the "superman" as an aim of society, this concept should be understood in a spiritual rather than in a physical sense, and as an extension of this idea, he postulated the goal of a spiritual "supernation."

Each of the four selections which follow deals with one of the challenges which confront the Jew in the modern world. In the *Law of the Heart* Ahad Ha-am points to what he regarded as the lack of spontaneity and the absence of an impulse for change among the Jewish people. They had, he felt, become a slave of the book, bound by the written word. What was needed, he believed, was a new and compelling urge to "revitalize the idea of the national renaissance."

The essay on Jewish culture, given as an address at a conference in Minsk in 1904, laments the dearth of creativity in Jewish literature, caused by the fact that the best minds among Jewish youth were turning to other fields, relinquishing Hebrew literature to "dullards and mediocrities." While Ahad Ha-am overstated the case for his own time, his analysis of the problem has contemporary relevance.

Our next selection, *Slavery in Freedom*, presents his reactions to a group of essays by prominent French Jews published by a French publishing house in celebration of its jubilee. Ahad Ha-am was very critical of the apologetic tone of these writers, of their denial of any identification with Jews in other lands, and of their insistence that Jews were simply a religious denomination and not a people. With irony and disdain he described these attitudes as "moral slavery" and their acceptance of the mission idea as "intellectual slavery." In comparison, Ahad Ha-am asserted the moral superiority of East European Jewry.

The essay on *Imitation and Assimilation*, like the one on *Slavery in Freedom*, is frequently quoted. It points to a problem which still exists in Jewish life—the danger of fragmentation, as Jews in different countries build their own characteristic type of Judaism based on local influences.

Ahad Ha-am's solution for these fundamental challenges was the building of a spiritual center in Palestine which would radiate to the Diaspora new teaching and new hope. This proposal was frequently attacked, particularly by the political Zionists, and in our final passage, written in 1907, he tried to defend his point of view.

1. Character of Judaism

. . . J U D A I S M conceives its aim not as the salvation of the individual, but as the well-being and perfection of a group, of the Jewish people, and ultimately of the whole human race. That is to say, the aim is always defined in terms of a collectivity which has no defined and concrete form. In its most fruitful period, that of the Prophets and the divine revelation, Judaism had as yet no clear ideal of personal immortality or of reward and punishment after death. The religious and moral inspiration of the Prophets and their disciples was derived not from any belief of that kind, but from the conviction of their belonging to "the chosen people," which had, according to their belief, a divine call to make its national life the embodiment of the highest form of religion and morality. Even in later times, when the Babylonian exile had put an end to the free national life of the Jews, and as a result the desire for individual salvation had come to play a part in the Jewish religious consciousness, the highest aim of Judaism still remained a collective aim. For proof of the truth of this statement there is no need to look further than the prayers in the daily and festival prayer-books, of which only a minority turn on the personal needs of the individual worshipper, while the majority deal with the concerns of the nation and of the whole human race.

Which of these two aims is the higher? This question has been endlessly debated; but the truth is that in this matter we cannot establish any scale of values. A man may attain to the highest level in his religious and moral life whether he is inspired by the one aim or by the other. But individual salvation certainly makes a stronger appeal to most men, and is more likely to kindle their imagination and to inspire them to strive after moral and religious perfection. If Judaism, unlike the other religions, prefers the collective aim, this is yet another instance of the characteristically Jewish tendency to abstractness and to the repudiation of the concrete form. So long as this tendency persists—so long, that is, as the Jewish people does not lose its essential character—no true Jew can be attracted by the doctrine of the Gospels, which rests wholly and solely on the pursuit of individual salvation.

The same tendency shows itself in yet another direction, and this perhaps the most important of all: I mean in regard to the basis of morality. That Jewish morality is based on justice, and the morality of the Gospels on love, has become a platitude; but it seems to me that not all those who draw this distinction fully appreciate its significance. It is usual to treat the difference as merely one of degree, the moral scale and its basis being the same in either case. Both doctrines, it is supposed, are directed against egoism; but the Christians claim that their religion has reached a higher point in the scale, and the Jews refuse to admit this claim. Thus Christian commentators point proudly to the positive principle of the Gospels: "Whatsoever ye would that men should do unto you, do ye even so to them," and throw it in the teeth of Judaism, which has only the negative principle of Hillel: "Do not unto your neighbour what you would not have him do unto you."

But if we look deeper, we shall find that the difference between Judaism and Christianity on this point is not one of less or more, but is a fundamental difference of view as to what is the basis of moral conduct. It was not by accident that Hillel put his principle in the negative form; it was because the positive formulation is repugnant to the Jewish conception of the basis of morality. We should have no cause for satisfaction if we found the doctrine in its positive form attributed to Hillel in some text or other; we should question the authenticity of a text which put into Hillel's mouth a pronouncement so out of harmony with the spirit of Judaism.

The root of the distinction lies here also, as I have said, in the preference of Judaism for abstract principles. The moral law of the Gospels asks the "natural man" to reverse his natural attitude towards himself and others, and to put the "other" in the place of the "self"—that is, to replace straight-forward egoism by inverted egoism. For the altruism of the Gospels is neither more nor less than inverted egoism. Altruism and egoism alike deny the individual as such all objective moral value, and make him merely a means to a subjective end; but whereas egoism makes the "other" a means to the advantage of the "self," altruism does just the reverse. Judaism, however, gets rid of this subjective attitude entirely. Its morality is based on something abstract and objective, on *absolute justice*, which attaches moral value to the individual as such, without any distinction between the "self" and the "other." On this theory a man's sense of justice is the supreme judge both of his own actions and those of other men. This sense of justice must be made independent of individual relations, as though it were a separate entity; and before it all men, including the self, must be equal. All men, including the self, are under obligation to develop their lives and their faculties to the limit of their capacity, and at the same time each is under obligation to assist his neighbour's self-development, so far as he can. But just as I have no right to ruin another man's life for the sake of my own, so I have no right to ruin my own life for the sake of another's. Both of us are men, and both our lives have the same value before the throne of justice.

I know no better illustration of this point of view than the following well-known *B'raita:* "Suppose two men journeying through the desert, only one of whom has a bottle of water. If both of them drink, they will both die; if one of them only drinks, he will reach safety. Ben P'tura held that it was better that both should drink and die, than that one should witness the death of his comrade. But Akiba refuted this view by citing the scriptural verse: 'and thy brother shall live with thee.' *With thee*—that is to say, thine own life comes before thy neighbour's" (*Bab M'zia,* 62a).

We do not know who Ben P'tura was; but we do know Akiba, and we may be sure that his is the authentic voice of Judaism. Ben P'tura, the altruist, does not value human life for its own sake; for him it is better that two lives should perish, where death demands no more than one, so long as the altruistic sentiment prevails. But Jewish morality looks at the question objectively.

Every action that leads to loss of life is evil, even if it springs from the purest sentiments of love and compassion, and even if the victim is himself the agent. In the case before us, where it is possible to save one of the two lives, it is a moral duty to overcome the feeling of compassion, and to save what can be saved. But to save whom? Justice answers: let him who has the power save himself. Every man's life is entrusted to his keeping, and to preserve your own charge is a nearer duty than to preserve your neighbour's.

But when a man came to Raba, and asked him what he should do when one in authority threatened to kill him unless he would kill another man, Raba answered him: "Be killed and kill not. What hath told thee that thy blood is redder than his? Perhaps his blood is redder" (*Pesahim*, 25b). And Rashi, who generally gets to the root of the matter with his instinctive understanding of Judaism, correctly explains thus: "The question arises only because you know that no religious law is binding in the face of danger to life, and think that in this case also the prohibition of murder ceases to be binding because your own life is in danger. But this transgression is not like others. For do what you will, there must be a life lost. . . . How do you know that your life is more precious than his in the sight of God? Perhaps his life is more precious."

If a question like this were put to a Christian priest, we may be sure that he would begin to expatiate in glowing terms on a man's duty to sacrifice his life for another, to "bear his cross" in the footsteps of his Messiah, so that he might win the kingdom of heaven—and so forth. But the Jewish teacher weighs the question in the scales of objective justice. As a life must be lost in any case, and nobody can say which of the two lives is more precious in God's sight, the plea that the law may be broken in order to save life does not entitle you to break the sixth commandment. You must therefore be killed, and not kill. But suppose the case reversed: suppose the question to be whether I can save another from death by giving my life instead of his. Raba would reply: "Let the other be killed, and do not destroy yourself. For do what you will there must be a life lost; and how do you know that his blood is redder than yours? Perhaps yours is redder." From the standpoint of Judaism every man's blood is as red as any other's; every soul is "precious in the sight of God," be it mine or another's. Consequently no man is at liberty to treat his life as his own property; no man may say: "I am endangering myself; what right have others to complain of that?" (Maimonides' Code, *Laws of Murder* XI. 5). Jewish history of course records many cases of martyrdom, which will remain precious and sacred memories for all time. But these are not cases of one life given for the preservation of another similar life; they are sacrifices of human life for "the sanctification of the Name" (the religious and moral ideal) or for "the good of the community" (the religious and moral aim).

And justice demands that we rise above sentiment not only in deciding between the self and another, but also in deciding between two other persons. Forty years ago Abraham Geiger drew attention to the unique character of the Biblical injunction "Neither shalt thou countenance a poor man in his cause." All other moral codes warn us only against favouring the rich and powerful; and the Gospels themselves favour the poor, and exaggerate their merits and the greatness that awaits them in the Kingdom of Heaven. All this is very well from the point of view of sentiment; but a morality based on justice rises above sentiment, and teaches us that, while charity is a virtue, and it is our duty to help the poor if we are able, we must not let compassion induce us to sin against justice by favouring the poor man in his suit.

According to Herbert Spencer, the pinnacle of moral development will be reached when the altruistic sentiment becomes a natural instinct, and human beings can find no greater pleasure than in working for the good of others. Similarly Judaism, in conformity with its own principles, looks forward to the development of morality to a point at which Justice will become an instinct with good men, so that in any given situation they will be able to apply the standard of absolute justice without any long process of reflexion. They will feel even the slightest deviation from justice instantaneously, and with the certainty of intuition. Personal and social considerations will not affect them in the slightest degree; their instinct will judge every action with absolute impartiality, ignoring all human relations, and making no difference between X and Y, between the self and the other, between rich and poor. Such is the moral ideal of Judaism; and because Judaism links the fulfilment of its moral aspirations with the advent of the Messiah, it endows the Messiah with this faculty of intuitive justice. The Talmud (Sanhedrin, 93b) says of the Messiah that "he will smell and judge," on the basis of the scriptural verse (Isaiah xi. 3): "And shall make him quick of understanding (Heb. 'smell') in the fear of the Lord; and he shall not judge after the sight of his eyes"; and Kimhi comments on this verse as follows: "Because the sense of smell is a very delicate sense, he gives the name of smell to the most delicate perception —that is to say, the Messiah with little scrutiny will feel which men are good, and which evil."

But this development lies hidden in the bosom of a distant future. For the present the human race still lacks the instinctive sense of justice, and even the best men are apt to be so blinded by self-love or prejudice as to be unable to distinguish between good and evil. For the present, therefore, we all need some touchstone, some fundamental principle, to help us to avoid weighting the scales of justice to suit our personal ends or inclinations. Hillel has given us such a principle: "Do not unto your neighbour what you would not have him do unto you." Altruism would substitute: "Do unto your neighbour what you would like him to do unto you." In other words, take the circle of egoism, and put the "other" at its centre instead of the "self"; then you will know your whole duty. But Judaism cannot accept the altruistic principle; it cannot put the "other" in the centre of the circle, because that place belongs to justice, which knows no distinction between "self" and "other." But in the circle of egoism there is no place for justice except in a negative form. It will certainly be just not to do as egoism would not be done by; but to do as egoism would be done by—that is something without any limit, and to make it obligatory is to tilt the scales of justice to the side of the "other" and against the "self."

Even that "great principle of the Torah" (as Akiba called it) 'thou shalt love thy neighbour as thyself" (Leviticus xixi. 18), though in form it appears to be positive, is in reality, if rightly understood, negative. If the Torah had meant that a man must love his neighbour to the extent of sacrificing his life for him, it would have said: "Thou shalt love thy neighbour more than thyself." But when you love your neighbour *as* yourself, neither more nor less, your feelings are in a state of equilibrium, with no leaning either to your own side or to your neighbour's. The true meaning of the verse is: "Self-love must not be allowed to incline the scale on the side of your own advantage; love your neighbour as yourself, and then justice will necessarily decide, and you will do nothing to your neighbour that you would consider a wrong if it were done to yourself." For proof that this is the real meaning we have only to look further in the same passage of Leviticus, where we find, (*ib.* 33-34): "And if a stranger sojourn with thee in your land, ye shall not do him wrong. The stranger that sojourneth with you shall be unto you as the homeborn among you, and thou shalt love him as thyself." Here it is evident that to love the stranger "as thyself" means to carry out the negative precept "ye shall not do him wrong"; and if the stranger is expressly placed on the same footing as the native, this shows that in relation to the native also the intention is only that self-love must not prove a stronger motive than justice.

But in the Gospels "Thou shalt love thy neighbour as thyself" is interpreted in an altruistic sense: it means that your own life is less important than your neighbour's. Hence there is some excuse for the Christian habit of attributing this verse to the Gospels, as though it had originally appeared in the New and not in the Old Testament. It is true that the meaning which they put on the verse belongs not to the Mosaic Law, but to the Gospels.

But it must be remembered that in addition to the relation of individual to individual there is another and more important moral relation—that of nation to nation. Here, also, some great principle is needed to keep without bounds that national egoism which is fraught perhaps with even greater danger to the collective progress of humanity than individual egoism. If we look at the difference between Jewish and Christian ethical teaching with this requirement in mind, we shall see at once that the altruism of the Gospels provides no sort of basis for international relations. A nation can never believe that its moral duty lies in self-abasement or in the renunciation of its rights for the benefit of other nations. On the contrary, every nation feels and knows that its moral duty is to maintain its position and to use its opportunities to create conditions in which it can develop its potentialities to the full. Hence Christian nations have not been able to regulate their relations with one another on the moral basis of their religion; national egoism has inevitably remained the sole determining force in international affairs, and patriotism, in the

Bismarckian sense, has been elevated to the position of the supreme moral criterion.

But the Jewish law of justice is not confined within the narrow sphere of individual relations. In its Jewish sense the precept "Thou shalt love thy neighbour as thyself" can be carried out by a whole nation in its dealings with other nations. For this precept does not oblige a nation to sacrifice its life or its position for the benefit of other nations. It is, on the contrary, the duty of every nation, as of every individual human being, to live and to develop to the utmost limit of its powers; but at the same time it must recognize the right of other nations to fulfil the like duty without let or hindrance. Patriotism—that is, national egoism—must not induce it to disregard justice, and to seek self-fulfilment through the destruction of other nations. Hence Judaism was able thousands of years ago to enunciate the lofty ideal "Nation shall not lift up sword against nation" (Isaiah ii. 4), because that ideal is no more than the logical consequence of the idea of absolute justice, which lies at the foundation of Judaism.

2. Are Jews a Chosen People?

. . . I T is admitted by almost everybody . . . that the Jewish people is pre-eminent in its genius for morality. No matter how it happened, or by what process this particular gift was developed: it is certainly a fact that the Jewish people early became conscious of its superiority to its neighbours in this respect. In the manner of those times, this consciousness found expression in the religious idea that God had chosen Israel "to make him high above all the nations," not in the sense of forcible domination—for Israel is "the fewest of all peoples"—but in the sense of moral development, "to be His own treasure . . . and that thou shouldst keep all His commandments": in other words, to realise through the ages the highest type of morality, and to bear for all time the burden of the most exacting moral obligations. There was no thought of the advantage or disadvantage of the rest of mankind; the sole object was the existence of the superior type. The Jews have retained this sense of election throughout their history, and it has been their solace in time of trouble. They have never tried—if we ignore a few exceptional cases—to increase their numbers by conversion: not, as their enemies say, out of narrowness, nor yet, as Jewish apologists plead in extenuation, out of extraordinary tolerance, but simply because it is characteristic of the superior type, as Nietzsche puts it, "never to consent to lower his duties to the level of duties for everybody, or to throw his responsibility on to others or admit them to a share in it."

It is indeed a unique feature of Judaism that it distinguishes its own adherents from the rest of mankind only by imposing on them a heavy load of duties and obligations, whereas it lets the non-Jews off lightly, allowing them to earn life eternal by merely fulfilling the most fundamental moral duties (embodied in the seven "Noachian laws"). It is only during the last century or so, since the French Revolution spread the doctrine of universal equality and fraternity, and made the general well-being the supreme ideal, that Jewish thinkers have begun to be ashamed of the idea of the election in its original sense, and have tried to adapt Judaism to modern thought by inventing the theory of "the mission of Israel," which is an attempt to reconcile the two ideas by making the one a means to the other. The Jews—so the argument runs—are the chosen people, but they were chosen to spread fraternity and well-being among mankind by teaching the world the rule of life embodied in the Torah which was entrusted to them for that very purpose. This compromise, entirely without foundation in fact, and entirely dependent on a belief in the supernatural, has been riddled over and over again by criticism, and there is no need here to go over the old ground again. But the Jews as a people have always interpreted their mission simply as the fulfilment of their own duties, and from the earliest times to the present day they have regarded their election as an end to which everything else was subordinate, not as a means to the happiness of the rest of humanity. While it is true that the Prophets expressed the hope that Judaism would have a good influence on the morality of the gentile world, their idea was that this result would follow automatically from the existence of a superior type of morality among the Jews, not that the Jews existed solely for the purpose of exerting themselves to bring this result about. The gentiles are to say "Come ye, and let us go up to the mountain of the Lord . . . and He will teach us of His ways, and we will walk in His paths." We are not told that the Jews are to say "Come, let us go out to the gentiles and teach them the ways of the Lord, that they may walk in His paths."

The idea here outlined could be expanded into a complete philosophy. For the spiritual tragedy of modern Jewish life is perhaps only a result of the contrast between the "chosen people" as it might be and as it is in fact. We still retain, though only as an instinctive feeling, the old belief in our unique genius for morality; we still feel that it is our mission as a people to be a super-nation in the moral sense. But on the other hand, now that we have left the ghetto and begun to participate in European culture, we cannot help seeing that our superiority is only potential. In actual fact we are not ahead of the rest of the world even in the sphere of morality. As a people in exile we have failed to fulfil our mission, because we have not been free to order our life in our own way. And possibly it is the sense of this contrast between what is and what might be that has unconsciously made Zionists of many who scoff at the idea of the "chosen people" and the moral mission and express their Zionism in purely economic and political terms. . . .

3. The Law of the Heart

T H E relation between a normal people and its literature is one of parallel development and mutual interaction. Literature responds to the demands of life, and life reacts to the guidance of literature. The function of literature is to plant the seed of new ideas and new desires; the seed once planted, life does the rest. The tender shoot is nurtured and brought to maturity by the spontaneous action of men's minds, and its growth is shaped by their needs. In time the new idea or desire becomes an organic part of consciousness, an independent dynamic force, no more related to its literary origin than is the work of a great writer to the primer from which he learnt at school.

But a "people of the book," unlike a normal people, is a slave to the book. It has surrendered its whole soul to the written word. The book ceases to be what it should be, a source of ever-new inspiration and moral strength; on the contrary, its function in life is to weaken and finally to crush all spontaneity of action and emotion, till men become wholly dependent on the written word and incapable of responding to any stimulus in nature or in human life without its permission and approval. . . .

The Haskalah writers of the last generation did not get down to the root cause of this tyranny of the written word. They put the blame primarily on the hard-heartedness and hide-bound conservatism of Rabbis who thought nothing of sacrificing the happiness of the individual on the altar of a meticulous legalism. Thus Gordon in *The Point of a Yod* depicts the Rabbi as

A man who sought not peace and knew no pity,
For ever banning this, forbidding that,
Condemning here, and penalising there.

These writers appealed to the moral sense of the common man against the harshness of the law. They thought that by painting the contrast in sufficiently lurid colours they could provoke a revolt which would lead to the triumph of the moral sense over the written word. But this was a complete mistake. There was in fact no difference between the attitude of the Rabbi and that of the ordinary man. When Vofsi pronounced the bill of divorce invalid, he may have been just as sorry for the victims as the assembled congregation, who, in the poet's words,

Stood all atremble, as though the shadow of death
Had fallen upon them.

It was not only the Rabbi who never doubted for a moment where the victory must lie in a conflict between the moral sense and the written word: the congregation did not dream of questioning the Rabbi's decision, still less of questioning the law itself. If they "stood all atremble," it was only as one might tremble at some catastrophe due to the unalterable course of nature. A normal people would react to a tragedy of this kind by determining that such a thing should never happen again; but a "people of the book" can react only by dumb sorrow, such as would have been occasioned by the heroine's falling dead at her wedding. To blame the written word, to revolt against the rigour of the law—that is out of the question.

Zangwill is nearer the truth in his *Children of the Ghetto.* In this novel there is an incident similar to that of Gordon's poem, but the treatment is very different. The Rabbi, Reb Shmuel, is himself the girl's father, and a very affectionate father. His daughter's happiness in her love for David is his happiness too. But when he discovers by accident that David is of the priestly family, and therefore cannot marry Hannah, who is technically a divorced woman because of a young man's stupid joke, his first words, in spite of his anguish, are "Thank God I knew it in time." All David's appeals to justice and mercy are in vain. It is God's law, and must be obeyed. "Do you think," says Reb Shmuel at the end of a long and painful scene, "I would not die to make Hannah happy? But God has laid this burden upon her —and I can only help her to bear it."

No: Vofsi and all his kind are not monsters of cruelty. They are tender-hearted enough; but their natural feelings have not free scope. Every sentiment, every impulse, every desire gives in without a struggle to "the point of a *yod.*"

Where the natural play of heart and mind is thus stifled, we cannot expect to find self-assertion or strength of purpose in any business outside the field of the written word. Logic, experience, common sense and moral feeling are alike powerless to lead men into new paths towards a goal of their own choice. Inevitably, as our experience has shown, this general condition puts obstacles in the way of the solution of any and every one of our problems. It has long been obvious to thinking men that there is no hope for any particular measure of improvement unless the general condition is put right first of all.

The paramount question is, then, whether there is any possibility of curing this long-standing disease; whether the Jewish people can still shake off its inertia, regain direct contact with the actualities of life, and yet remain the Jewish people.

It is this last requirement that makes the question so very difficult. A generation ago the *Haskalah* movement showed how the process of awakening could be brought about. Leaving the older people alone, it caught hold of the young, and normalised their attitude to life by introducing them to European culture through education and literature. But it could not make good its promise to bring humanism into Jewish life without disturbing the Jewish continuity: to that its products bear ample witness. Coming into Jewish life from outside, *Haskalah* found it easier to create an entirely new mould for its followers than to repair the defects of the Jewish mould while preserving its essential characteristics. Hence there can be no complete answer to our question until a new and compelling urge toward normalisation springs up amongst us from within, from our own Jewish life, and is communicated to the younger generation through education and literature, so that it may fuse with the humanism of *Haskalah* and prevent the latter from overwhelming and obliterating the Jewish mould.

A native-born urge of this kind has recently come into play in the form of the idea which we call *Hibbat Zion*, though that name is inadequate to express the full meaning of the idea. True *Hibbat Zion* is not merely a part of Judaism, nor is it something added on to Judaism: it is the whole of Judaism, but with a different focal point. *Hibbat Zion* neither excludes the written word, nor seeks to modify it artificially by addition or subtraction. It stands for a Judaism which shall have as its focal point the ideal of our nation's unity, its renascence, and its free development through the expression of universal human values in the terms of its own distinctive spirit.

This is the conception of Judaism on which our education and our literature must be based. We must revitalise the idea of the national renascence, and use every possible means to strengthen its hold and deepen its roots, until it becomes an organic element in the Jewish consciousness and an independent dynamic force. Only in that way, as it seems to me, can the Jewish soul be freed from its shackles and regain contact with the broad stream of human life without having to pay for its freedom by the sacrifice of its individuality.

4. The Questions of Jewish Culture

THERE is no need to demonstrate the existence of an original Hebrew Culture. So long as the Bible is extant, the creativity of the Jewish mind will remain unchallengeable. Even those who deny that the Jewish nation still exists must admit that when it did exist it was a creative nation; they must admit, too, that the old Jewish nation has left a legacy which bears the indelible impress of its original genius. This being so, those of us who believe (or rather feel) that the Jewish nation still exists have a right to believe, without further evidence, that it is still capable of original creative work. No doubt the difficult conditions of life in exile have had their effects, in the field of culture as in other fields; but the Hebrew genius has neither changed fundamentally nor ceased to function. . . .

The complete, or almost complete, sterility of Hebrew culture dates only from the modern period of assimilation and emancipation and it does not mean that we have suddenly lost our original creative faculty. It is due simply to the development of a tendency to sink our national individuality in the pursuit of assimilation. We have voluntarily and of set purpose tried to cease being original and to become merely imitators; and as a natural consequence the most gifted Jews have found no scope for their talents in Jewish life, and have deserted it for other fields of activity.

But at the same time these very men are themselves the best evidence of the inexhaustible fund of creative power that we still possess: for try as they will to hide their Jewish characteristics, and to make their work a faithful reflex of the spirit of the people whose livery they have adopted, it is apparent to the critical eye that they very rarely succeed. In spite of themselves there is something distinctively Jewish about all their work, something which differentiates it from the work of their non-Jewish colleagues. There can therefore be no doubt that, if all these dispersed forces were re-united in the service of Jewish culture, this culture would today be one of the richest and most original in the world. But that thought, so far from comforting us, should only deepen our sense of loss. We give everything and get nothing; we scatter our talents in every direction, to enrich the enemies who persecute us; and we ourselves are none the richer for all the achievements of our most brilliant sons. "There is an evil which I have seen under the sun, and it is heavy upon men: a man to whom God giveth riches, wealth, and honour . . . yet God giveth him not power to eat thereof, but a stranger eateth it."

But we have gone so far along the road of national self-effacement that we are no longer even conscious of the evil. Indeed so far from regretting the dissipation of our cultural strength, we are positively beside ourselves with joy and pride when a Jew achieves distinction in the outside world, and we lose no time in reminding the world that he is one of us—though he himself may be very anxious to let that fact be forgotten. If, as occasionally happens, an incident of this kind provokes some of us to moralise ruefully on the hard lot which condemns us to fertilise other people's gardens while our own is neglected, there is a chorus of protest from Jews of the "enlightened" and "broad-minded" type. They tell us, with haughty contempt, that we are sinning against "humanity." What, they say, does it matter to us whether a man works for his own people or for another? The important thing is that he is doing something for "humanity." That is the only ideal of the future; and to profess any other is to convict oneself of pettiness and narrow-mindedness.

That is certainly a "broad" view, but it overlooks the fact that depth is no less important than breadth, and for all its breadth it is purely superficial. Does it really make no difference to the quality of a man's work whether it is done among his own people or among strangers? In the one case he works in the native environment to which he owes his earliest impressions and the formative influences that have determined the bent of his mind and character; in the other he is a stranger in a strange land, in which he cannot make himself truly at home except by artificially tearing himself in halves, with the inevitable result of a lack of wholeness in his character and his work.

Thus even from the broadly human point of view the dispersal of our cultural powers involves a certain amount of loss, and may legitimately be regretted. In any case, however, those of us who are nationalists need not be ashamed to express our concern at the seriousness of the loss from the point of view of the Jewish people. The most convinced and most cosmopolitan of liberals will admit that an individual has the right to further his own particular purposes by any legitimate method which does not run counter to the interests of humanity and progress; and what holds good for the individual holds good for the nation. We have a right, then, to ask ourselves not what humanity loses by our loss, but what it gains, and what it would lose if the primary benefit of our own men of genius accrued to ourselves and not to others —in other words, if those who owe their birth and their inspiration to the Jewish people were to make their contributions to human culture as members of that people and not as members of another.

Take, for example, the case of Antokolski, whose premature death we still mourn. We need make no secret of the fact that for us there is a touch of bitterness in the homage which is paid him all over the world, and especially in Russia. It was for Russia that Antokolski worked while he lived, and it is Russia that gets the glory now he is dead; while we can only reflect sadly how much he might have given to his own people, and how low we have sunk when men like him have to go elsewhere to find scope for their genius.

Let nobody say that such reflections are a crime against humanity and progress. If Antokolski had devoted his genius, or at least some considerable part of it, to the service of his own people's culture, and had portrayed Jewish life, of which he undoubtedly had a more sympathetic understanding than of the non-Jewish life to which he actually went for his subject, how would humanity and progress have suffered?

No doubt it is easy to answer with the oft-repeated assertion that Jewish life is too circumscribed to provide material for creative work of genius. But if we leave generalisations and come to concrete cases, this answer will not hold water. For example: Antokolski wanted to make a statue of a blood-thirsty tyrant, a dreadful monster of violence and cruelty, who, none the less, had a spark of human feeling and was always torn between crime and remorse. Could there be a more perfect example of such a tyrant than Herod? Yet Antokolski went to Russian history and made a statute of Ivan the Terrible. This obscure tyrant is almost unknown outside his own country, and is scarcely intelligible except to a Russian; whereas Herod is a figure of some importance and influence in world history, and Antokolski certainly knew all about Herod before he had so much as heard of Ivan the Terrible. Can it be said that the Russian tyrant is a subject of richer interest and more universal appeal than the tyrant of Judaea? Or take another instance—Antokolski's statue of the Russian Chronicler, Nestor. For this type of a scholar-recluse the sculptor went back to a Kiev monastery in the eleventh century, although he had seen much better examples in the Jewish life of Vilna, where he was born. The "perpetual student" so brilliantly depicted by Bialik has a much wider and more human appeal than the Russian monk, as well as being closer to Antokolski in spirit. Though he does not immure himself in a monastery, he is as remote as any monk from the hubbub of life, and he has no interest in anything except reading books, and possibly writing them. As a child Antokolski must have listened awe-struck to stories of the great recluse who had lived in Vilna a century earlier, studying and writing from one year's end to another, with never a moment's relaxation. The child's imagination must have been fired by the Gaon of Vilna; but the great artist forgot him, and had to go wandering away to the strange world of a mediaeval Russian monastery in search of something that he might have found in the Jewish life of his native town. Was this so essential to the progress of art and the welfare of mankind that we have no right to complain of our loss? And yet some of us have gone so far as actually to congratulate the Jewish people on having given Antokolski's genius and his work to Russia, and even to describe his insistent search for spiritual beauty behind the beauty of external form—surely a Jewish trait if ever there was one—as essentially characteristic of Russian art!

Nor is Antokolski the only Jew of genius who has used his genius in the service of others. It is just the same with all our greatest artists, thinkers and writers. They leave our humble tenement as soon as they realize that their exceptional abilities will unlock the doors of palaces. And when they become famous, we gaze at these great men from afar, and share in the pride and joy of their escape from the dark cavern into the sunlit world. But even this miserable pride is stigmatised by the anti-Semites as the unpardonable impudence of a servant who presumes to claim an interest in his master's property. We are bled white for their enrichment, and then they turn round and reproach us with having no contribution of our own to make to modern culture. It is the old story over again. The world has even annexed our God, and then reproaches us with having lost Him.

Then there is the other side of the shield. While our best and most original minds are lost to us, and reveal their Jewish characteristics, despite themselves, in non-Jewish fields, those who remain behind are mostly the smaller fry; and they have not the stamina to resist being swept off their feet by the surrounding tide of non-Jewish culture. Thus what they produce in the field of Jewish culture is for the most part entirely lacking in originality; it is nothing but endless and indiscriminate copying of non-Jewish models. . . .

The term "Jewish literature" is often used in a wide sense, to include everything written by a Jewish writer in any language. If we were to accept that definition, we could not complain of the poverty of Jewish literature, which would include, for example, Heine's love lyrics, Borne's crusade against political reaction in Germany, and Georg Brandes's critical essays on every literature in the world except the Hebrew. But the definition is fundamentally wrong. A people's literature is the literature written in its national language. A writer using a language other than that of his own people may no doubt betray his own national temperament, even if his subject has no connection with his own people's life (and this is in fact true of the great Jewish writers just mentioned, and of others); and he may even influence the affairs of his own nation by writing about them in a foreign language. Yet as literature what he writes belongs not to his own people, but to the people in whose language it is written. North America produces a great number of books, some of them of high literary value, to say nothing of a vast periodical literature; yet, strictly, North America has no literature of its own, because it has no language exclusively its own. There is no clearly recognisable border-line between American and English literature, and the latter, being more fully developed and richer, includes everything written in the English language. The same is true of the Swiss. What they write belongs to the literatures of the three great nations whose languages they speak and write, and they have no literature of their own (if we ignore what little has been written in the German-Swiss dialect).

Jewish literature, then, is the literature written in our own language; it does not include books written by Jews in other languages. In so far as such books deal, in whole or in part, with the affairs of other nations, they belong to the literatures of the nations in whose languages they are written; and the best of them have their place (though not always the place they deserve) in the histories of those literatures, along with the works of the non-Jewish writers. But in so far as such books deal exclusively with matters of Jewish interest, they constitute a sort of literary ghetto; and this ghetto, like any other, has no significance for the gentile world, and is regarded by the Jews as something of a purely temporary character, with no prospect of a permanent place in Jewish life. This ghetto literature is read and enjoyed for a time by Jews in the country in which it is produced, but it has not the abiding hold on their interest and affection that a national literature acquires. Thus, for example, the name of Levanda is almost forgotten, and his sketches of Russo-Jewish life, which were so popular among Russian Jews twenty years ago, are scarcely in demand today; whereas Smolenskin's novels, which are similar in subject and much inferior as literature, are still as popular and as widely read as though they had only just appeared. I can find no explanation except that Smolenskin wrote in Hebrew, and Levanda in Russian. This is not an isolated instance; and it shows that Jews regard as their own literature only what is written in their own language. . . .

That being so, it has to be recorded that our national literature is in a very bad way. There is no need to demonstrate this at length. Anybody qualified to judge must admit that the only department in which contemporary Hebrew literature has reached a high level is that of self-advertisement. Take it at its own valuation, and you might suppose that it was achieving wonders and producing a masterpiece every day of the week. In fact, the puffs are the only masterpieces. It is almost a case of *vox et praeterea nihil*.

Before the *Haskalah* period we had a national literature of truly original character. It had no doubt its weak points, and many hard things can be said about both its form and its content (though most of its critics have exaggerated its faults). But at any rate it was undeniably our own. It bore the hallmark of the Jewish genius; it was a faithful expression of the Jewish heart and mind; it was the collective work of all the best intellects in every period of Jewish life. But since our modern exodus from the ghetto, since we began to dissipate our energies in every direction, Hebrew literature, like every other branch of our national culture, has fallen under a blight. The men of genius leave their poverty-stricken people and bestow their gifts on those who are rich enough without them; while Hebrew literature becomes the happy-hunting-ground of dullards and mediocrities, who behave with all the unrestraint that a man may permit himself in his own bedroom. Such good books as are written by the few writers worthy of the name are good only because they are more or less like what is good in other literatures. From first to last, modern Hebrew literature can scarcely point to a single work which can claim to be an original and distinctive expression of the Jewish point of view. It is almost all translation and imitation, and for the most part indifferent stuff at that. The translations are not close enough to the originals, and the imitations are too close. What they have in common is that they are all imported, not home-grown. A literature such as this, which is essentially nothing but a purveyor of foreign ideas and sentiments presented in a much inferior form, cannot appeal to us as something that belongs to our own Jewish life.

It is a shameful confession to have to make, but for anything written in our time that remotely resembles original Hebrew literature we have to go to the literature of *Hasidism*, which, with all its childishness, does present here and there a profound and truly Hebraic idea. That is more than can be said of the *Haskalah* literature.

5. Slavery in Freedom

I HAVE before me as I write a new French book, . . .
called *La Gerbe*. It was issued last year by the publisher of the
Archives Israelites, to commemorate the fiftieth anniversary of
that publication. . . . It is in vain that we look for any sign of
genuine rejoicing, of such "exaltation of spirit" as would be
proper to this jubilee festival. Through the whole book, from
beginning to end, there runs an undercurrent of grief, a dark
thread of lamentation.

First of all let us hear the editor himself, the central figure of
the celebration, give his account of the achievements of his publication. "In the year 1840," he tells us, "fifty years after the
promulgation of the principles of 1798, the Jews possessed rights
on paper; but in practice their rights were non-existent." And
then he asks in a parenthesis, "Do they exist fully even in 1890?"
After this question, which calls for no answer, he goes on to re-
count his battles against prejudice, and tells how he has tried
unceasingly to spread the great principle of "social assimilation
(*la fusion sociale*) with all its corollaries." What he says amounts
to this, that even the second jubilee after the principles of '98
has not brought the desired happiness; that hatred of the Jews
has revived even in France, despite the principles of '98, and
despite all the battles against prejudice and all efforts to promote
assimilation. And so—our respected editor promises to continue
to fight and strive. . . .

The writers in *La Gerbe* . . . are certainly men of parts and distinction, and it is not for such men as these to turn back in fright at the sight of the enemy—still less to let others see that they are afraid. They know how to control themselves and make a show of looking at all these things from above; they know how to comfort themselves and their readers with pleasant hopes and fair promises, which read sometimes like little prophecies. One of the writers promises us on his word that this is the last battle between the Jews and their enemies, and it will end in complete victory for us, to be followed by real peace for all time. The great Revolution of '89 is always on their tongues. They refer again and again to the "rights of man" (*les droits de l'homme*), or, as some put it, "the new Ten Commandments" which that Revolution promulgated; and each time they express the hope —a hope which is also a sort of prayer—that the French people will not forever forget those great days, that the French people will not, *cannot* turn back, that the French people is still, as of old, the great, the enlightened, the glorious, the mighty people, and so forth, and so forth.

Whether these prophecies will be fulfilled or not is a question with which we are not here concerned. But in the meantime it requires no very penetrating vision to discern from them, and from the pages of *La Gerbe* generally, the true spiritual condition of the French Jews at the present time. There is here none of that "exaltation" which some would fain discover, but the exact opposite. Their condition may be justly defined as spiritual slavery under the veil of outward freedom. In reality they accepted this slavery a hundred years ago, together with their "rights"; but it is only in these evil days that it stands revealed in all its glory.

The writers of *La Gerbe* try, for instance, to prove to us and to our enemies that the fortunes of the Jews in every country are inextricably bound up with those of its other inhabitants, or even with those of humanity as a whole; that the troubles of the Jews in any particular country are not, therefore, peculiar to them, but are shared by all the other inhabitants, or even by humanity as a whole; . . .

This trick of exciting sympathy with the Jews on the ground that it will benefit other people is very familiar to us here also. Our Russian Jewish writers, from the time of Orshansky to the present day, are never weary of seeking arguments to prove that the Jews are a milch cow, which must be treated gently for the sake of its milk. Naturally, our French *savants* do not condescend to use this ugly metaphor. They wrap up the idea in a nice "ideal" form. But when all is said, the idea is the same there as here; and a terrible idea it is, sufficient in itself to show how far even Western Jews are from being free men at heart. Picture the situation to yourself. Surrounded by armed bandits, I cry out "Help! Help! Danger!" Is not every man bound to hasten to my help? Is it not a fearful, an indelible disgrace, that I am forced to prove first of all that my danger affects other people, affects the whole human race? As though my blood were not good enough, unless it be mingled with the blood of others! As though the human race were something apart, in which I have no share, and not simply a collective name for its individual members, of whom I am one!

This slavery becomes more and more apparent, when the writers in *La Gerbe* come to deal with the internal affairs of Judaism. Valiantly they champion the cause of our religion against its rivals, knowing as they do that this is permitted in France, where neither the Government nor the people cares very much about such discussions. But when they have to disclose the *national* connection between the Jews of France and other Jews, or between them and their ancestral land, a connection in which it is possible to find something inconsistent to a certain extent with the extreme and zealot patriotism which is in vogue in France, then we discover once more their moral slavery —a spiritual yoke which throttles them, and reduces them to a condition of undisguised embarrassment.

One of the contributors, the distinguished philosopher Adolphe Franck, expresses the opinion that every Jew, *without distinction of nationality*, who enjoys the fruits of emancipation in any country, is bound to be grateful, first and foremost, to the Frenchmen of the Revolution, and must therefore regard France as his *first fatherland*, the *second* being his actual birthplace. And here our philosopher finds it his duty suddenly to add: "Jerusalem is [for the Jew] nothing more than the birthplace of his memories and his faith. He may give it a place in his religious service; but he himself belongs to the land of his birth." This way of regarding Jerusalem is a very trite commonplace, which our Western thinkers grind out again and again in various forms. Not long ago another philosopher, a German Jew, published a new volume, which contains a scientific article on the Book of Lamentations. Now, a *scientific* article has no concern with questions of practical conduct; and yet the author finds it necessary to touch in conclusion on the practical question, whether at the present day we have a right to read this book in our synagogues. He answers in the affirmative, on the ground that the Christians too read it in their churches three days before Easter. "If we are asked, 'What is Zion to you, and what are you to Zion?' we reply calmly, 'Zion is the innermost kernel of the inner consciousness of modern nations.'" This answer is not perhaps so clear as it might be, even in the original; but the writer's object is perfectly clear. We have, therefore, no right to be angry if our French philosopher also adopts this view. But when we read the whole article in *La Gerbe* and find the author concluding that the Jews have a special "mission," which they received *in Jerusalem*, which they have not yet completely fulfilled, and for the sake of which they live, and *must live* till they do fulfill it completely, then we shall have a serious question to put. The duty of gratitude, we argue, is so important in our author's view, that he would have every Jew put France before the country of his birth—France, which was nothing more than the cause of our obtaining external rights, which we might have obtained without her, if only we had deserted our "mission." That being so, does it not follow *a fortiori* that Jerusalem, which gave us this very "mission," the cause and object of our life, has a claim on our gratitude prior even to that of France? Even so great a philosopher as our author could not, I think, find a logical flaw in this argument: and yet he could write as he has done. Is not this moral slavery? . . .

But this moral slavery is only half the price which Western Jews have paid for their emancipation. Beneath the cloak of their political freedom there lies another, perhaps a harder, form of slavery—intellectual slavery; and this, too, has left its mark on the book which we are considering.

Having agreed, for the sake of emancipation, to deny the existence of the Jews as a people, and regard Judaism simply and solely as a religion, Western Jews have thereby pledged themselves and their posterity to guard with the utmost care the religious unity of Israel. But emancipation demanded certain practical changes in religious matters; and not everybody could make this sacrifice. Hence people "of the Jewish persuasion" have split into various sects; the unity of the religion, on its practical side, has vanished. There remains, then, no other bond than that of religion on its theoretical side—that is to say, certain abstract beliefs which are held by all Jews. This bond, apart from the inherent weakness which it has in common with every spiritual conception that is not crystallized into practice, has grown still weaker of recent years, and is becoming more and more feeble every day. Scientific development has shaken the foundations of every faith, and the Jewish faith has not escaped; so much so that even the editor of *La Gerbe* confesses, with a sigh, that "the scientific heresy which bears the name of Darwin" is gaining ground, and it is only from a feeling of *noblesse oblige* that he still continues to combat it. What, then, are those Jews to do who have nothing left but this theoretical religion, which is itself losing its hold on them? Are they to give up Judaism altogether, and become completely assimilated to their surroundings? A few of them have done this: but why should they not all adopt the same course? Why do most of them feel that they cannot? Where is the chain to which they can point as that which holds them fast to Judaism, and does not allow them to be free? Is it the instinctive national feeling which they have inherited, which is independent of religious beliefs or practices? Away with the suggestion! Did they not give up this feeling a hundred years ago, in exchange for emancipation? Yet the fact remains that it is not in their power to uproot this feeling. Try as they will to conceal it, seek as they will for subterfuges to deceive the world and themselves, it lives none the less; resent it as they will, it is a force at the centre of their being. But this answer, though it satisfies us, does not satisfy them. They have publicly renounced their Jewish nationality, and they cannot go back on their words; they cannot confess that they have sold that which was not theirs to sell. But this being so, how can they justify their obstinate clingings to the name of Jew—a name which brings them neither honor nor profit—for the sake of certain theoretical beliefs which they no longer hold, or which, if they do really and sincerely maintain them, they might equally hold without this special name, as every non-Jewish deist has done?

For a long time this question has been constantly troubling the Jewish thinkers of Western Europe; and it is this question which drove them, in the last generation, to propound that new, strange gospel to which they cling so tenaciously to this very day—I mean that famous gospel of "the mission of Israel among the nations." This theory is based on an antiquated idea, which is at variance with all the principles of modern science, as though every nation had been created from the first for some particular purpose, and so had a "mission" which it must fulfill, living on against its will until its Heaven-sent task is done. Thus, for example, the Greeks were created to polish and perfect external beauty; the Romans to exalt and extol physical force. On this hypothesis, it is not difficult to find an answer to our own question—an answer not inconsistent, on the one hand, with emancipation, and, on the other hand, with the unity of Judaism. The answer is this: Israel as a people is dead; but the Jewish Church still lives, and must live, because the mission of Israel is not completely fulfilled, so long as absolute monotheism, with all its consequences, has not conquered the whole world. Till that victory is achieved, Israel must live in spite of itself, must bear and suffer and fight; to this end it was created—"to know God and to bring others to that knowledge." . . .

It is perhaps superfluous to deal at length with this theory, which, indeed, it is difficult, in our day, to treat seriously. We are forced, despite ourselves, into a smile, a smile of bitter irony, when we see distinguished men, who might have shown their sorely tried people real light on its hard and thorny path, wasting their time with such pleasant sophistries as these; trying to believe, and to persuade others, that a whole people can have maintained its existence, and borne a heavy burden of religious observance and an iron yoke of persecutions, torments and curses for thousands of years, all for the purpose of teaching the world a certain philosophy, which is already expounded in whole libraries of books, in every conceivable language and every conceivable style, from which who will may learn without any assistance from us: and especially at the present time, when the number of those who wish to learn grows less every day, nay, when we ourselves are every day forgetting our own teaching.

It is, indeed, surprising that such a thinker as Munk, and even the older thinkers of our own day, could and still can believe in the mission of Israel in the sense explained above. But we shall be less surprised if we remember that Munk wrote in the "forties"

and that the older contributors to *La Gerbe* are for the most part
children of that earlier generation which educated them—children of an age in which the idea of a "final cause" was intelligible
and current as a scientific theory. It is, however, a strange phenomenon, and more difficult to explain, that the same position
should be adopted by thinkers and writers of the present generation. These men, who know and admit that "the scientific heresy
which bears the name of Darwin" is gaining ground, that is to
say, that the world is accepting gradually a scientific theory
which does not admit the existence of purpose or end where it
seems most obvious—how can these men still cling to a doctrine
which demands belief in the missions of nations generally, in
the mission of Israel in particular, and above all, in such a wonderful mission as this? There can be but one answer. They are
compelled to do so, because they can find no other way of reconciling Judaism with emancipation. In the first place, Israel has
no right to be anything but a Church consecrated to Heaven;
in the second place, this heavenly bond has become too weak;
and in the third place—and this is the important thing—they feel,
in spite of it all, that Jews they are, and Jews they want to be.
And so, in order to conceal the contradiction between these
"truths," they are forced to take refuge in this antiquated theory.
On all other questions of conduct or of scholarship they belong
to their own generation; but on the Jewish question they cannot
move from the position which their fathers took up fifty years
ago. As though these fifty years had brought no change of idea
and outlook into the world!

Thus this intellectual slavery also is a result of political freedom. If not for this freedom, emancipated Jews would not deny
the existence of the Jewish nation; they would not have to climb
up to Heaven, on an old and rickety ladder, to seek there what
they might have found on earth. It might be maintained, indeed,
that even then there would have been thinkers who inclined to
look for some "mission" for their people, or, to speak more
accurately, for some spiritual aim suited to its spiritual characteristics. But then they might have found a different aim—not,
perhaps, a finer one, but still one that would have gained acceptance more readily, one more in accordance with the ideas of
modern times and with the truths of logic and of history. For
instance, they might have argued thus: Here has our people

been wandering over the face of the earth for some two thousand years, in the course of which we do not find that it has ever consciously invented any new thing of importance, has ever beaten out any new highway on the tract of life. Its part has been always that of the huckster; it has peddled about all kinds of goods, material and spiritual, of other people's making. All the good work which the Jews did for the world's culture in the Middle Ages was at bottom nothing but huckstering and peddling: they picked up learning in the East, and gave it to the West. "Yes," replies Munk, in extenuation, "because the mission of Israel does not lie in making new discoveries." Well, so let it be! But now that we see that Israel was fitted to be, and in fact has been, a huckster of culture, surely common sense will tell us that this is the occupation for Israel to follow now, if some spiritual aim is wanted. Now, therefore, that we have acquired culture in the West, let us return and carry it to the East. And, if we are so very fond of teaching, it is surely better for us to go where there is a more evident lack of teachers, and where it is easier to find attentive pupils.

But the truth is that if Western Jews were not slaves to their emancipation, it would never have entered their heads to consecrate their people to spiritual missions or aims before it had fulfilled that physical, natural "mission" which belongs to every organism—before it had created for itself conditions suitable to its character, in which it could develop its latent powers and aptitudes, its own particular form of life, in a normal manner, and in obedience to the demands of its nature. Then, and only then, we may well believe, its development might lead it in course of time to some field of work in which it would be specially fitted to act as teacher, and thus contribute once again to the general good of humanity, in a way suited to the spirit of the modern world. And if then philosophers tell us that in this field of work lies the "mission" of our people, for which it was created, I shall not, indeed, be able to subscribe to their view; but I shall not quarrel with them on a mere question of names.

But alas! I shall doubtless be dead and buried before then. Today, while I am still alive, I try mayhap to give my weary eyes a rest from the scene of ignorance, of degradation, of unutterable poverty that confronts me here in Russia, and find comfort by looking yonder across the border, where there are Jewish professors, Jewish members of Academies, Jewish officers in the army, Jewish civil servants, and when I see there, behind the glory and the grandeur of it all, a twofold spiritual slavery— moral slavery and intellectual slavery—and ask myself: Do I envy these fellow-Jews of mine their emancipation?—I answer, in all truth and sincerity: No! a thousand times No! The privileges are not worth the price! I may not be emancipated; but at least I have not sold my soul for emancipation. I at least can proclaim from the housetops that my kith and kin are dear to me wherever they are, without being constrained to find forced and unsatis- factory excuses. I at least can remember Jerusalem at other times than those of "divine service": I can mourn for its loss, in public or in private, without being asked what Zion is to me, or I to Zion. I at least have no need to exalt my people to Heaven, to trumpet its superiority above all other nations, in order to find a justification for its existence. I at least know "why I remain a Jew"—rather, I can find no meaning in such a question, any more than if I were asked why I remain my father's son. I at least can speak my mind concerning the beliefs and opinions which I have inherited from my ancestors, without fearing to snap the bond that unites me to my people. I can even adopt that "scientific heresy which bears the name of Darwin" without any danger to my Judaism. In a word, I am my own, and my opinions and feelings are my own. I have no reason for concealing or denying them, for deceiving others or myself. And this spiritual freedom —scoff who will!—I would not exchange or barter for all the emancipation in the world.

6. Imitation and Assimilations

L o n g ago, in the days of the Prophets, we Jews learned to despise physical force and to respect only spiritual power; and as a result the superior might of our persecutors has never, in our subsequent history, induced in us an attitude of self-effacement. It required some great spiritual force, such as we have occasionally encountered in the life of another people, to bring about entire self-abandonment and a desire for complete absorption in an alien form of life. Knowing this, our national leaders have tried to isolate us from the spiritual life of other nations, so as to allow no opportunity for imitation; and this policy of segregation has been responsible for driving many away from Judaism. Circumstances have, however, sometimes been such that the policy could not be carried out; and whenever this has happened, whenever the barriers have been broken down and there has been freedom of intercourse between the Jews and the rest of the world, it has become obvious that the apprehensions of the patriots were groundless and their policy of segregation unnecessary. We Jews have not merely a tendency to imitation, but a positive genius for it. Whatever we imitate, we imitate thoroughly; we very soon manage to make ourselves masters of what we started to copy in a spirit of pure self-effacement. And at that stage our leaders of thought show us how to make use of what we have borrowed for the purpose of our own self-expression; so that the imitation automatically ceases to be self-effacing, becomes competitive, and in the result positively strengthens the Jewish consciousness.

Long before the Hellenising Jews of Palestine tried to substitute Greek culture for Judaism, the Jews in Egypt had come into close contact with the Greek way of life and thought; yet we do not find any movement towards complete assimilation on their part. On the contrary, they used their knowledge of Greek life and thought for the purpose of revealing the distinctive spirit of Judaism, of showing the whole world its beauty, and of vindicating its superiority to the proud philosophy of Greece. Starting, that is, from imitation of the self-effacing type, they succeeded in making what they borrowed so thoroughly their own that they were able to use it for competitive purposes.

If those who made the Greek Septuagint translation of the Bible for the Egyptian Jews had at the same time translated Plato into Hebrew for the Jews of Palestine, thus familiarizing our people with the Greek spirit of its own land and through the medium of its own language, it is highly probable that a similar process of transition from self-effacing to competitive imitation would have taken place in Palestine, but on an even higher plane, and with consequences even more important for the development of the Jewish spirit. In that case there would have been no dangerous Hellenising movement in Palestine, and perhaps there would have been no need of the Maccabees and of the whole chain of events which had its source in that period. Perhaps— who knows?—the whole course of human history might have been entirely different.

But the Seventy did not translate Plato into Hebrew. It was only at a much later date, in the Arabic period, that the Jews became familiar with Greek culture in their own language—and then not in their own land. But even though the contact was made on foreign soil, self-effacement soon gave place to competition, with remarkable results. Language, literature, religion— all underwent a revival and in combination helped to express the distinctive spirit of Judaism through the medium of the newly-acquired culture. So complete, indeed, was the absorption of this culture that the Jews of that period could not believe that it was in fact a foreign culture, or that Judaism could ever have existed without it: and they must needs find an ancient legend to the effect that Socrates and Plato had learnt their philosophy from the Hebrew Prophets, and that the whole of Greek philosophy had been stolen from Jewish books which had been lost at the time of the destruction of Jewish independence.

Since that time we have again gone through two successive periods, a long one of complete segregation, and a short one of complete self-effacement. But again we are coming to recognize that salvation lies along neither of these two roads, but along a third road that lies between them: that of the enrichment of our national individuality by means of imitation of the competitive kind.

It is not only in these latter days of Jewish nationalism that signs of this recognition have appeared. Evidence of it could be found, some considerable time before the rise of nationalism, on the one hand in the production in European languages of a literature dealing with Judaism and Jewish values, and on the other hand in the movement for the reform of the external ob-servances of Judaism. This latter movement, it is true, is widely held to be a long step on the way to complete assimilation. But that view, though it is shared by some of the Reformers them-selves, is mistaken. If self-effacement had reached the stage of complete indifference to the maintenance of any link with the past, and of a genuine desire to be absorbed in the foreign life, there would no longer be any incentive to adapt the inherited tra-dition to modern requirements; the natural course would be to leave it severely alone till it vanished of itself, meanwhile carrying it on for a time without change, out of mere force of habit and respect for the past.

Geiger asserts that anybody who writes Hebrew in our days is not really expressing himself, but is unconsciously living for the time being in the vanished world of the Talmud and the Rabbis, and thinking their thoughts. What Geiger says in fact is true of most of the Jewish scholars of the West, as their Hebrew style proves, because the link between them and their ancestral language has already ceased to exist. But it is not true of the Hebrew writers in Eastern Europe and Palestine. Hebrew is still a part of their very being; they write Hebrew because they want to express their real selves; and they are anxious to improve the language and to make it as fully adequate a medium of expression for themselves as it was for their remote ancestors.

When, therefore, we find Geiger and his school spending all

their time and energy in reforming the religious side of our Jewish inheritance, though completely indifferent to the improvement of our language, we may regard it as certain that on the religious side their Jewish individuality still lives. It is a shrunken and one-sided individuality, but it is not dead. Whether they themselves admit it or not, they are in fact trying to express their Jewish personality while they imitate non-Jewish models.

Absorption, then, is not a danger that we need fear; what we have to fear is fragmentation. Each Jewish community, in its efforts to enrich its Jewish individuality, is bound to imitate, in the sense of competitive imitation, the culture of the particular country in which it lives; and consequently there is a danger that in course of time these differing cultural environments will produce such a degree of diversity as will reduce us from a single nation to a number of separate tribes, as we were at the beginning of our history.

Experience gives ground for this apprehension. The East-European Jews, for example, first learnt western culture from the Jews of Germany; the modernising influence was not that of their own non-Jewish surroundings, but that which was at work among the German Jews. They imitated the German Jews absolutely, regardless of the difference of conditions in their own countries, as though they had been wholly German themselves. But after they had gone some way along the road of Haskalah and had become conscious of their new strength, they abandoned self-effacing imitation of the German Jews for competitive imitation, and began to develop on lines conditioned by the different cultural conditions of the countries in which they lived. Similarly, the Jews of France still provide the pattern on which the Jews of the Orient model themselves; but here again this is only a temporary state of things, which will end when the Oriental Jews become conscious of their new strength. Every Jewish community which has developed by imitation of another shakes off that influence as it becomes more self-reliant; and so the danger of fragmentation is always on the increase.

There is one way out of this danger, and only one. To weld the scattered Jewish communities together, in spite of the disintegrating effect of the differing local influences to which they are subjected, we need a centre which will exert a strong pull on all of them, not because of some fortuitous and temporary relation, but of its own right, because it is what it is. Such a centre will in some measure impose itself on every community in the diaspora, and will serve them all, despite their diversities, as a transmuting and unifying force.

In the early period of our history the military prowess of David and the wise statesmanship of Solomon combined to create a rallying-point for the scattered tribes in the Temple. Now that we are an aged people, no one man, whether soldier or statesman or financier, can possibly create the new centre of which we are in need. Whether they like it or not, all those who want us to remain a single nation will be compelled to accept the logic of history and to look eastwards to what was our centre and our model in days gone by.

7. A Spiritual Centre

. . . FIFTEEN years ago there appeared for the first time an idea that afterwards occasioned endless expenditure of ink. "In Palestine," I wrote, "we can and should establish for ourselves a spiritual centre of our nationality." My literary experience was not then extensive, and I overlooked this important consideration: that in putting before the public an idea which does not accord with the general view, one must not merely put it in a logically clear and definite form, but must also reckon with the psychology of the reader—with that mental apparatus which combines unrelated words and ideas according to the requirements of its owner—and must try one's utmost to avoid any word or expression that might afford an opening for this process of combination. I confess now that in view of this psychological factor I ought to have felt that the formula "a spiritual centre of our nationality" would provide a good opening for those who wished to misunderstand, although from the point of view of logic it is quite clear and precise.

"Centre" is, of course, a relative term. Just as "father" is inconceivable without children, so "centre" is inconceivable without "circumference"; and just as a father is a father only in relation to his children, and is merely so-and-so in relation to the rest of mankind, so a centre is a centre only in relation to its own circumference, whereas in relation to all that lies outside the circumference it is merely a point with no special importance.

When we use the word "centre" metaphorically in relation to

human society, it necessarily connotes a similar idea: what we mean is that a particular spot or thing exerts influence on a certain social circumference, which is bound up with and dependent on it, and that in relation to this circumference it is a centre. But since society is a complex of many different departments, there are few centres which are universal in their function—that is, which influence equally all sides of the life of the circumference. The relation between the centre and the circumference is usually limited to one or more departments of life, outside which the two are not interdependent. Thus a given circumference may have many centres, each of which is a centre only for one specific purpose. When, therefore, the word "centre" is used to express a social conception, it is accompanied almost always—except where the context makes it unnecessary—by an epithet which indicates its character. We speak of a literary centre, an artistic centre, a commercial centre, and so on, meaning thereby that in this or that department of life the centre in question has a circumference which is under its influence and is dependent upon it, but that in other departments the one does not exert nor the other receive influence, and the relation of centre and circumference does not exist.

Bearing in mind this limitation, which is familiar enough, and applying it to the phrase quoted above—"in Palestine we can and should establish for ourselves a spiritual centre of our nationality"—we shall find that the phrase is capable of only one interpretation.

"A *centre* of our nationality" implies that there is a national *circumference*, which, like every circumference, is much larger than the centre. That is to say, the speaker sees the majority of his people, in the future as in the past, scattered all over the world, but no longer broken up into a number of disconnected parts, because one part—the one in Palestine—will be a centre for them all and make them all into a single, complete circumference. When all the scattered limbs of the national body feel the beating of the national heart, restored to life in its native home, they too will once again draw near to one another and welcome the inrush of living blood that flows from the heart.

"Spiritual" means that this relation of centre and circumference between Palestine and the lands of the diaspora will of necessity be limited to the spiritual side of life. The influence of the centre will strengthen the Jewish national consciousness in the Diaspora; it will restore our independence of mind and self-respect; it will give to our Judaism a national content which will be genuine and natural, unlike the substitutes with which we now try to fill the void. But all this cannot apply outside the spiritual side of life, in all those economic and political relations which depend first and foremost upon the conditions of the immediate environment, being created by that environment and reflecting its character. Whilst it is true that in all these relations the effects of the changed outlook (such as the reinforcement of our sense of national unity and power of resistance) will show themselves to some extent, yet essentially and fundamentally these departments of life in the diaspora will not be linked with the life of the centre. For it is absolutely inconceivable that Palestine could radiate economic and political influence throughout the length and breadth of the Diaspora, which is co-extensive with the globe, in such a way and to such an extent as would entitle us to say, without inexact use of language, that Palestine was the centre of our national life in these departments also.

When I first used the phrase under discussion, I knew beforehand that I should excite the wrath of the *Hoveve Zion* (who held the field in those days). But looking at the matter, as I did, solely from the point of view of logic, I was sure that the brunt of their anger would fall on the word "centre"; for the use of that word involved a negation of the idea of a return of the whole Jewish people to Palestine, and so clipped the wings of those fantastic hopes which even then, in the days before the first Basle Congress, were proclaimed as heralding the end of the *galut* and a complete and absolute solution of the Jewish problem in all its aspects. The epithet "spiritual" seemed to me so simple and clear, as a necessary logical consequence of the assumption involved in the word "centre," that it never remotely entered my mind that here might be the stumbling-block, and that I ought at once to file a declaration to the effect that, although the centre would be spiritual in its influence on the circumference, yet in itself it would be a place like any other place, where men were compounded of body and soul, and needed food and clothing, and that for this reason the centre would have to concern itself with material questions, and to work out an economic system suited to its requirements, and could not exist without farmers, labourers, craftsmen, and merchants. . . .

But my amazement soon died away when I remembered the "psychological apparatus." This apparatus was bound to fasten on some word or other in order to make my unpopular theory appear absurd; and since the word "centre," if the critics dwelt on it and led the minds of their readers to analyze its meaning, was calculated not to serve that end, but, on the contrary, to make it clear where the absurdity really lay, they found it best to put all the emphasis on "spiritual." "A *spiritual* centre! Now do you understand what these people want? They care nothing for a material settlement, for colonies, factories, commerce; what they want is to settle a dozen *batlanim* in Palestine to carry on the business of spiritual nationality."

Great indeed is the power of human psychology. This interpretation of my views gained currency, and is accepted to this day as a matter of course. Even those Zionists who read my views in the original, and have not learnt them from the voluminous pamphlet literature of recent years, are quite certain that that is what spiritual Zionism means. It has availed them nothing to read immediately afterwards, in the same article, that the spiritual centre must be "a true miniature of the Jewish people," and that in the centre there will appear once more "the genuine type of a Jew, whether it be a Rabbi or a scholar or a writer, *a farmer or a craftsman or a business man.*" It has availed nothing, because psychological factors dominate not only the judgment, but also the memory.

. . . [In] my opinion the whole point of the material settlement—whether its architects realise it or not—is to provide the foundation for that spiritual centre of our nation which is destined to arise in Palestine in response to the insistent urge of the national instinct; whereas our material problem will not be solved by the acquisition of a home of refuge, because in the great centres of Jewish population the natural increase will always offset the loss due to transfers to the Jewish home, so that in the ordinary course of nature our numbers cannot be reduced by emigration. But it does not by any means follow that we ought not to do anything here and now for the spiritual rebirth. We cannot wait for it to come about automatically when the material settlement in Palestine is sufficiently far advanced. We must admit that that would mean waiting a very long time. A score or a hundred agricultural settlements, however well established, will not of themselves save the Jewish soul, in the sense of bringing about a re-union of our scattered spiritual forces and their concentration in the service of our national culture. For that we shall need a national centre in the fullest sense, with all the manifold and expanding interests, demands and activities that that term connotes. Can we sit and wait for the realisation of this great vision—which nobody expects to come very quickly —and meanwhile allow the process of spiritual decay to go on unchecked?

I maintain, then, that Zionism cannot confine itself to the material work of rebuilding Palestine. We must advance along both lines at the same time. While making every effort to create a large Jewish settlement on sound lines, we dare not neglect to do what is necessary to make Palestine a permanent and freely developing centre of our national culture, of our science and scholarship, our art and literature. While gradually assembling the skilled labour that is needed to repair the ruins of our country and restore its past glories, we must also assemble the forces of heart and mind and brain that will repair our spiritual ruins and restore the Jewish people to its rightful place of honour in the comity of human culture. The establishment of a single great school of learning or art in Palestine, or a single Academy of language and literature, would in my opinion be a national achievement of first-rate importance, and would contribute more to the attainment of our aims than a hundred agricultural settlements. These agricultural settlements are merely so much building material for our future home; they cannot of themselves provide the driving power for a revolution in Jewish life. But a great cultural institution in Palestine, attracting to itself a large number of gifted Jewish scholars, for whom it would provide the possibility of carrying on their work in a Jewish atmosphere, free from repressions and not unduly subject to extraneous influences—such an institution could even now become a source of new inspiration to the Jewish people as a whole and bring about a true revival of Judaism and Jewish culture.

I am well aware that this is reversing the usual order of things. The normal and natural development of a nation's life proceeds from the lower to the higher stages. A nation's first care is to make its economic and political position secure; only when that has been satisfactorily accomplished does it turn its mind to less material concerns and produce whatever it is capable of producing in the domain of the spirit. But we Jews are not a new-born nation, just beginning to climb the ladder of progress rung by rung. We climbed the lower rungs of the ladder thousands of years ago, and had reached a high level of culture when our natural progress was forcibly arrested. The ground was cut away from under our feet, and we were left hanging in mid-air, carrying a heavy and valuable load of accumulated culture, but without any sort of basis for healthy life or free development. So things went on for centuries. The Jewish people remained miserably poised between heaven and earth, struggling with all its might to preserve its cultural inheritance and not to fall below the level it had reached in its more prosperous days. And now, when we have some hope of coming down to earth again and building our life on solid natural foundations, are we to be told that we ought to jettison our burden of culture, so as to be better able to concentrate on the material tasks which normally take precedence, and afterwards start again, in the customary fashion, from the bottom of the ladder? . . . Intellectually we emerged from childhood three thousand years ago, and we need an adult's diet; but the circumstances in which we are placed compel us to go to nursery school again and master the alphabet of national life. What are we to do? The answer is that we must start from both ends at once—that is to say, build from the bottom and from the top at the same time. Of course this is not the normal method of nation-building. But then our life is altogether abnormal, and however we may build, the structure will be something without precedent. So it is of no use to look to other nations for guidance. We must do what our peculiar circumstances compel us to do, relying on the strength of will and the patience which have miraculously kept us alive till now and will see us through in the future.

We must, however, realize from the outset that this reconcentration of our scattered spiritual energies is not an easy matter, to be taken in our stride. The establishment of a home of refuge for Jewish culture perhaps demands preparation no less elaborate, and resources no less ample, than does the establishment of a home of refuge for persecuted Jews; and besides preparing for the future, we have a great deal of current work to do. We are all familiar with the division of Zionist opinion on the question of the attitude of Zionism to the current problems of the Diaspora. My own opinion is that efforts to improve the economic and political position of Jewish communities in the Diaspora are not strictly within the province of Zionism. Work of that kind of course has to be done, and it is useful as a means of obtaining some temporary alleviation of the position, however slight. It has an undoubted claim on all those who are in a position to help. But life in exile, at its best, will always remain life in exile—that is to say, the opposite of that free national life which is the object of the Zionist movement; and a single movement cannot concern itself with two opposites. The case of cultural work is not analogous. The creative Jewish genius remains the same throughout history, and it has continued to function and to be true to itself even in the dispersion. Every spark of it that breaks away and floats into the outside world is an irreparable loss to our nation. To regain these lost sparks, to keep them at home for the benefit of our own culture is essentially Zionist work, because by adding immediately to our spiritual assets it helps to pave the way for the larger cultural enterprise on which we shall embark after the establishment of the centre in Palestine, when the work of these returned wanderers will serve as the starting point for an advance into higher realms of achievement.

This is a complicated and difficult task, and it unquestionably needs a strong and well-knit organization. The business of such an organization should be to acquire the necessary resources, to take measures for the conservation of our spiritual energies, to support every cultural activity which promises to be of benefit, and, above all, to work for the gradual realisation of the main aim—the establishment of the spiritual centre in Palestine . . .

FOR FURTHER READING
Books by Ahad Ha-am

Selected Essays of Ahad Ha-am edited by Leon Simon (Philadelphia: Jewish Publication Society, 1962). With an excellent introduction by the translator.

Ahad Ha-am: Essays, Letters, Memoirs edited by Leon Simon (London: East and West Library, 1946). Includes all the material in the Jewish Publication Society edition (above) plus additional writings.

Books about Ahad Ha-am

HERTZBERG, Arthur, "The Agnostic Rabbi—Ahad Ha-am," in *The Zionist Idea*, (New York: Atheneum, 1977). Introductory essay by Arthur Hertzberg and five translated essays by Ahad Ha-am.

GLATZER, Nahum N., editor, *Modern Jewish Thought: A Source Reader* (New York: Schocken, 1977). This is one of the many anthologies available which include contributions by Ahad Ha-am. Includes a brief introduction with a translation of an important essay.

"Ahad Ha-am" in *Encyclopedia Judaica*, Volume 2: 440–448, (Jerusalem: 1972). A thorough overview of his life and thought.

AARON DAVID GORDON
(1856–1922)

EDITOR'S NOTE

Aaron David Gordon was one of the most remarkable personalities to arise in modern Palestine during the first two decades of this century. He was the central figure in the emerging labor Zionist movement and the symbol of the advanced social ideals of the new community.

Like Ahad Ha-am, Gordon was born in a small village in the Russian Ukraine in 1856. For a time his father was in the timber business and the family lived in the middle of the Ukrainian forest. Gordon, therefore, grew up in close contact with nature and developed a love for the soil and the natural life. After his marriage, he became an official in the office of a relative, the noted Baron Joseph Günzberg, and remained in this position for twenty-three years. But Gordon was unhappy with the pettiness of the other officials and with what he considered the parasitism and unnatural form of Jewish life in the Diaspora. In 1904, at the age of forty-eight he emigrated to Palestine where he sought employment as a common laborer, a difficult undertaking for a frail, middle-aged Jew at that time. Most of the Jewish employers preferred cheap Arab labor to that of inexperienced idealistic Jewish workers. After working in various settlements such as Petah Tikvah and Ein Ganim, he finally came to live in Degania, the new cooperative settlement in the Galilee.

Gordon was regarded as the spiritual father of the workers. The example of this white-bearded man, hoe in hand, working joyfully side by side with younger men, the purity of his ideas and his personal idealism inspired his entire generation.

For the first decade after his death it was Gordon, the man, who was remembered—the guide and mentor who helped so many in those difficult years of the Second Aliyah. With the passing of time, however, more attention has been given to his writings. His essays on the need for a regeneration of Jewish life in Palestine and the importance of labor in the life of the Jew were widely read. In recent years there has been an increasing interest in his theoretical writings on religion.

Gordon was not a systematic writer. There is much that is repetitious in his essays. But many of his pieces have an enthusiastic, lyrical quality which reflects the soul of the man. In Gordon's view, the purpose of the writer is not to be an educator or "teacher of life" but rather to listen to the "innermost voice" of the people and to give expression to the "deepest individuality in their soul." Many of his essays, therefore, reflect the era in which he lived—the period of the Second Aliyah when the ideal of Jewish labor was still new and the theories of socialism, Marxism and Jewish nationalism were vying for acceptance. Others are timeless, dealing with aspects of religion and the need for what he called "cosmic unity." From among his essays we have chosen a number of passages presenting his concept of Jewish nationalism and several others on his religious views.

In all his essays, Gordon was deeply concerned with the sense of alienation which he felt to be characteristic of modern man—his sense of loneliness and isolation, his lack of contact with nature. In Gordon's view, the essential task of his generation was to overcome this loneliness and alienation by relating man to the organic wholeness of the cosmos.

In our first selection, Gordon emphasizes the role of the nation in this process of inner renewal. To him the nation was an organic cosmic unit created by nature itself, "the most important link uniting the individual with the larger world" and the "primary force in the development of human nature." Thus Gordon could not accept Marxism as a philosophy because it aimed at reconstructing the social order rather than at bringing about an inner change in every human being. To achieve the cosmic unity which is the aim of his philosophy, the majority of the people must be engaged in productive labor. Labor must become the chief ideal of the Jewish people, of the educated and uneducated alike. In his view there need be no conflict between intellectual growth and the life of nature through work.

Once the regeneration has taken place in Palestine, there will also occur a revival in the Diaspora. Gordon, therefore, urged a pioneering movement among Jewish youth in each nation, the establishment of *kevutzot* and the revival of Hebrew as a bond between Palestine and Jews in other lands.

Though Gordon was not observant of religious forms, he did not subscribe to the view current in his time that religion was a thing of the past. To him religion meant an awareness of the cosmic unity of all reality. Thus he saw great value in the *Yom Kippur*, even for those not otherwise observant, as a day which "brings strength to the individual personalities who gather together and blend their voices in a sea of voices."

His spiritual orientation is also revealed in the passage on immortality. Gordon had no sympathy with what he regarded as the petty desires of men to leave their names as a memorial in books or scientific discoveries. What is eternal in the individual personality is the hidden vital impression that it leaves in life. One's aim should be to strengthen the "creative spirit of life."

The final selection sets down some of the distinctive ethical and religious features of Judaism in contrast to Christianity—the lack of any mediator between the Jew and his creator, the emphasis on study in place of a "fixed established faith" and Judaism's concern for family purity.

8. The Nation

THIS is the essence of the problem: the regeneration of the Jewish people in Palestine. What form the revival shall take, how it shall be created, that alone must be clarified.

First of all we should understand that our national regeneration is a matter of creation. It is not restricted to the establishment of a new social order or even to a renewed social spirit. It embraces a task immeasurably greater, a purpose infinitely deeper. It must begin at the very source of life, at the very roots of nature itself. It delves down to the well-springs of existence and demands a spirit and order which emanate from life itself.

The collective life of man like that of other animals is founded, essentially, upon the family. Out of this smaller unit has developed the larger organism, the larger family—the nation. . . .

The complete revelation of natural collective life is achieved within the nation, the large family. Although the nation originated human relations and human life, the nation itself shows an arrested development at the stage of primitive man. Nor is the nation aware of the evil of its retarded state. Imperfect as the individual may be, he is, nevertheless, conscious of his shortcomings and of the need for perfecting himself. But the prime force in the development of human nature and of life—the nation —is not concerned with its own development, or with its own perfection. Some hold that the nation is above such considerations. Restrictions that limit the individual in his acts—theft, cheating, forgery, evil ways, murder, abominations—are not only tolerated by a nation but they serve to add to its reputation for heroism and for glory. There is another view maintained especially today. There are those who see in the concept "Nation" a remnant of ancient days, a force that checks human salvation, a thing of evil which self-respecting people must uproot from their heart and destroy.

We, who belong to a people that has suffered more than any other, that has been torn up from its soil, alienated from nature, yet continues vigorous; we, a nation which has not been destroyed by two thousand years of misfortune, we consider that in our aim for a complete regeneration there can be no other possibility for attaining the life we seek except to base it wholly upon its natural foundation. We must return fully to nature, to creative work, to a sense of order, and to a spiritual life, in short, to family-nationhood. More than others we must be concerned, indeed, we are charged with the task of the regeneration of the nation. We must direct it toward the development of the human spirit, toward the search for truth and righteousness in its relation with other peoples and with all mankind. We must reinstate the nation to its former strength. Our national renaissance is not mere national freedom or rejuvenation: our national revival is like a resurrection of the dead, an event that has no parallel. For such an achievement in general, and for our nation in particular, one rule must govern: either there is complete achievement or none at all. The full power of the creativeness of the human spirit has not yet been realized. The human spirit must grow in proportion to the growth of human consciousness. This cannot take place without a thorough regeneration of the nation. The nation may be likened to a funnel: at its wide receiving end endless existence is poured in, while through its concentrated, restricted end the funnel empties its contents into the soul of man. The nation, therefore, is the force which creates the spirit of man. It is the link which unites the life of the individual to the life of mankind and to the world at large.

There are no gaps in nature. The cosmic order of the expansion of life starts with the individual, proceeds to the family, then to the nation and from the nation to the race, and throughout to the whole of humanity.

This is the basis of our idea, the idea of our revival and redemption; it is founded on this dual concept: human-nation,

nation-man. Where there is no "nation-man" relation, there is no "man," no individual man. Who should be more aware of this than we Jews? At the cost of untold suffering we have acquired the privilege of being the first to sponsor this creative principle. Out of the misfortunes and the purgatory which we have suffered, we generated a secret light. This light we shall direct into the open.

In truth, this is an idea for the future, possibly for a very remote future but from the very beginning of our efforts for national revival and redemption we must hold to this idea as to a guiding star, a star for lighting our path.

Some may consider that the essence of the idea belongs to the realm of the imagination. Possibly. I shall not argue the point. Who knows whether the human spirit is on the ascendant or on the decline! I do not question the basic principle in the idea, but I doubt whether there will be an upward swing of the human spirit. Yet this much is clear to me: there is no other way for the renewing of life, for the regeneration of man. No, there is no other way.

Our renaissance demands an exalted spirit, a vigorous idea that will overwhelm and pervade the whole of man with the strength of a religious conviction; its force must be powerful enough to revolutionize his world and to regenerate the spirit of man.

9. Nationalism and Socialism

. . . L E T us consider for a moment these two—nationalism and socialism—at closer range. In nationalism there is a cosmic moment, a moment when you may say that the spirit of the physical nature of a people's homeland becomes fused with the spirit of the people. This is of the utmost importance. This is the source of the greatest riches of a nation; herein lies the difference between a nation that is a collective body—alive, creative —and a society that is a mechanical unit, moving and working. To illustrate in a measure how important is the cosmic moment in nationalism, one may look at the community of the United States of America. Consider this: a wholly independent entity, vast, rich—a human collective—great, alive, energetic, powerful. But is this collective a nation? Is it a specific, particular, individual nation? It seems to me difficult to give a positive answer to this question. The United States is independent politically, and in many other respects, but from the point of view of national individuality of this human society, it is to this very moment an English colony in spite of the long period of several centuries that this society has been in existence in America. Who knows how many hundreds of years must elapse before it will be a specific nation, wholly American? (From just this very condition may come the fact that there is so much of the mechanical in this community.) To be sure, there are certain differences, possibly even great differences, between the English and the Americans, but there is not here the basic difference which marks different nations, as for example, the German and the French.

Herein lies the strength of the cosmic moment in nationalism; far otherwise is it with socialism.

Socialism was born out of the development of science and technique on the one hand, and out of capitalism on the other. It rests entirely upon technique and action, while nationalism rests upon life and creation. Socialism, therefore, is so clear and smooth, so easily understood in all its phases, so very convenient for use in explaining everything in the life of man! This cannot be said of nationalism any more than it can be said of life itself. For this reason, socialism based the progress, the regeneration of human life upon the improvement of the social system, not upon the improvement and regeneration of the human spirit. Clearly, we have a mutual, reciprocal action here; no thinking mind will deny this. But the difference lies in what we emphasize most, what we consider are essentials. Socialism has made the external life, the objective elements of life most important, and holds that these will improve not only life but man as well. It did not sufficiently take into account the subjective factors of man. . . . At bottom, materialism is not the objectionable feature of socialism —for there are in socialism non-materialistic factors—rather it is the mechanical element in socialism that is the objectionable consideration. This mechanistic quality is felt in all the acts and party life of socialist disciples and in everything that they write. Sometimes you seem to see within it breadth, light, song, but when you examine it all closely, you find that it is the breadth of a vast array on a great battle front, not the breadth of the world; the flight is of an airplane, a perfected Zeppelin, with all its tumult, its noise, not the flight of an eagle, not even of a little free bird. The song is of a phonograph, of a perfect recording machine; it is not the song of a living human soul.

Not without purpose did the original founders of socialism definitely oppose nationalism, for they saw in it a direct contradiction to socialism. Life, however, demands a slow, imperceptible transition from socialism to nationalism in a new form adapted to the new spirit and to the new thought of our day. One may say perhaps that this is the weakness of the socialist movement: it does not consciously follow this course; rather, it aspires to the pursuit of its mechanical, partisan trends. . . .

I think it is worthwhile for every one of us Jews—indeed, to feel it as an obligation upon us—to sit a moment alone, each in his own corner, to free himself of all influences, of all external influences, and from the influences of our own past in order to ask ourselves with the utmost simplicity, seriousness, and truth, this question: what essentially are we seeking in our national work? Particularly, what are we seeking in Palestine? Why should we separate ourselves from the nations among whom we have lived all our days, go far from the lands where we were born and which have left their impress upon our spirit? Why should we not participate wholeheartedly with those nations who are engaged in great work for the future of humanity? Why not completely assimilate with those nations? What hinders us? Religion in our day is no great barrier. Today one may live without religion. He who insists upon religion as a basic factor in life may hope that in the not too dim and distant future there will be complete religious freedom among the nations. To say that we cannot assimilate is sheer sophistry. Why did all the ancient people assimilate? Why cannot we, if we but will it, if we but agree to it, if we do not stubbornly oppose it with all our might? What a specious argument for supporting the idea that idle negation, an inability to die is the foundation for the existence of a nation!

In reality, we saw that assimilation among us, at least until recently, was growing stronger and stronger in spite of all this fallacious reasoning. Why then should we swim against the current? Why should we not permit the current to bear us wherever it will?

Some say, nationalism. But the question arises: what is nationalism, and what is our peculiar nationalism that is not alive and yet does not let us die? Wherein is its strength? We have no land. The language? But we have no one living language; we have several non-national tongues. Religion? But gradually religion is losing its influence—and what will those who are not religious answer? What then is this peculiar, stubborn something that one cannot put a finger on, that does not want to die and does not let us die?

It seems to me that the moment a Jew is really himself, he will not be ashamed to admit that there is within him a certain something which fights for his individual existence, which seeks a method for revealing itself in an individual form.

This is our national individuality—that cosmic moment together with the historic moment already mentioned—which is one of the fundamental principles of the personal "I" in each one of us. . . .

The cosmic moment in national independence is not ours in the Diaspora; that we must seek in Palestine. In the Diaspora the historic moment operates within us; it upholds us and prevents our dying, but it is unable to give us life. There in the Diaspora we have of necessity no national or creative life. From a creative standpoint we are parasites physically, and, perhaps, to a greater degree, spiritually. There our national individuality naturally is restricted, has shrunk, is all but destroyed. Unable to draw sustenance directly from its life-source, it necessarily feeds upon its own past, and continues to shrink more and more; or it feeds upon the life-source of others and so gradually wastes away and dies in the spirit of others. There our youth seeking some meaning in life is strongly attracted to socialism which has no cosmic moment at all; this explains the obviously astonishing phenomenon that socialism which arose out of the life of others is, in a measure, much more popular among us, has among us more enthusiastic disciples than among the nations that gave it birth and in whose midst it has, indeed, a more normal soil than among us. . . .

10. Labor

T H E redemption of the land and labor. Can you imagine that there is anyone who will not see that here there are two sides to but one question? The point is so clear, so simple—who can fail to understand this?

Our sages have said, however, that it is just the simplest of things that men accept only with the greatest difficulty. Truly one sees this very clearly in Palestine; that is, of course, if one has been endowed with clear vision. Here, for example, we see Jewish labor and hear that it is an obstacle to the revival of the Land. We find here saviors of the Land whose highest wisdom dictates the use of non-Jewish labor in the redemption of the Land. . . .

This is the language of the penny-wise, the language of the ideal of the coin, of cold figures; it is the current language of the settlements in Palestine. This is a firmly rooted ideal here, since aside from the practical and idealistic features of the proposition, it brings good returns on the investment. From this you can gather the rest.

Surely, we must be lenient in our judgment. For, no matter how bitter we may feel toward our farmers and their deeds in the present, heaven forbid that we forget what they were and what they did in the past! We must not shut our minds to the situation that we are beneficiaries of all that they did and of all that they became. . . .

A people that was completely divorced from nature, that

during 2000 years was imprisoned within walls, that became inured to all forms of life except to a life of labor, cannot become once again a living, natural, working people without bending all its will-power toward that end. We lack the fundamental element; we lack labor, but labor by which a people becomes rooted in its soil and in its culture. To be sure, not every individual among other peoples exists by labor. Many among such peoples despise labor and search for a way of life that can maintain itself on the labor of others. But the majority of a living people works in normal fashion; work is ingrained in their lives, and so it is carried on as an organic function. A living people always possesses a great majority to whom labor is its second nature. Not so among us. We despise labor. Even among our workers there are those who work because of necessity and with the continual hope of some day escaping from it and leading "the good life." We must not deceive ourselves. We must realize how abnormal we are in this respect, how alien labor has become to our spirit, and not alone to the individual life, but also to the life of the nation. . . .

To me the thing is clear and simple. All this should teach us that from now on our chief ideal must be labor. We were defeated through lack of labor—I do not say that we sinned—for we ourselves were not responsible for the situation. Work will heal us. In the centre of all our hopes we must place work; our entire structure must be founded on labor. If only we set up work itself as the ideal—rather, if only we bring into the open the ideal of labor, shall we be cured of the disease which attacked us. We shall then sew together the rents by which we were torn from nature. Labor is a lofty human ideal, an ideal of the future. A great ideal in this sense is like the healing sun. Even if it be true that history is not concerned with pointing a moral nor with disseminating knowledge, yet everyone with vision can and should learn from history. Our condition in the past, our situation in the present can teach us that we must take the lead in this— we must all work.

We have grown used to hearing the complaint that we have no longer the man-power to accomplish great deeds. What of those Jews who went to the slaughter by the thousands and tens of thousands rather than betray their people and their God? Do not say that the fathers were better than their sons, for this is not so. Those Simons and Reubens who today in Palestine are absorbed in gathering pennies while the life of their nation now hanging by a thread is of no concern whatsoever to them—these same Simons and Reubens in those terrible days in the Diaspora were the very ones who gave their lives as sacrifices for their people. For another spirit was then over them—over the whole nation. There is no need of bringing evidence of this from afar; near and very powerful evidence is at hand. These same Reubens and Simons now in Palestine—were they not different, and not so many years ago, either? Did they not themselves come here in the name of an ideal? Did they not aspire to labor and did they not work hard and undergo great suffering and make enormous sacrifices? Then a different spirit was upon them; that spirit, however, has fled.

Let us begin with the creation of a new spirit. Let us begin at the stage to which they first came and upon which we have come to lay the foundation. Let us begin and we shall find our way. . . .

11. Education and Labor

. . . THERE is a good deal of talk, possibly also much thinking among us, concerning the subject of education. Considerable information regarding the matter is being gathered; much, too, is being done in the field. But I doubt if any of it is of a creative character. (Now I emphasize education as distinct from teaching.) A very hard, a very great task confronts the teacher as educator—a far greater task than the teaching of secular or religious science. The teacher as an educator—if he really is prepared for his profession—must first of all be a philosopher with a full, individual world-outlook; that is, before he can educate man, he must know man; he cannot know man except through the man that is within him, except through his own, inner world. He must, too, be a son of nature, for his task is not alone to train man as a social and a national product, but, primarily, as a cosmic phenomenon, for as far as the pupil is concerned, his world is within himself. Education is not attained through books or through oral instruction. The educator must be the book or the living image, so that the student without any instruction from the educator must see and realize what the educator has created and creates of himself and of his talents. Such an example gives the student an idea to what he may aspire in his own development. The educator must, therefore, be alive, a man whose life is a never-ending creation. True, not every real educator can reach this goal, but it seems to me that every educator should strive toward this aim and should look upon it as an ideal governing him.

How much of life, of life from its source, could teachers draw from the labor movement in Palestine! How much thought could they pour into the movement if they but realized that the ideal of labor concerns them fully as much as it does the laborers themselves! What an influence they could wield on their environment, on their student body—a silent influence unmarked by propaganda, but an influence drawn from life itself! What spiritual sustenance this would bring to the laborers, and what power this would add to the slender movement that is so much in need of freshness and of light! But more important, a bond would be created, or would be realized, connecting the school—be it elementary or advanced—with life, for life would become a powerful influence in the school and the school, too, in turn, would influence life. We should then see the relation between labor and the university, and the subject of a university would not be so distant an objective for Palestine.

There was a time, and not so long ago at that, when all our people, young and old, knew that learning must be without thought of any ulterior motives, that learning "must not be used as a spade wherewith to dig, nor for a crown wherewith to aggrandize thyself." Not infrequently in those days did we find in an ordinary worker or in a cart-driver and such, a man learned in the Torah. Today, our people, young and old, know that learning for its own sake is a thing of the past. It is looked upon as something impractical or worse. Yet I dare ask those who can really think and feel if this ideal is only an impractical ideal? Indeed, is the purpose of education to create a "civilized" man who will seek physical and spiritual pleasure from the day's culture; that is, will he derive physical and spiritual satisfaction from accomplishments attained by others? Is not culture in itself a wealth which enriches a man so that he is forbidden to draw on what belongs to others? Or should the doubtful benefit prevail, which certain cultured men bring to the "civilized" of their own class, who then are permitted to live richer lives than those the industrious laborer of fair earning capacity can indulge in, when there are millions of people who are not allowed enough bread to eat in exchange for their labor? Should it not be the duty of the educator to influence his students rightly along these lines; especially, should they not get this from our educators who teach mainly in the name of spirit, of Judaism, of the Torah?

Regardless of what men of polished minds and of cultured souls may say, learning for its own sake is a great moral value which Judaism has esteemed and has cultivated to the highest degree. Teachers should accept this value, revive it, and make it live once more. They should impress their pupils with the clear and simple truth that learning, secular and religious, should be acquired for its own sake, that a right-minded man graduated from an intermediate or a higher school—more properly, because he has graduated—is under obligation to work and not to live on work done by others.

Here I turn to my comrades in ideals and work. They must clarify fully for themselves what their relations are toward labor. If they look upon labor as a force that must absorb the entire man, leaving him no possibility for fulfilling his higher needs, his thirst for knowledge and for art, then their idea toward labor is not the kind that will broaden, deepen, or enrich life; on the contrary, it is one that will darken and narrow it. Men with such ideas hold to the common belief that labor is a necessary evil to be avoided by those who have sufficient intellectual ability to earn a living by some easier method; labor is to be endured only by those who have no talent for finding other means of making a livelihood. But if my comrades look upon labor with the idea that it can regenerate life, then they will clearly realize that labor involves a transvaluation of values—that life demands this change, if we really wish to live. As long as we hold to the banal notion that work and culture are mutually opposed to one another, that a worker should not be a highly cultured man, and again, that a highly cultured man cannot be a laborer, then the whole philosophy of labor is worthless. What good is an ideal which does not elevate the spirit but drags it down? This we must realize: the underlying concept of labor is such that it will add to life and light, not detract from them. Labor holds that university graduates, and, in general, any educated man—even he who has received the highest form of training—ought also to work. This does not imply that whoever works should not graduate from a university or should not be a highly cultured man. True culture is of such great wealth that it should not be denied to those who work by the sweat of their brow if they are endowed with intelligence and with talent, for to such spiritual poverty is a far greater hardship than material poverty. Moreover, real culture is the light which we need to illumine the path of our ideals.

12. The Work and Revival in the Diaspora

T H E work for Palestine in the Diaspora is a pioneering task, a preparation of human material together with fund-raising for the necessary means for immediate settlement in Palestine. There is need of regeneration in whatever lands our people now live. The regeneration of the spirit and the body through physical labor, through agricultural labor more especially, the awakening of a national consciousness, of creativeness, and of the revival of the Hebrew language in speech and in thought is also a pioneering task even if its immediate objective is not Palestine.

We must grasp the idea in all its phases. Since we are torn up by the roots from Palestine, and in the Diaspora have become enslaved and persecuted, we have been alienated from nature, from living a natural form of life, and from all productive labor. Our economic and spiritual life are anomalous. Our national spirit has drawn sustenance for its life in exile only from remnants of the past or from the tables of others.

Now that we aspire to return to a national, a human and individual regeneration at one and the same time, we must correct all this, and to a great extent, create all this anew. First of all, we must of course strike roots in Palestine by means of our own labor upon its soil, and we must revive our national language. Who knows how many years, how many generations will have passed before the whole nation will return, or whether it ever as a whole will be restored to the Land? We must, therefore, be mindful, too, of our people in the Diaspora, that they also shall be regenerated and by the self-same means as in Palestine—through the return to nature, to work, and to the national language. It is essential that the Jewish people striking roots in Palestine should send the sap of life to its branches that stretch into other lands, just as those branches must transmit a part of their good to the roots which are in Palestine.

In proportion as progress in our revival advances in Palestine, to that degree will the lands of other nations lose their character of lands of exile for us. They will become lands to dwell in, lands where our people will live under the same conditions that other nationals live in countries outside their own. For at such a time, Jews dwelling in those countries will not merely be acted upon, and be influenced by others, but will in their turn act upon and influence others. Not only will this situation not turn the heart of the people of the Diaspora away from Palestine, but on the contrary, it will strengthen and deepen in their heart—in the heart of men of understanding—the need for living in Palestine, the fountain-head of our individual life, and of our creativeness.

Such conditions will be a source of blessing, a source of mutual interaction between Jews who are in Palestine and those who are in other lands; not only that—it will also be a source of influence between our nation and other nations.

The sum of all this lies here: to educate, to regenerate the Jew one must begin at the beginning—with man. The Jew cannot fully be a man without fully being a Jew. The mistake of the assimilationist comes from his thinking that the less Jew he is the more man he is. On the contrary, he is less a man—and to that very extent is he less a Jew. There is no such creature as "man" in the world. There are Russians, Germans, Englishmen, and so on. . . . And to the degree that the Jew destroys the natural Jewish foundation in his soul, he substitutes therefor an unnatural, national foundation. In other words, he becomes an unnatural Russian, German, and so on. You cannot in rebuttal cite the fact that there are assimilated Jews of great ability, for who knows how much such men would have gained in depth of soul, in originality, had they developed their Jewish foundation instead of having destroyed it?

It is obvious that even in the lands of the Diaspora, Jews must look to labor, to nature; they must strive to recreate their own lives. We should engage in all forms of labor, especially in the till-ing of the soil; we should avoid the exploitation of the labor of others; we should inject the spirit of the family into our eco-nomic life—these are the things we must strive to attain even in the Diaspora; even here there is room for Kvutzot, for Moshavei-Ovdim, and so on.

Our thinking, too, must be wholly our own, bearing the im-press of our own soul, of our Hebrew language. In the Diaspora, no less than in Palestine must we bend all our energies toward making Hebrew a living tongue—the expression of the word and the thought of the Jew—if we wish the complete regenera-tion of the nation wherever it may live. The language will be the strongest living bond between the nation in Palestine and the parts of the nation in other lands; it will be the most powerful defence against assimilation.

We should not close our eyes to the fact that Yiddish is dying out. Only a blind man, or one who deliberately shuts his eyes, can fail to see this. The various native tongues are gradually re-placing it. Youth is speaking more and more Russian, Polish, German, and so on. In America, too, where Yiddish apparently is flourishing, the second generation speaks English. The Jewish jargon persists only because of the stream of immigrants who came from lands where European culture had not penetrated all Jewish ranks. Whoever wishes to satisfy the demands of his national feeling will prefer Hebrew over Yiddish.

Is this—the renascence of the nation in the Diaspora, its trans-formation into a working, a creative people, and the revival of the Hebrew tongue among that people—is all this within the realm of the attainable? The deepest emotion responds: "Yes"—of course, in the second, third, or fourth generations. All this is difficult, perhaps in a manner hard to estimate in advance; indeed, it may not be grasped until it is seen balancing on the borders of the possible and the impossible while still remaining within the limits of the possible. Essentially, this is the nature of every-thing that serves as an object of creative effort—that it seems to rest on the borderline dividing the possible and impossible until the creative spirit renders it possible.

How bring all this about? One can say little. It is a local question to be settled by each country. All that we must realize is that it is a pioneering work. We must raise in each country of the Diaspora a pioneering movement for manual labor, particularly for farming, and for the use of the Hebrew tongue—a great, general movement, especially among the youth, not alone for Palestine, but also for those other lands. Out of such a movement will rise a steady stream toward Palestine. Those unable to go to Palestine will remain in the various lands as pioneers for work on the soil and for developing Hebrew speech. The major consideration is this: that all must work, all must learn Hebrew, especially the youth.

Very difficult is this work in the beginning. For aside from the hardships inherent in the task, it is hard for an individual to be an exception to the rule. It is not easy to fight against one's environment, against accepted public opinion, and against the attitude of the community towards one who does not follow the beaten path. When an individual who comes from a non-laboring class decides to live by the work of his own hands, he is looked upon by his community in most countries as one who stepped down from a higher level to the lowest rung of the social ladder; the community acts toward him in accordance with this judgment. And when one tries to make Hebrew his regular spoken language in the lands of the Diaspora, is he not considered by the community as very queer, if not foolish, or mad? As in all beginnings at pioneering work this is the role that must be played by the few exceptional individuals. Much, however, of this difficulty in pioneering work can be lessened when these individuals unite into one group. Such a group will slowly draw to itself those who sympathize with its aims. In this way the movement will expand from a narrow to a wide circumference; then the movement will become a living stream which will draw and bear all upon its current.

In some such form as this do I picture the work of regeneration in the lands of the Diaspora. Let no one be alarmed lest this type of work will interfere with the work for Palestine, since in any event each community is forced to be concerned with the vital task of the present in those lands. Here we are merely clarifying the point that this essential, communal work must be carried on in a form acceptable to us—in a form of regenerative work, and not in a form that maintains a state of decay.

To conclude: those who seek the revival of the nation in the lands of the Diaspora will find the path to labor in this direction, and will know what to do. Life and work will be their teachers. The major consideration is the will to turn the course of work into the channel of a truly national and human regeneration.

13. The Meaning of Religion

... RELIGION, at bottom, is the pure, the human relationship toward the essence of existence in all its phases; it is the expression of the living, eternal question; it renews itself at all times; it is a vital force guiding life. It is not a freezing, congealing element. Accordingly, the form of religion reflects the form of pure, national life. It is like an expression of lofty harmony in the national soul. It is a kind of melody that blends all voices of the soul of a nation so that they express themselves in the symphonic harmony of national life.

The feeling is sometimes realized during a national, religious festival. No other celebration, individual or communal, can attain the musical quality that pervades a national, religious festival—needless to say, when those who participate are sincerely national and religious.

Pure, natural life, a life amid nature and with nature, a life expressing the sense of higher unity and higher responsibility—this is true religion. This living expression, this expression in practice, in life, is an acknowledgment of God—a deeper acknowledgment than an intellectual one. When, for example, Buddha, the apparent atheist, demands from man and more especially from himself (and carries out that demand) conduct in accordance with a superior, ethical code—this, in itself, is an unconscious recognition of God, greater than that of an avowed believer. By and large, there is in the spiritual attitude of Buddha toward nature and toward life, more of God than is found in the faith and conduct of certain religious priests.

Religion was not clarified either by the light shed on it from ancient thought flowing from religious feeling or by the light of new thought, seemingly probing every purpose. Those engaged in clarifying the essence of religion are accustomed, for one thing, to see the focal point of their observation in the objectives of religion. Their explanation runs along these lines: to declare the existence of God is to declare the existence of religion: to negate the existence of God is to negate the existence of religion. Since there is no proof of the existence of God, positive or negative, through the power of the mind, it follows that religion is a concept suspended in mid-air—something that lacks meaning. This conclusion was reached by substituting the form of religious expression for religion itself, the insignificant for the significant. It is not unreasonable to assume that more than religion has stagnated—the concept of religion has stagnated. When we are faced by the concept of religion, we think of something fixed, static, that took shape thousands of years ago—for instance, the duty imposed on a religious believer to have faith in miracles and in marvels. All of it is tinged with something of opinions and of acts which the mind cannot accept, which cannot develop, renew itself, give rise to new thought and to a new spirit. Indeed, modern thinking relegates religion to mythology, a lullaby harking back from the childhood of the race and still able to put older children to sleep even today. In truth, these moderns consider that religion has become so antiquated that it would be a good idea to cast it out of the world as something intoxicating and corrupting.

This threadbare concept of religion and of God influences the whole trend of thought and of emotion more deeply than we are accustomed to think it does. I believe one may be permitted to say that this debased concept has greater influence than vital thought or living emotion for persuading a thinking, feeling man either with certainty or with naivete that God is dead, without realizing that it is only the outmoded, passive concept of God that is dead, not God, the Unseen, Whom he meets in everything he thinks and feels, Whom he cannot grasp, nor overtake, with Whom he deals in all he senses, thinks, speaks, yet does not know what He is or whence He came. The Unseen will never die though all the scientists definitely calculate that all is revealed, is known, is clear; that the foundation of the world is set in blindness, darkness, death, (they talk of "dead matter"); that only man lives, knows, is aware of all things. Our knowledge does not accept the idea that the foundation of the world rests in blindness or that the sense of superior responsibility is based or will persist in this concept. Hence you may conclude that religion, too, will not die while there is a human soul in the world, a sense of human responsibility, and a longing for human life.

14. Yom Kippur

I ASK myself and I wonder further if there is anyone who may be asked: what is the Day of Atonement to us, to those who do not observe religious forms?

The nation set one special day aside devoted to meditating upon itself as a nation; it set the day aside for its sons, a day for the contemplation of the self, and as members of a definite people, for weighing the values of life, for the complete devotion to the most lofty demands of the spirit of humanity. Private affairs and accounts cease—prayers and supplications for a livelihood are very few on *Yom Kippur* and *Rosh Ha-Shonah*. Important accounts and serious matters were the order of the day—accounts of national, human, and universal significance. Divisions existing among individuals were ended; the withdrawal of each person within his own sphere of interest stopped. All individuals felt themselves members of a single, sublime organism, a single nation. As units of one exalted personality, they came to take stock of themselves, with their lives, and with their world. The individual personality, the unit, grew and rose to higher levels with the growth of the exalted personality as that in turn developed with the growth of the units. Herein is the core of the matter: the individual as an individual is able to take stock of himself every day or any day he feels so disposed. But as in every national deed, especially of a religious, national character, strength is important, the strength which is increased when the individual personalities gather together. The light that is poured on that personality because of the fullness of light in the exalted personality is also significant. So, too, is the lofty melody important that is imparted to the individual voice when it blends in a sea of voices composing the sublime, human, cosmic choir.

I am not asking myself the origin of *Yom Kippur* or its ancient form. I do not ask whether the majority of the nation looked upon *Yom Kippur* from this point of view in preceding generations or whether it considers it in this light today. Facing me is a fact and a possibility. The fact is that during many generations it was a day that the whole nation dedicated to repentance, to prayer, and to heartfelt worship. It was possible for the spiritual men of the nation to make their reckoning lofty. I ask again what is the significance of this day to us, to those who do not observe the forms of their religion?

I ask: is this day for us only a heritage from the past, a remnant from antiquity? Do we not really need this day, need it but in its national form? If the day will cease being what it is, and will become an ordinary day like other days, will it not involve a great human and national loss, a decline that will entail no elevation for us, for all of us, sons of this nation?

As long as we were penned in within walls, ragged, and cut off from the great life of the world, from man, and from his broad and abundant life, we took what our ancestors bequeathed us. We had faith in it; we gave our lives for it. When the walls of the ghetto fell, when we saw the world and all that is in it at close range, when we came to know man and his life, when we received with all this what others gave us, we realized that the traditions of our fathers did not harmonize with those which grew and developed within us. Did we begin to investigate this to any extent? Did we attempt to analyze fully, to ponder deeply the question: what really has become antiquated, unsuitable; what became utterly useless or decayed? In the final analysis, did we ask: what has been obscured or obliterated in form only, while its essence is seeking a more fitting, a more noble form, since it is alive, fresh, and only aspires to a lofty regeneration?

During all our long exile we existed on the strength of our religion; we not only existed but we suffered and were sustained time and again by its power. By its strength we lived; often we lived heroically. Is it possible, can the mind entertain the possibility that such a condition is created merely out of the subtleties of the imagination? out of the ramblings of an ignorant soul without any living, fundamental core? Has the accepted idea been sufficiently examined and critically analyzed—has it been sufficiently founded in logic and in the human spirit—that with the loss of the basis for blind faith there follows also the loss of the basis of religion?

(Unfinished)

15. The Immortality of the Soul

. . . T H E man who comprehends eternity, that is, the infinity that exists in all the life of the world, both in space and in time, who sees that the very secret of existence is eternity—such a man is naturally, logically, and vitally compelled to acknowledge that he who comprehends all this, who consciously expresses all this, is also a part of the same eternity; from every point of view, he himself is eternal. If, however, the individual asking this question were free of any personal interest and inspired only to comprehend the truth and the eternity in himself and in existence, he would ask the question differently, in a more fundamental form: did his individual soul live before his birth, before his appearance into this world, in an individual form? He would then see clearly that eternity does not begin in time, for the eternity he seeks is the same eternity that was in life and in existence before his birth and will continue in the life and in existence after his death. He will realize that he, in his individual form, is only one of the waves of which eternity is composed. He would then seek eternity not after death but in his very life. He would seek the secret of eternity in the fleeting second. Human life would perhaps then take on a different content and a different form. Maybe it would then be worthwhile to live—perhaps even to die.

One of the forms of the secret yearning of man for eternity is the aspiration of the majority of mankind—especially of those who, to a certain extent, have made some imprint on life—to leave their name as a memorial in life after their death. One wishes to preserve his memory in books which he has written; another, in artistic creations; a third, in scientific discoveries, a fourth, in ideas, thoughts and opinions which he has uttered; a fifth, in deeds and accomplishments which he has performed or undertaken. The important point is that all this be sufficiently noted, emphasized, and always that it bear the name of its author. Men in all generations and for all time should know that at such a place and in such a time there lived this man who composed, created, discovered, meditated, performed, undertook a certain thing.

How petty is all this! How superficial! How long can an individual, be he ever so great, remain in the memory of generations to come, as a definite, recognized, outstanding individual? At most, a few generations, possibly a few hundred years. Beyond that, only the name remains; it makes no difference to anyone whom it designates, for, properly speaking, it has become an abstract name for an abstract personality. In the end, after thousands of years, the name becomes blurred. Doubt arises whether there ever lived such a man; perhaps his creation represents a popular, a collective expression. What man knows who Homer was, or Buddha, or Moses, and so on? Who can picture them to us in their real, living, individual, and not in their abstract form? Does not doubt arise as to their very existence? Even within the period since scientific history has been written, who can predict for us what will happen along this line when tens of thousands of years and more shall have passed? When hundreds of thousands of years, millions of years, have passed, who will mention the names of Copernicus, Spinoza, Kant, Tolstoy, and so on? What is such a number of years compared to eternity? Less than a drop in the ocean.

Here again is revealed the same fundamental viewpoint that is present in the yearning for eternity discussed above. The individual personality is a passing wave in the eternal sea of life and of existence. What is eternal in the individual personality is the hidden, vital impression that it leaves in life, that is eternal to the degree that it aids in strengthening the regenerative, the creative spirit of life. That which the individual personality leaves behind after death will influence life only to the extent that it failed in its aim during life. Further, what the individual personality leaves will affect life to the extent that it had not reached into or been accepted by the hearts and minds of its contemporaries, or to the extent that this "something" had failed to emerge from its hidden cell. One may compare this to a man who died leaving a pregnant wife that bears him a posthumous child; in a wider sense, this may be likened to those distant stars whose light reaches the earth after they are extinguished and are no longer what they were. Yet their light, too, will finally perish and die. . . .

A few more words about necrologies, and so on. Men wish to honor that which leaves them never to return; they are forced to consider that he who has left will have no further existence. All that was the "he" has gone to the source, to the eternal source of creation, and that "he" has entered into such association and such relationships as those who remain alive cannot conceive. Before them lies an eternal secret which they must treat as an eternal secret. If they wish to do him honor, that honor should be paid in silence. Let each one withdraw into his corner, to the seclusion of his own soul; let him meditate or weep in solitude over the fate of him who has passed, over the fate of all mankind. Is not this enough?

So I used to act. I have honored silently all those who have passed on, and so would I wish that others should act toward me. Those who wish to honor me, let them do it silently. For at least one year let them not speak or write aught concerning me.

Matters of which I have written should be discussed only if there yet remains in them, and to the extent that there is still in them, a living value; that is to say not a literary nor a journalistic value, but a vital value for the life that is being regenerated.

16. A Word on Differences Between Judaism and Christianity

I F one wishes to consider Judaism at its source, down to its roots, one must realize this especial phase of it: that everything —morality, religion, all the world of man—depends on the idea that man is created in the "image of God." "And God created man in His image, in the image of God created He him. Male and female, He created them." This is the spinal cord of Judaism.

One need not seek far, if one wishes the truth, to find that everything of real value in Christian morality is in its essence entirely Jewish. That which was in Judaism a mystery, a thing given to the heart of each man, became in Christianity a revealed fate, a clear manifestation, a minted coin.

The difference that marks the two in the ethical field is also to be found in the religious sphere. The revelation of God in "Thou shalt not look upon any idols," and the revelation of God in the form of man who himself is to bear the sins of humanity, differentiates clearly the two faiths. Christianity constricts man, constricts the image of God, by constricting God and the absolute unity of God. God needed an aid, and man a mediator between himself and his Creator. Man became a wretched creature, neither able nor given the right to help himself in seeking for his improvement. An exalted life is given to man ready-made; this he must accept as it is handed down to him. Judaism, on the other hand, sees the exalted life of man achieved through the very labor required to gain this state, through his very attempts to pave the road that is to lead to his goal. For life also is a complete unit; therefore, an active search for a higher life is a higher life.

The difference is obvious in the primary principle given to man by the two religions as a basic rule by which man must govern his practical life. Christianity lays this down as a first principle in the form of a great affirmation than which there is nothing greater, in the form of an exalted love which, in reality, is the Biblical command: "Thou shalt love thy neighbor as thyself." This in Judaism comes as a positive conclusion from the negative admonition which preceded it in: "Thou shalt not steal," and, too, "Thou shalt not hate thy brother in thy heart." "Thou shalt not seek revenge, nor bear enmity against him." Here is an outburst of light, rising from the spirit after it had been purified of the imperfections of life to the end that: "And thou shalt love thy fellow-man as thyself." In clearer form it was handed down by Christianity as a dominating principle, a something definite which is neither followed nor preceded by anything else, a condition which requires no preparation and is not capable of any further development.

During that very same period Judaism put into the mouth of its Hillel an utterance as a foundation for all its law, a very simple rule in the form of a light negative: "What is hateful to you, thou shalt not do unto your fellow-man . . . Everything else is a commentary. Go and acquire knowledge."

The ethics of Judaism is expressed not only in the first and most important part of the rule: "What is hateful to you, thou shalt not do unto your fellow-man," but also in its second part: "Everything else is a commentary. Go and acquire knowledge!" Go, thou, complete your study; perfect yourself.

Whether Hillel considered it to be so or not, this is the chief characteristic of Judaism as distinguished from Christianity which gives to man a fixed, an established faith. Here in the entire relationship to the heathen who came to ask him the law of life, one feels a powerful yet modest spiritual loftiness. You sense in all the devotion of Hillel to the written and to the traditional law, in all his recognition of the need a person has who comes to live in accordance with those conditions, and to learn the law governing that life, that in the end the most important principle in his eyes is the free-will of man which molds life, that free-will is life itself and therefore the law of life; and secondly, in "Go and acquire knowledge!" you realize that you yourself can create the form; you yourself can attain the state of: "My body I gave to those who smote me and my cheek to those who plucked off the hair," or you can attain to an even higher estate. But you will attain it yourself. Such words are not at all a command, for they are the entire content of life, the full creation of a man's life in his own way and according to his own loftier image. It is no wonder, then, that Judaism has never been rightly understood, especially since Christianity has apparently revealed to mankind a great light—such a light as the world had not seen before.

Judaism seems to impart a light hidden in many lanterns, one within the other. Man's life-work is to take the light out of each lantern and reveal it gradually. At first, man sees the light only in accordance with the strength of his own eyes, but he knows the light is hidden and he must open and remove one lantern after the other. This work is difficult. Judaism really gives man certain rules, but these are in the main rules of preparation, rules in a negative form, rules warning man how to keep away from all forms of contamination. For the task is very delicate and requires that the tools for the task—thought, feeling—be absolutely pure. The task is hard. Judaism tells us that the Torah was begotten in pain, but it represents to the full the life of its spirit, and life teaches man. He thereupon opens and removes lantern after lantern, and by so doing, accustoms his eyes to the light. Then, with all his entire being he adapts himself fully to the growing light and learns how to govern his life by it.

What has Christianity done? It has taken the hidden light out of all the lanterns and has given it to anyone who seems to want it. Everyone shouted: "Light, light!" At first it seemed to the near-sighted ones that redemption had really come to wretched humanity. The results, however, are well known. Eyes unaccustomed to the light became blind. In place of feeling and thought, there came imagination and words. The will that could not adapt itself flared up so that it burned alive all who were not inspired in the same way. It taught man in the name of a supreme love to plant falsehood and hate with all their concomitants.

Christianity admits that man lives in the world to fulfill the Supreme Will. This is the whole content of the life of man. Love for all men and for all living creatures is also, in truth, an expression of that same attitude of complete self-denial of the human ego before the Supreme Will; hence, the altruism, the substitution of one's own ego for another's, properly speaking, for the fulfillment of the Supreme Will in contrast to all individualism whether personal or national. Here, too—out of this passivity—comes the theory of non-opposition to evil. This is not the same as feeling the evil of another, of feeling his misfortune, his ugliness as if it were a very defect in one's own soul, as if it were your own pain, seeking neither revenge nor hate, but suffering, and seeking a remedy, or feeling that the only remedy lies in secret sorrow. In not opposing evil, you feel a sense of security or so it should be, for this has been decreed by the Supreme Will which knows better than man what is good and what is evil. Only the passive will, in sight of the Supreme Will, can influence for good the doer of evil.

It is clear that this absolute self-denial, this thorough obliteration of the human form was bound to arouse in Christianity itself an internal rebellion. When the modern age dawned with its exact science and free, clear thought, it generated many opposing currents, among them radical currents.

But the hypnosis of hatred for the Jew arising from a sacred source, from the source of Supreme Love, is so great that instead of placing the basic contradiction where it belongs, Christianity lays it at the door of Judaism. In general, it is not difficult to see that in those cases where Christianity comes to prove and to reveal the weakness of Judaism, it only uncovers and proves, in reality, the weakness of Christianity.

Judaism teaches that man is primarily an active force—that is his human form—and not a force acted upon. Man, all mankind, creates the world in the image of God and fulfills his mission in life by exalting his essence to the highest degree. As the purpose of man does not lie in self renunciation, but in the exaltation of this self, so also is the purpose of life. This purpose of life, then, is neither monasticism nor asceticism but purification, naturalness, and sanctification.

This attitude gives rise to the deep and constant anxiety for purity in the family relationship and for the hard struggle against perverted sexual desires. Not without cause does this struggle go on, for sexual desire and all that it involves, all the relationships it fosters form a Gordian knot within which are united and entangled the most delicate and the coarsest threads of man's life, a fact that is known to everyone who is familiar with the psychology of man and his life. Here lie the weakness and the strength, the impurity and the holiness of man; here, rightly considered, are the roots of many, many phenomena of man's life and spirit—negative and positive phenomena which seem far distant from this sphere.

I am not here to decide that Judaism has completely solved the problem or cut this knot. In truth, it is a matter of the spirit of man bound, to a great extent, to the body of man, to his physical make-up, whether that be healthy or not. On the whole, this is one of the chief, one of the greatest and deepest questions of the world—perhaps, if I may say so, one of the riddles of the world.

To the extent, however, that it is possible to solve this problem by a national and religious formula, especially when one considers that the solution was given at a time when other nations living within the same region were all of them plunged in lewdness—in their faith and their religion—it is permissible to conclude that Judaism gave the most correct and the most beautiful solution to this problem.

In truth, we have also seen that this family purity—that of the man as well as of the woman—was strictly observed by the Jews through all misfortune and persecution down to the present generations, the generations marked by imitation and self-abasement.

Deep and pure love does not cease with marriage, but in reality it actually begins with marriage. It is not correct to say that this pure, profound human emotion dies or that it never existed, that its foundation lies only in the imagination. The superficial attitude towards the tender feeling causes it to fade, to become weakened because it is wasted, penny by penny, before a suitable mate is found. . . .

FOR FURTHER READING
Books about Aaron David Gordon

"Aaron David Gordon" in *Encyclopedia Judaica*, Volume 2: pp. 790–793, (Jerusalem: 1972). Includes a biography with excellent overview of his philosophy.

HERTZBERG, Arthur, in *The Zionist Idea*, pp. 368–386, (New York: Atheneum, 1977). Includes an introductory essay and translations of six central essays.

SELTZER, Robert M., *Jewish People, Jewish Thought* (New York: Macmillan, 1980). Although there is just a brief description of Gordon's works, this book provides excellent background material.

GONEN, Jay Y., *A Psychohistory of Zionism* (Mason/Charter, 1975). Includes several fascinating references to A.D. Gordon.

ABRAHAM ISAAC KUK

(1865–1935)

EDITOR'S NOTE

Abraham Isaac Kuk, the first Chief Rabbi of Palestine, a leading Jewish mystic and Orthodox religious thinker, is by now a legend in Israel. His passionate love for *Eretz Yisrael*, the holiness which he saw in the Jewish nationalist movement, his broad sense of tolerance for the non-religious *halutzim* (pioneers), and his recognition of their contribution to the upbuilding of the land, endeared him to all segments of the Palestinian community.

Kuk was born in 1865 and grew up in a typical small town in northwestern Russia. He served for several years as rabbi in the town of Boisk where he urged Orthodox Jews to support the idea of a return to Zion. In 1904 he himself settled in the Holy Land, serving as rabbi of Jaffa and the surrounding agricultural settlements. While on a visit to Europe in 1914 the World War broke out and Kuk had to remain in Europe until the end of hostilities. In 1919 he accepted the invitation to become Chief Rabbi of Jerusalem, and in 1921 he was chosen to be Chief Rabbi of all Palestine.

Kuk's writings are even less systematic than those of Gordon. His books consist of thoughts, *pensées*, epigrams and a series of jottings on various phases of Jewish religion and nationalism. They often express a mood, rather than analyze a problem, and at times are difficult to understand.

Kuk wrote many works, a number of which are as yet unpublished. Except for occasional selections, most of his books have not been translated from the Hebrew. They cover a wide range of subjects from technical *halakhic* problems to rhapsodic expressions about God, man, redemption, national survival, the land of Israel, literature and art.

We begin with several passages in which he describes some of the elements of the mystical experience—the sense of unity, the experience of freedom and the resolution of conflicts. Kuk portrays the inner life of the spirit as the living source of constant creation, of flashes of insight. The path to mystical enlightenment alternates between radiance and darkness, joy and travail, exhilaration and depression. In the mystical experience there is a heightened sense of being alive in the midst of a vast and vibrant world.

We then turn to his world view which is not a systematic philosophy but a depiction of religious consciousness. The love of God is the basis of Kuk's thought. He is not concerned with proofs for the existence of God but rather with the testimony of faith. God is essentially the Unknowable. He is the center toward whom all energies and thoughts are directed.

Kuk's faith in God led him to a belief in progress. He could see no limit to the ultimate achievements of mankind. In poetic language he affirms the worth of the human being and the human soul. In spite of new scientific discoveries, he believed man to be the focus of the expanding and growing universe.

The third selection deals with the concept of prayer which, Kuk feels, is an "absolute necessity for us and for the whole world." Man's soul is in a constant state of worship. It longs for the spiritual enoblement and ultimate perfection which God has made possible for us.

The rituals and practices of Judaism, however, are based not only on a love of God, but also on a love of Israel. Kuk was an ardent Jewish nationalist. To him, feelings of national loyalty were as sacred as religious impulses. The whole nation at Sinai agreed to keep the Torah and there are, therefore, nationalistic as well as religious reasons for observing the *mitzvot*. They give the Jewish people its distinctiveness and help the nation to survive. Kuk, therefore, appealed to secular Jewish nationalists to observe the customs of Israel because of their reverence and affection for the nation.

For Kuk, there is an undying love in the heart of the Jew for his land—a love which existed even before Israel became a nation. *Eretz Yisrael* therefore is an organic part of Jewish nationhood. It is not merely an instrument for establishing national unity, but is the only place where the original creativity of the Jew can reassert itself. As Buber has pointed out, no one among the interpreters of Jewish nationalism understood the uniqueness and eternity of the relationship between the Jewish people and their land as did Kuk. For him it is a "land of holiness" which has a unique power to transform the Jew. Here thoughts are purer, the imagination clearer and the mind prepared for holiness.

Israel has a special genius for holiness and the world is waiting for what Kuk called the "light of Israel." To him God chose the Jewish people to "cleanse the whole world from all impurity and darkness."

In our final selection, Kuk reasserts the fact that Israel is a chosen people, different from all other nations. Though there is a spiritual decline in our time from the holiness of the past and the Jews of the Diaspora have become alienated, the return to the Holy Land would renew Israel's holiness. Kuk regarded his own era as the first stage in the final redemption of the Jewish people.

17. The Experience of Mysticism

Expanses, expanses
Expanses divine, my soul doth crave.
Enclose me not in cages,
Of matter or mind.
Thru heavenly vastness my soul doth soar
Unfenced by walls of heart
Or walls of deed—
Of ethics, logic or mores—
Above all these it soars and flies,
Above the expressible and nameable,
Above delight and beauty.
Exalted and ethereal.
Lovesick am I—
I pant, I pant for my Lord,
As a deer for river banks.
Oh, who can my anguish relate?
Who lyre be, to sing my agony,
To voice my bitterness,
The endless pain of expression?
I thirst for truth, not concepts of truth.
Lo, I ride above the heavens,
Wholly absorbed within the truth
Wholly pained by travail of expression;
How can I the great truth articulate
Which my heart overfills?
Who can to multitudes uncover,
To nations and individuals
The total fulness that is creation,
The sparks of light and warmth

Which my soul doth contain.
I see those flames arising.
Bursting thru all firmaments.
Who perceives them?
Who of their vigor can relate?
I am not one of God's elected heroes,
That found all worlds within them
And did not care if others
Their riches knew or not.
These herds of sheep that walk erect,
Will it matter if they know the height of man?
Is then aught harmed by ignorance?
But, I am to this world enchained.
The living, they are my friends.
My soul with them is interwined;
How then illumination share with them?
For all that I relate
Doth only hide my radiance,
Becloud my inner light.
Thus, great is my pain and anguish.

*   *   *

Mystical apprehension is founded on the inner conviction of almightiness, the absence of limitation on the possibilities of infinite power. Objective cognition is, on the other hand, built on the knowledge of the limitation of power in accordance with the circumstances in which power manifests itself in this world. In each sphere, the form of one or the other cognition enjoys absolute sovereignty. There is no limit to one's power in the inner world; there is no freedom in the outer physical world.

*   *   *

In every second, in the smallest instant of time, we create, consciously and unconsciously, an endless multitude of creations; if we can only learn to perceive them, bring them within the borders of clear cognition, accustom ourselves to include them within the framework of expression suitable for them, then their splendor and majesty will be revealed and their power in all the phases of life will become visible.

*   *   *

For in them the secret of the higher life is revealed; all rational labor, all systematic work, all laws and judgments, religious precepts and verdicts, profound conceptions and maxims of logic derive the spirit of their life only from the shadows of the shadows of the radiance of these great flashes.

* * *

Thereupon, there follows the recognition, how everything is dark and devoid of any value in comparison with the light of the Infinite; how the endless depths which separate the Creator from the created render seemingly impossible any kind of relation between them. Then everything is dried up and emptied of meaning.

And out of this travail of the soul and out of this deep insight into the nothingness of all things and the majestic fulness of their Source and the power of the exalted existence of the Supreme Light, its positive phases and its brightness begin to fill all the chambers of his soul. . . . And he begins to ascend, the confidence of his soul and the sense of the eternity of his life is intensified and he is uplifted to higher spheres, until he recognizes his frustration and wretchedness, and, with a broken spirit, he succumbs to despair; thereupon, the spirit returns to shine for him. It comes and goes like flashes of lightning.

* * *

All being whispers a secret to me: I have life, take, please take —if you have a heart and in the heart there is blood, that the poison of despair has not sullied;

But, if thy heart be uncircumsized and my beauty holds no charm for you—Being whispers to me—away, away from me, forbidden am I to thee!

If every gentle twitter, every flash of beauty, not the splendor of holy song but the stream of foreign fire in thee arouse—away, away from me, forbidden am I to thee.

And a living generation will arise
That will sing to beauty and life;
And youth without end
From the dew of heaven will derive.

And a living people will attend to the flow of the secrets of being from the splendors of Karmel and the Sharon, and out of the tenderness of song and the beauty of life—the light of holiness will rise to overflowing; And all being will murmur to him, My chosen one, I am for thee intended!

18. World View

God

The essence of our knowledge of the Deity is this: that He is One, the Creator and the Revealer of Commandments. And all the varied faculties of the spirit are only so many aids to the solution and the detailed description of this knowledge; their purpose is to clarify it and present it in a form that will be at once the most ideal, noble, rational, practical, simple and exalted.

How shall man obtain a conception of the majesty of the Divine, so that the innate splendor residing within his soul may rise to the surface of consciousness, fully, freely, and without distortion? Thru the expansion of his scientific faculties; thru the liberation of his imagination and the enjoyments of bold flights of thought; thru the disciplined study of the world and of life; thru the cultivation of a rich, multifarious sensitivity to every phase of being. All these desiderata require obviously the study of all the branches of wisdom, all the philosophies of life, all the ways of the diverse civilizations and the doctrines of ethics and religion in every nation and tongue.

*　　*　　*

I'm filled with love to God;
I know, my heart's desire,
My innermost love,
Isn't called by any name.
How can a name call forth,

What's more than even All,
More than the Good,
More than the Substance,
More than the Being.
And I so love,
I say, I do, do love
The Lord of all.
He dwells, the Endless Light,
In human names
Expressions given Him,
Articulations and designations,
When man's soul is uplifted on high.
I cannot sate my soul
With love that comes from logic's bonds,
From worldly search and research
In light of existence,
To human eyes revealed.
Within our souls lights divine arise
In multiform shapes, according to our minds.
The One, Eternal Truth,
Before the One,
In depths of Holy Truth,
Revealed is He.
Within us dominant,
Ruling our inner soul,
The soul of all creation.

*   *   *

Progress

The world is destined to rise above the need of cultivating the
soil, which, in its present form, bears the aspect of the ancient
curse. . . . The spirit of man will rise and the earth will respond with the great blessing of abundant fruitfulness, so that
"loaves of bread and garments of silk will spring out of the
ground," and the varied toils of man will assume a more refined
aspect.

Symbolic of this ascent is the light revealed in the observance
of *Shemittah*, the Sabbath of the land, when no toil is permitted,
all competition between men ceases, the blessing of God thru
the fruit of the soil is sufficient unto all men and the human heart
recognizes the confraternity of all living creatures. Indeed, both
the Jubilee and *Shemittah* years are heralds of a new world, which

is not yet ready; they foretell a higher good, deriving from the illumination of a higher spirituality.

It is reasonably to be inferred that there is a spark in every soul which aspires ever upward and is uplifted thru the light of exalted grace that flows down perpetually. . . . Every universal ideal has its soul, which is progressively uplifted. . . .

The world is always being uplifted because its roots are constantly being filled with the light of wisdom. . . .

Understandably, there is a higher force which impels it to ascend—a force the action of which began when it was still contained within its source, before the descent into reality. And the observed evolution from the bottom upward is one phase of the general phenomenon of all creation treading the path of Repentance.

*   *   *

The Soul

The soul sings all the time; joy and sweetness are her garments; highminded tenderness envelops her. Man must raise himself to the heights of the loftier reaches of his soul, learn to recognize her spirit-steps and her wing flaps that are filled with the majesty of the holy of holies. Let him be ever on the alert, to listen to her message of holiness. . . .

The soul thinks without thought, acts without action. Thru her, only thru her do we ascend the steps, to which all the secret depths of the life of existence impel us. Then shalt thou delight thyself in the Lord! This is the secret of the thirst and the mystery of the satisfaction.

It is possible to feel the motions of the soul that in its hidden depths is joined unto the exalted worlds, whence it derives the secret of its life, its radiance and its splendor.

The more one sanctifies himself, removing himself from sin and inclining himself to nobility and spirituality, the more his soul reveals itself to him; its light begins to suffuse his inner being; he becomes conscious of an irresistible demand issuing out of his whole self to isolate himself in the source of his life.

In the body, the soul is not enclosed, but held, as by the end of a shoe string, like a bird capable of traversing the heavens, that is held back by a thin silken thread.

*   *   *

Behold how much truth and poetry there is in the phenomenon of the centrality of the soul of man in relation to all of being. This phenomenon is by no means lessened by the discovery of the vast and infinite dimensions of the cosmos, the starry universes, the constantly evolving nebulae; on the contrary, this poetry is enriched and enlarged thru this vastness and magnificence. Wherever the light of life is revealed to cognition, there is an embodiment of ethical and esthetic aspiration, and the center is revealed.

*   *   *

19. On Prayer

PRAYER is the ideal of all the worlds. All of being aspires toward the source of its life; every flower and blade of grass, every grain of sand and clod of earth; the things which throb visibly with life and those in which life is concealed; the smallest beings of creation and the largest, the angels and holy seraphs of heaven, all the particularity of being and all its universality—everything longs and aspires, craves and yearns for the perfection of its high, holy, pure and mighty Source. Man absorbs all these yearnings at all times and occasions, becoming thru them uplifted and ennobled in holy desire. When the time comes for the unfolding of the sacred desires in prayer, waves of light issue in freedom and holy reflection to the wide expanses of the divine. Man uplifts all creation with himself in prayer, unites all being with himself, uplifts and exalts the All to the source of blessing and the source of life.

Prayer is an absolute necessity for us and for the whole world, also the most sacred kind of joy; the waves of our soul beat ceaselessly on the shores of consciousness. We desire of ourselves and of the world the kind of perfection that the limitations of existence render impossible of attainment. In our despair and frustration we may turn against our better judgment and against our Creator. But before this cancer of the spirit has had time enough to grow in our midst, we come to pray. We give utterance to our thoughts and uplift ourselves to a world of absolutely perfect existence. Then our inner world too is rendered absolutely perfect in truth, and restful joy fills our consciousness. . . .

The source of fear is the awareness of limitation, of the inexorable laws which determine the character of the world, bringing all things to their destined aim and purpose. This awareness brings to mind the glory of the Creator incarnated in the fulness of His worlds; thence, the mind moves on to contemplate the quality of freedom of the human individual, which makes it possible for man to wander in confusion in the realm of action, marring and destroying the beauty and majesty of the processes of the universe. Thereupon, a fear of action descends upon the worshipper which deepens into a fear of greatness, an awe of the heavenly majesty; this mood grows in exaltation by degrees, reaching down to the roots of the soul, softening the hard quality of coarse matter and adjusting one's life to the absorption of the gentle sweetness of the light of holiness, in the fulness of its splendor, in accordance with the extent of the soul and its capacity. Now the worshipper is prepared to take another step on the road of exaltation, to contemplate the nature of the unlimited, the light of holiness which surrounds the eternal worlds, without measure and limitation; to behold where the light of true Grace dwells and whence it flows to all the corners of existence, dispensing goodness and blessing, light and life, and lending sweetness and holy splendor to every action and gesture that it inspires. Then, love appears. . . .

When we desire any object in prayer, we must bear in mind that our intention is to remove darkness and evil from the world and to strengthen the goodness and light of the fulness of Divine life; the appearance of which does not merely correct one fault, but all faults and all defects for all failings are remedied by it; in the exaltation of our soul, we desire only complete and absolute perfection.

20. The Rituals of Judaism

T H E whole hierarchy of Jewish law and custom, including the extra burdens of rabbinic ordinances and folkways which the Jewish people voluntarily assumed, is the detailed expression of the inner love of the people of Israel to the Name of God, the Torah, the nationhood and the land of Israel—all of which are inseparably intertwined. Inner love and sacred yearning seek to expand and break out thru whatever channels are close at hand. The most natural way to express religious feeling among the people of Israel is to impress the seals of love, joy, reverence, and pious trust on the forms and ways of personal and group life. This was the genuine feeling of the nation as a whole, from the beginning until the end, so long as its spirit was healthy and strong; its custodian is the vital and virile part of the nation, the geniuses of piety and learning. The Torah and all its commandments in their minutest details, as expressed in thought and deed, form a great and mighty Divine poem, a poem of confident trust and love. Every commandment and law has a unique musical quality that the congregation of Israel perceives and appreciates. It evokes the blossoms of reverent joy and song within us. It is for us to remove the warts from the ears of our sons, "the thorns and thistles that surround the noble flower," so that the waves of song will echo in their hearts as well, uplifting their souls with the same natural exaltation that is common to all in whom the spirit of Judaism is properly developed.

Thus, we observe lovingly the customs of Israel that have no basis in Divine Revelation, because of our reverence and affection for our nation—an affection that is sacred, derived from a high, divine source. The basic principle in the observance of the commandments of our Sages is the fact that the whole nation has accepted them, so that the honor of the nation, its historical influence and its eternal, divine quality are incarnate in them. Therefore, whatever is more ancient is more beloved since the will and the general character of the nation are revealed in it.

In the heart of every single Jew there is hidden a wonderful vital force, which impels him to attach himself to his nation, the life stream of which flows within him. This subconscious impulse makes him share the powerful yearning of the national soul for the pure and uplifting light of truth and divine equity—a yearning that cannot but find its fulfillment in time in the actual world. All practices, commandments and customs are nothing but so many vessels, containing a few sparks of this great light from above, and in proportion to the spiritual power inherent in these vessels, their purity and fitness in thought and their exactitude in expression—the light concealed in them grows and expands.

21. Sacred and Secular

W E have two overall values in life: the sacred and the secular. We in our own era, suffer from the malady of such exaggerated overemphasis of the secular that it spreads over the entire breadth of life and darkens the sacred light within us. The concept of the sacred has become so weak among members of this generation that it has become synonymous for them, with every image of feebleness and weakness; while in truth, all power and all strength can only be found stored within it.

This malady of severing the concept of the sacred from thought and from life, attached itself, to our sorrow, with the noble movement with which we live in our time—the movement of national rebirth, Zionism and its branches. To begin with, individuals came with a great deal of spirit in them, but who, nevertheless, in their lives, were detached from the foundations of the sacred in Israel, and with the power of the secular concepts of national values which were close to their hearts and minds, they enlarged, broadened and deepened the idea of return to Zion and the national rebirth and Zionism. While there was sufficient strength in that secular concept to be the subject of publication, of propaganda, and of the winning of adherents in a certain sense for a limited time, the secular could not endow eternal life by any means. And therefore after a relatively short period of time passed for the movement in its secular form, we already sense in it, despite its enlargement, an air of dessication and disintegration. We sense the pangs of this ailment, the secular sickness that has spread in a frightening form through the entire breadth of our movement of rebirth.

It is understood that if this movement were secular by nature, the elimination of the sacred from its values would not have affected it, just as it does not affect many other secular groups and movements in the world. But since the source and foundation of the movement and our entire national rebirth comes, in truth, from the sacredness of the holy of holies when it emanates from the source of holiness and is based on the whole foundation of the holiness of the people, the holiness of the land and the holiness of its soul which draws from the word of God which is in the Torah—the source of all sacred values in the world and life —then its secular content is not suitable for it and does not measure up to its quality or character and therefore we feel weakness in all the parts and branches of our movement, all the more after the passing of several years since its initial appearance.

While the secular is able to serve the sacred, to strengthen and to bolster it, to prepare and give it a firm foundation in the practicalities of life, heaven forbid, that it oversteps its bounds and stands in its place.

A bitter error is committed by those theorists who think that the new national movement will suffice for us in place of the sacred, and therefore are prepared to expel from their homes the sacred or to enlarge the secular concepts over the sacred. This is a deception that will never take root and will be unable to find a position of permanence for generations, not among the life of Jews or among life in general, not in the purview of the congregation of Israel and not in the purview of the great thinkers of Israel and the people of spirit among the nations.

The sacred must return to its status in our national Zionist movement, for only with it is the source of life. And then, too, it will revive through its strength, the secular values which were prepared and will be prepared to be of support. And this will be the path of repentance which will cure us from our sickness and will bring closer to complete redemption speedily and in our time. Amen.

22. The Land of Israel

E R E T Z Yisrael is not something apart from the soul of the Jewish people; it is no mere national possession, serving as a means of unifying our people and buttressing its material, or even its spiritual, survival. Eretz Yisrael is part of the very essence of our nationhood; it is bound organically to its very life and inner being. Human reason, even at its most sublime, cannot begin to understand the unique holiness of Eretz Yisrael; it cannot stir the depths of love for the land that are dormant within our people. What Eretz Yisrael means to the Jew can be felt only through the Spirit of the Lord which is in our people as a whole, through the spiritual cast of the Jewish soul, which radiates its characteristic influence to every healthy emotion. This higher light shines forth to the degree that the spirit of divine holiness fills the hearts of the saints and scholars of Israel with heavenly life and bliss.

To regard Eretz Yisrael as merely a tool for establishing our national unity—or even for sustaining our religion in the Diaspora by preserving its proper character and its faith, piety, and observances—is a sterile notion; it is unworthy of the holiness of Eretz Yisrael. A valid strengthening of Judaism in the Diaspora can come only from a deepened attachment to Eretz Yisrael. The hope for the return to the Holy Land is the continuing source of the distinctive nature of Judaism. The hope for the Redemption is the force that sustains Judaism in the Diaspora; the Judaism of Eretz Yisrael is the very Redemption.

Jewish original creativity, whether in the realm of ideas or in the arena of daily life and action, is impossible except in Eretz Yisrael. On the other hand, whatever the Jewish people creates in Eretz Yisrael assimilates the universal into characteristic and unique Jewish form, to the great benefit of the Jewish people and of the world. The very sins which are the cause of our exile also pollute the pristine wellspring of our being, so that the water is impure at the source. Once the unique wellspring of Israel's individuality has become corrupt, its primal originality can express itself only in that area of loftiest universal creativity which belongs to the Jew—and only in the Diaspora, while the Homeland itself grows waste and desolate, atoning for its degradation by its ruin. While the life and thought of Israel is finding universal outlets and is being scattered abroad in all the world, the pristine well of the Jewish spirit stops running, the polluted streams emanating from the source are drying up, and the well is cleansing itself, until its original purity returns. When that process is completed, the exile will become a disgust to us and will be discarded. Universal Light, in all its power, will again radiate from the unique source of our being; the splendor of the Messiah who is to gather in the exiles will begin to be manifest; and the bitter lament of Rachel weeping for her children will find sweet and glorious consolation. The creativity of the Jew, in all its glory and uniqueness, will reassert itself, suffused with the all-encompassing riches of the spirit of the greatest giant of humankind, Abraham, whom the Almighty called to be a blessing to man.

A Jew cannot be as devoted and true to his own ideas, sentiments, and imagination in the Diaspora as he can in Eretz Yisrael. Revelations of the Holy, of whatever degree, are relatively pure in Eretz Yisrael, outside it, they are mixed with dross and much impurity. However, the greater is one's yearning for an attachment to Eretz Yisrael, the purer his thoughts become, for they then live in the air of Eretz Yisrael, which sustains everyone who longs to behold the Land.

In the Holy Land man's imagination is lucid and clear, clean and pure, capable of receiving the revelation of Divine Truth and of expressing in life the sublime meaning of the ideal of the sovereignty of holiness; there the mind is prepared to understand the light of prophecy and to be illumined by the radiance of the

Holy Spirit. In gentile lands the imagination is dim, clouded with darkness and shadowed with unholiness, and it cannot serve as the vessel for the outpouring of the Divine Light, as it raises itself beyond the lowness and narrowness of the universe. Because reason and imagination are interwoven and interact with each other, even reason cannot shine in its truest glory outside the Holy Land.

Deep in the heart of every Jew, in its purest and holiest recesses, there blazes the fire of Israel. There can be no mistaking its demands for an organic and indivisible bond between life and all of God's commandments; for the pouring of the spirit of the Lord, the spirit of Israel which completely permeates the soul of the Jew, into all the vessels which were created for this particular purpose; and for expressing the word of Israel fully and precisely in the realms of action and idea.

In the hearts of our saints, this fire is constantly blazing up with tongues of holy flame. Like the fire on the altar of the Temple, it is burning unceasingly, with a steady flame, in the collective heart of our people. Hidden away in the deepest recesses of their souls, it exists even among the backsliders and sinners of Israel. Within the Jewish people as a whole, this is the living source of its desire for freedom, of its longing for a life worthy of the name for man and community, of its hope for redemption —of the striving toward a full, uncontradictory, and unbounded Jewish life.

This is the meaning of the Jew's undying love for Eretz Yisrael —the Land of Holiness, the Land of God—in which all of the Divine commandments are realized in their perfect form. This urge to unfold to the world the nature of God, to raise one's head in His Name in order to proclaim His greatness in its real dimension, affects all souls, for all desire to become as one with Him and to partake of the bliss of His life. This yearning for a true life, for one that is fashioned by all the commandments of the Torah and illumined by all its uplifting splendor, is the source of the courage which moves the Jew to affirm, before all the world, his loyalty to the heritage of his people, to the preservation of its identity and values, and to the upholding of its faith and vision.

An outsider may wonder: How can seeming unbelievers be moved by this life force, not merely to nearness to the universal

God, but even toward authentic Jewish life—to expressing the divine commandments concretely in image and idea, in song and deed. But this is no mystery to anyone whose heart is deeply at one with the soul of the Jewish people and who knows its marvelous nature. The source of this Power is in the Power of God, in the everlasting glory of life.

23. The Rebirth of Israel

THE world and all that it contains is waiting for the Light of Israel, for the Exalted Light radiating from Him Whose Name is to be praised. This people was fashioned by God to speak of His Glory; it was granted the heritage of the blessing of Abraham so that it might disseminate the knowledge of God, and it was commanded to live its life apart from the nations of the world. God chose it to cleanse the whole world of all impurity and darkness; this people is endowed with a hidden treasure, with the Torah, the means by which the Heaven and the Earth were created.

The Light of Israel is not a utopian dream, or some abstract morality, or merely a pious wish and a noble vision. It does not wash its hands of the material world and all its values, abandoning the flesh, and society and government to wallow in their impurity, and forsaking the forces of nature, which fell in the Fall of Man, to remain in their low estate. It is, rather, a raising of all of life.

No people has yet grown sufficiently in mind and spirit to be able to appreciate the sacredness of the universe, the joy in God's greatness, the enthronement of Creation from its very beginning to its very end, completely enveloped, as the world is, by the infinite goodness, the mighty strength, and the perfect purity of the One God.

All the peoples, as we well know, are under the influence of their varying civilizations. We know the exact value of each; we can estimate how much of light and darkness are intermingled in their respective ideals and aspirations. In the course of our history we have conquered the most oppressive and sinister forces of paganism, and we are now engaged in overcoming lesser manifestations of the darkness.

An ancient Jewish heresy, in which pagan influence was present, announced the abolition of the specific commandments of the Torah, while it haughtily and magniloquently took over religious and ethical values from Judaism. Such darkness stems from the inability of the non-Jewish mind to grasp the full meaning of the splendor of the exalted Divine order, which unites Heaven and Earth, body and soul, creed and deed, image and action, individual and society, this world and the world to come, the beginning and the end of Creation, the grandeur of eternity and the joy of Heaven and Earth and all their hosts. But a time will come when even the lowest of the world's depths will be cleansed of its filth, even the worst of its crookednesses will be set straight, and even the slightest perversion will be corrected. Then light will shine for the righteous.

The world of the gentiles is tattered and rent. In its view the body is divided from the soul, and there is no inner bond and identity between matter and spirit, no basic unity between action and idea. At present, before the Light of Israel becomes manifest, the doctrine of Communism represents the highest spiritual ascent of gentile culture. But how poor is a world in which this black evil has raised its head and pretends to be its highest aspiration. What a treasure chest of wickedness is hidden in this most fearful lie, which has such a dangerous exterior sheen of purity! How pitiable are the spiritual streams out of the Jewish world of true holiness which are pouring into this swamp of wickedness! How much more incandescent the Light will have to become in order to redeem the rays which have fallen into darkness! But they will be redeemed, once and for all, with the redemption of the Holy People.

Redemption is continuous. The Redemption from Egypt and the Final Redemption are part of the same process, "of the mighty hand and outstretched arm," which began in Egypt and is evident in all of history. Moses and Elijah belong to the same redemptive act; one represents its beginning and the other its culmination, so that together they fulfill its purpose. The spirit of Israel is attuned to the hum of the redemptive process, to the sound waves of its labors which will end only with the coming of the days of the Messiah.

It is a grave error to be insensitive to the distinctive unity of the Jewish spirit, to imagine that the Divine stuff which uniquely characterizes Israel is comparable to the spiritual content of all the other national civilizations. This error is the source of the attempt to sever the national from the religious element of Judaism. Such a division would falsify both our nationalism and our religion, for every element of thought, emotion, and idealism that is present in the Jewish people belongs to an indivisible entity, and all together make up its specific character.

But, mistaken as is the attempt to divide these indivisible components of the Jewish spirit, it is an even greater error to imagine that such a sundering could possibly succeed; it is, therefore, pointless to wage a bitter and ill-conceived war against those who are loyal to only one aspect of the Jewish character. If the only bar to separating the various spiritual elements that are present within the congregation of Israel were that this is prohibited by the law of the Torah, then we would indeed be dutybound to resist this to the very end. But since such a sundering is an absolute impossibility, we can rest assured that its protagonists can err only in theory, but not in practice. No matter what they may think, the particular element of the Jewish spirit that they may make their own, being rooted in the total life of our people, must inevitably contain every aspect of its ethos.

Our quarrel with them must be directed only to the specific task of demonstrating their error and of proving to them that all their effort to fragmentize the higher unity of Israel is foredoomed to failure. We who represent the integrity of the Jewish will and spirit must react in a deeply natural way, by merely analyzing the opposing positions to show that any individual element of the Jewish spirit cannot help but include all the values that the "sunderers" hope to forget and destroy. Once this truth is established, our opponents will ultimately have to realize that they were wasting their efforts. The values they attempted to banish were nonetheless present, if only in an attenuated and distorted form, in their theories, and the result of their labors could only be spiritual hunger, narrowed horizons, and the loss of any true sense of direction. One path alone will then be open to our adversaries; to acknowledge the truth proved by experience and to cleave to the entire living and holy content of the fully manifest Light of Israel. Their souls will then no longer be tortured by nebulous and ghostlike ideas from which they could neither free themselves nor find in them clear illumination of the spirit. They will then realize that nationalism, or religion, or any other element of the spirit of Israel, can realize itself only in the context of a Jewish life that is full, stirring, and entirely true to every shade of its essence.

24. Lights for Rebirth

O U R national life, both intrinsically and in its relationship to all mankind, has had a long career. We have existed for a long time, and we have, therefore, expressed ourselves in many ways. We are a great people, and our mistakes are equally great; therefore, our woes and the consolations to follow them are both on the grand scale.

It is a fundamental error to turn our backs on the only source of our high estate and to discard the concept that we are a chosen people. We are not only different from all the nations, set apart by a historical experience that is unique and unparalleled, but we are also of a much higher and greater spiritual order. Really to know ourselves, we must be conscious of our greatness. Else we shall fall very low.

Our soul encompasses the entire universe, and represents it in its highest unity. It is, therefore, whole and complete, entirely free of all the disjointedness and the contradictions which prevail among all other peoples. We are one people, one as the oneness of the universe. This is the enormous spiritual potential of our innate character, and the various processes of our historical road, the road of light that passes between the mountains of darkness and perdition, are leading us to realize the hidden essence of our nature. All the mundane sine-qua-nons of national identity are transmuted by the all-inclusiveness of the spirit of Israel.

It is impossible to lop off any branch from the great, leafy tree of our life and to give it an existence of its own. Every fiber of our being would be roused to opposition and, in total self-awareness, we would react with all the inner strength at our command. The long road of our history has been determined by the hope for complete renascence of ourselves and of everything that is ours. Nothing can be ignored—not a single line in the image of our people dare be erased.

Yes, we are stronger than all the cultures of the ages and more enduring than all the permanencies of the world. Our longing is to reawaken to life in the amplitude of our ancestors—and to be even greater and more exalted than they were. We have made great moral contributions to the world, and we are now ready to become its teacher of joyous and vibrant living. Our spirit is unafraid of the passing ages; it gives birth to these ages and puts its stamp upon them. The power of our creativity is such that it impresses the most sublime spirituality on the practical stuff of life. As life evolves toward higher forms, this creative power increases, and the process of its fashioning the world into tangible expressions of the spirit becomes ever more marvelous to behold. All this will reach its highest fulfillment when our Jewish life is renascent in all its facets.

Society today is in a state of movement and tumult; but how poor and stultifying is this age, and how vast is the void that remains in the heart, after all the high-pitched emotions of wars and rumors of wars—for all of this is bereft of ultimate purpose and represents only the passing life of one or another group of men. Nor is there much greater value even to broad social revolutions, especially when these are attended by major upheavals which inflame the heart and confuse the mind. Without an ultimate spiritual ideal which can raise the whole of man's striving to the level of the highest forms that reason and sublime emotion can conceive, no movement can be of any value, or long endure.

But let us return to the Divine purpose, which is to realize the general good through the perfection of every person and group. It is not enough to exemplify this ideal at a moment of high emotion. To approach the estate of spiritual wholeness and to be assured of survival, a society must express the ideal clearly in every aspect of its soul. That which is beyond the reach of language will be said, in all its force, by the future all-encompassing and eternal divine order.

True, in the days of our decline the sparks of spiritual light are dim, and they are present, for the most part, in the memories embodied in our traditional way of life, in all the religious commandments and rules which stem from the past and look toward the future. But these conserve enormous vitality, and the dust that spiritual callousness has allowed to collect on them will be shaken off by a really serious movement of national renascence. The fiery sparks will become visible; they will join in becoming a great divine flame, warming the world and illuminating its uttermost reaches.

Our present is but a translated shadow of our great past; it is always turned toward the lofty future, a future that is so exalted that it lights up the present and gives it dimensions of active power unwarranted by its real estate, which is one of waiting and longing for the future. Everything depends on the value of the past and the future: Some pasts and futures can give light and warmth only to the most immediate present, and others are great enough to make of the present, which lives by their power, an age that is truly alive and creative. Our past is a great one, and our future is even greater, as is evidenced by our striving for the ideals of justice that are latent in our souls. This great force inspirits our present and gives it full life. From the deep range of our memories we draw many examples, a particular kind of wisdom and creativity, a unique outlook on the world, *mitzvot*, traditions and customs—all suffused with spiritual content, love, and gentleness, and nurtured by the dew of life, heroism, and majesty—by our own gentleness, our own heroism, and our own majesty.

Apart from the nourishment it receives from the life-giving dew of the holiness of Eretz Yisrael, Jewry in the Diaspora has no real foundation and lives only by the power of a vision and by the memory of our glory, i.e., by the past and the future. But there is a limit to the power of such a vision to carry the burden of life and to give direction to the career of a people—and this limit seems already to have been reached. Diaspora Jewry is therefore disintegrating at an alarming rate, and there is no hope for it unless it replants itself by the wellspring of real life, of inherent sanctity, which can be found only in Eretz Yisrael. Even one spark of this real life can revive great areas of the kind of life that is but a shadow of a vision. The real and organic holiness of Jewry can become manifest only by the return of the people to its land, the only path that can lead to its renascence. Whatever is sublime in our spirit and our vision can live only to the degree that there will be a tangible life to reinvigorate the tiring dream.

As the world becomes spiritual and the spirit of man develops to higher levels, the demand becomes ever stronger in man that he live in accordance with his true nature. This call contains much truth and justice, and it is incumbent upon the moral leadership that they purify it and direct it into the right channel. Man increasingly discovers God within himself, in his correct impulses; even those inner drives which appear on the surface to stray from what is conventionally held to be the true road, man can raise to such a high level that they, too, contribute to the ultimate good.

On awakening to life, the community of Israel will rediscover its courage and dignity. The purity and holiness that is used to demonstrate in submission is ever more being displayed through the courage of the soul in deeds of national heroism. These two states will become one, and, in their uniting, heroism will become all the greater because it will have been made sweeter by holiness.

There is an eternal covenant which assures the whole House of Israel that it will not ever become completely unclean. Yes, it may be partially corroded, but it can never be totally cut off from the source of divine life. Many of the adherents of the present national revival maintain that they are secularists. If a Jewish secular nationalism were really imaginable, then we would, indeed, be in danger of falling so low as to be beyond redemption.

But Jewish secular nationalism is a form of self-delusion: the spirit of Israel is so closely linked to the spirit of God that a Jewish nationalist, no matter how secularist his intention may be, must, despite himself, affirm the divine. An individual can sever the tie that binds him to life eternal, but the House of Israel as a whole cannot. And of its most cherished national possessions—its land, language, history, and customs—are vessels of the spirit of the Lord.

How should men of faith respond to an age of ideological ferment which affirms all of these values in the name of nationalism and denies their source, the rootedness of the national spirit, in God? To oppose Jewish nationalism, even in speech, and to denigrate its values is not permissible, for the spirit of God and the spirit of Israel are identical. What they must do is to work all the harder at the task of uncovering the light and holiness implicit in our national spirit, the divine element which is its core. The secularists will thus be constrained to realize that they are immersed and rooted in the life of God and bathed in the radiant sanctity that comes from above.

Despite the grave faults of which we are aware in our life in general, and in Eretz Yisrael in particular, we must feel that we are being reborn and that we are being created once again as at the beginning of time. Our entire spiritual heritage is presently being absorbed within its source and is reappearing in a new guise, much reduced in material extent but qualitatively very rich and luxuriant and full of vital force. We are called to a new world suffused with the highest light, to an epoch the glory of which will surpass that of all the great ages which have preceded. All of our people believes that we are in the first stage of the Final Redemption. This deep faith is the very secret of its existence; it is the divine mystery implicit in its historical experience. This ancient tradition about the Redemption bears witness to the spiritual light by which the Jew understands himself and all the events of his history to the last generation, the one that is awaiting the Redemption that is near at hand.

The claim of our flesh is great. We require a healthy body. We have greatly occupied ourselves with the soul and have forsaken the holiness of the body. We have neglected health and physical prowess, forgetting that our flesh is as sacred as our spirit. We have turned our backs on physical life, the development of our senses, and all that is involved in the tangible reality of the flesh, because we have fallen prey to lowly fears, and have lacked faith in the holiness of the Land. "Faith is exemplified by the tractate *Zeraim* (*Plants*)—man proves his faith in eternal life by planting."

Our return will succeed only if it will be marked, along with its spiritual glory, by a physical return which will create healthy flesh and blood, strong and well-formed bodies, and a fiery spirit encased in powerful muscles. Then the one weak soul will shine forth from strong and holy flesh, as a symbol of the physical resurrection of the dead.

FOR FURTHER READING

Books by Abraham Isaac Kuk*

The Lights of Penitence, The Moral Principles, Lights of Holiness, Essays, Letters and Poems translation and introduction by Ben Zion Bokser (Ramsey, NJ: Paulist Press, 1978). Translation of Kuk's major works with a lengthy biography and introduction. Highly recommended.

Lights of Return translated by Alter B.Z. Metzger (New York: Yeshiva University Press, 1978). An important translation of this central work with a preface and notes; part of "Studies in Torah Judaism" series.

Books about Abraham Isaac Kuk

"Abraham Isaac Kook" in *Encyclopedia Judaica* (Jerusalem: 1972). Includes biography and overview of Rabbi Kook's philosophy.

WEINER, Herbert, *9½ Mystics: The Kabbala Today* (New York: Macmillan, 1969). Chapter 10, "The View from the Root Above" is about the closest disciples of Rabbi Kook.

Surname is frequently spelled Kook.

GERMAN
JEWISH
THINKERS

HERMANN COHEN

(1842–1918)

EDITOR'S NOTE

With Hermann Cohen we enter a world different from that of the first three thinkers in this book. While Ahad Ha-am, Gordon and Kuk grew up in Eastern Europe and were primarily self-educated, Hermann Cohen was a west European thinker, a renowned philosopher who brought his academic training and scholarship to bear in analyzing Jewish thought. The first three were Jewish nationalists; Cohen was an anti-Zionist interested in the religious consciousness of the Jew. Probably the greatest exponent of Jewish thought since the enlightenment and the most important Jewish philosopher since Maimonides, Cohen was the philosophical spokesman for liberal Judaism.

Born in 1842 in the small town of Coswig, Germany, he was the son of a cantor and Hebrew teacher. Though Cohen studied for a time at the Rabbinical Seminary of Breslau, he gave up his plan to enter the rabbinate, turning instead to philosophy as his life's work. In 1873 he was invited to teach at the University of Marburg where he soon became a full professor of philosophy. (No mean accomplishment for a Jew in Germany at that time!) His brilliant contributions to the renewal of Kantian philosophy led to the recognition of the neo-Kantian "Marburg School" and brought fame to the university and to Cohen.

During this period Hermann Cohen had drifted away from Jewish life. In his own philosophy he found no original role for religion. The "idea of God" was to him the bridge between the natural sciences and ethics and was to be identified with the realization of morality in the Messianic Age. It had little in common with the traditional God concept.

After 1880, disillusioned by the rise of anti-Semitism in Germany, he began to return to Judaism. After his retirement from the University of Marburg in 1912 Cohen came to Berlin to lecture at the *Hochschule für die Wissenschaft des Judentums*, the school of higher Jewish learning, and devoted himself to developing his philosophy of religion. His earlier ideas underwent a change, and he now assigned to religion an important role of its own. The mature thinking of his last years is to be found in his great work *Religion der Vernunft aus den Quellen des Judentums* (*Religion of Reason Based on the Sources of Jadaism*), published posthumously (1929), and in a number of outstanding essays collected in three volumes entitled *Jüdische Schriften* (*Jewish Writings*) (1924) with a preface by Franz Rosenzweig. These works have not yet been translated and most of the passages presented are available in English for the first time. They were selected and translated by Ephraim Fischoff, rabbi in Lynchburg, Virginia and author of the chapter on Cohen in the companion volume of this series.

The first three selections dealing with Cohen's theological outlook are rather technical. They reveal a profound philosophical mind in contact with Jewish sources. In his view, Jewish monotheism is distinctive not so much because of its emphasis on the unity of God, but because of God's uniqueness or singularity. God cannot be compared or equalled to anything else in the world. Thus Judaism is not only incompatible with a belief in many gods but also with pantheism which equates God and nature. This otherness of God also excludes the possibility of an intermediary between God and nature, or between God and man, as in Christianity.

In the second selection Cohen explains how this concept of a unique God helps us to understand the existence of nature and of the human world. Though Divine Being is the only true Being, God does not stand outside all relationship to the world and to man. "Creation is a necessary attribute of God." Cohen's understanding of creation, however, is not the literal account of the Bible of a single event in time, a "creation out of nothing." Creation is rather an enduring process, a continuing "renewal of the world."

Revelation, too, Cohen did not interpret in the traditional sense as an isolated historical event on Mount Sinai dealing with definite laws and ordinances. To Cohen, revelation is a purely spiritual concept which began before Sinai and continues to the present day. It is a consequence of God's uniqueness and of creation. It is the source of a unique morality which manifests itself in the heart and spirit of all mankind.

In our fourth selection, Cohen describes the Sabbath as a genuinely original social institution, and as "the quintessence of the monotheistic ethic." The Sabbath affirms the "equality of human beings irrespective of their diverse social positions." It is an expression of sympathy with human suffering and an attempt to redress the balance of an imperfect world. This essay, a landmark in its time, presented a new approach for the investigation of Jewish religious practices.

Cohen's essay on the Day of Atonement also illustrates the importance of ethics in Judaism. The emphasis in the liturgy on purely ethical transgressions and the necessity of seeking forgiveness from one's fellow man before turning to God illustrate this.

Each of the other essays reveals the warm emotional attachment which the philosopher felt toward Judaism. His study on the Hebrew prophets indicates his strong sense of justice and grows in part out of his socialistic bent. Cohen, like Ahad Ha-am, Leo Baeck and Kaufmann Kohler, regards prophetic ethics as one of the finest achievements of Judaism.

Cohen discusses the importance of the Hebrew language in prayer, the deficiency of translations and the need for establishing chairs of Jewish studies at various German universities in an essay entitled *Two Suggestions for Securing Our Survival*. To accentuate the different aspects of his thought, we have divided this selection into two parts.

His emphasis on *The Importance of Jewish Unity* must be understood in the context of his times. Cohen was not a Jewish nationalist and when he writes about the "community" with which he is connected, he is referring to a religious community of believers.

In the final selection Cohen expresses the Jewish attitude toward death. He gives the spiritual meaning of immortality as historical survival in the unification with the ancestors of the group.

25. The Unity or Uniqueness of God

What Is the Real Meaning of the Uniqueness of God?

I N Greek speculation the concept of the unity of God led directly into pantheism. Thus this opened the way for the important insight that *unity cannot be the adequate expression for the authentic concept of monotheism.*

To be sure, the Biblical sources do not contain any methodical philosophy. Yet they do contain the germinal beginnings of religious speculation. How could this be otherwise, since they aim to reveal the truth of God? But how could the idea of God come to expression save through thought, which takes a position opposed to that of sense perception. Consequently if the effort was to be made, by using the instrumentalities of thought to teach what God is, as contrasted with the gods and no less with heaven and earth, then the idea of the unity of God must already have been present even in these oldest sources. This was necessary if the spiritual God was to be revealed as the God of Truth, in contrast to the manifoldness of plural gods and of the senses.

At this oldest fork in the path of the human mind it also is apparent that religious speculation does not just imitate philosophy but that it follows its own road even in regard to the general concepts of thought. It therefore rejects the concept of unity, which is the most general organ of thought, setting in its place *uniqueness,* and proceeds to conceptualize the new God through this notion.

God is unique—this is the new idea with which monotheism comes into the world. This conception enters into opposition to the general line of thinking which recognized only unity and appears to have no use for the concept of uniqueness. The world has unity, but this comprises an infinity of worlds. It may be asked, what more could the concept of uniqueness intend than is already contained in the concept of unity? The latter view may be tenable as far as the world is concerned. But is the concept of unity adequate in respect to God? Is the meaning of the unity of God merely that the plurality of gods comprises a unity? Even to pose such a question reveals that for monotheism unity will not suffice; for it God must become the Unique One.

Yet this seems to place monotheism in an inescapable paradox. For what is the meaning of this uniqueness of God? Clearly God may not form a unity with the world. Indeed His singularity seems to deprive the world of all rights, notably the right to become the content of thought. For God alone may be the only proper content of thought. Does it then really follow that monotheism would appear simply as a nihilism, vis-a-vis all thinking about nature? Does not man also belong in the realm of nature? And does the singularity of God in any sense then imply the nothingness of man, as well as of nature in its totality?

If this were the case, then there would indeed be no escape from pantheism, and monotheism would have to capitulate to it. Hence if monotheism is to maintain itself against pantheism, and if Xenophanes with his first word about the One God were not also to have spoken the last word concerning God, then the uniqueness of God must have another significance than merely the negative one—that God alone must be the sole content of thought.

The biblical sources do not contain any speculation regarding the nature of thought. Nevertheless it is clear that they do pursue thought, as contrasted with sense perception, and that they attempt to comprehend thought, in respect to its real content and object. This becomes unmistakably clear in regard to an idea which is just as much one of the chief organs of thought as the previously mentioned concepts of unity and identity. This is the concept of *being*.

It was Xenophanes who had excogitated the unity of the cosmos but he had transferred this unity to that of a singular God. Then came Parmenides who firmly related this unity to the cosmos, which he no longer transformed into deity. Rather did he transform cosmos into that other basic concept of thought, namely being. Henceforth the problem of philosophy was to be not cosmos but being; thereafter thought and being became interchangeable concepts of philosophical speculation.

Once again it must be regarded as miraculous that the primeval monotheistic thinking of the Bible, which does not operate with ratiocination, nevertheless posed the problem of being. Can this be doubted in view of the fact that the new God is not designated by any other expression than that of Being?

How Monotheism Differs from Polytheism and Pantheism

When Moses, on the occasion of God's first revelation to him at the burning bush raised the questions: "When the children of Israel shall inquire of me 'who is the God that has sent you to us? And what is His name?", God answered him thus: "I am that which I am. So shalt thou say to the children of Israel: 'I am' has sent me to you." There is probably no greater miracle in the history of the spirit than that revealed in this verse. For here, a primeval language which is as yet without any philosophy, emerges and haltingly pronounces the most profound word of all philosophy. The name of God is "I am that which I am." This signifies that God is Being, that God is the I, which denotes the Existing One. It is also quite characteristic that this Being is not represented as neuter but as a personal pronoun, as I. But does it lose hereby the conceptual value of Being when it becomes an existing I, an existing subject?

Earlier we asked about the meaning of the term unique or singular when applied to God. We now perceive that the unique God actually signifies the unique Being or more precisely the Uniquely Existent One. Thus we are brought around once again to the question as to whether monotheism becomes a nihilism when applied to the world and particularly to man. Does the unique God, in the sense of the Uniquely Existing One, destroy every type of being? Or is it that only, in regard to the meaning of Being, the unique Being of God makes a distinction between Himself and all other beings in the world, including the world of man?

It is obvious that from the beginning monotheism undertook to oppose not only polytheism but also pantheism. God and the world could not form a unity in view of the fact that God is unique.

But the uniqueness of God means the unique being of God. Does the fact that God is the unique being therefore reduce the world and man to *non-being?* Is monotheism really equivalent to a nihilism with respect to the world and man?

The revelation to Moses of the unique God was accompanied by a charge to his people. To regard the unique God as entailing a nihilism of the illogical sort just mentioned would, therefore, be not only a logical contradiction but also a psychological one.

To regard singularity when applied to God as reducing the world and man to non-being, is to extend unconsciously the idea of unity and its self-generated transformation into identity, an extension which carries over into the concept of uniqueness the contradiction of identity, or polarity.

Now such a contradiction exists in regard to the concept of unity but not in regard to the concept of uniqueness. We would rather maintain that uniqueness actually eliminates such a contradiction, and indeed that the concept of a unique God actually demands one being for the world and man, albeit this being would not be of the same type as the unique being of God.

From the being of God, however, it is possible to derive the other type of being appropriate to the world and man; it is in this derivation that the uniqueness of the divine being is elevated to its *positive* significance.

26. Creation

THE concept of the uniqueness of God, as contrasted with that of the unity of God, has the merit of making possible a direct relationship to nature and the world of man. With the concept of the uniqueness of God, nature does not remain a riddle to the human mind, which man then endeavors to solve only by the assumption that God realizes Himself in nature and hence that He is simply identical with nature. This doctrine of pantheism must be regarded as just an intellectual escape from the incomprehensibility and insolubility of the existence of nature. Unless nature is interpreted as the expression and fulfillment of God, it would seem to be left to accident.

The idea of the unique God rescues the human mind from such desperation. For this view nature does not remain a riddle of chance, nor does a solution for this predicament have to be sought in such an enigmatic type of God concept which eradicates the distinction between God and nature. With the concept of the singularity of God, there is indeed provided an explanation for the existence of nature.

Just as the concept of being as such serves as the presupposition for the scientific investigation of becoming, i.e., of events in nature, so, too, the uniqueness of Divine Being is the necessary and fruitful presupposition for understanding the problem of nature and the human world.

It is an essential element in the concept of the unique God

that nature and the human world achieve one existence. God and nature are not two different powers which may exist side by side, much less on equal status; rather the unique being of God entails conceptually the existence of nature. *Creation is a necessary attribute of God.*

Consequently creation does not present any contradiction to reason, even as the uniqueness of God cannot do so. Nor is creation a mystery, which sets apart the religious mode of knowledge from that available to the general enterprise of science. Rather is creation a thoroughly rational concept within the logic of being. Just as the singularity of God is in harmony with the logical concept of substance, so too creation is in congruity with the concept of being that is appropriate to the unique God.

The Hebraic Interpretation of Creation as Renewal

Accordingly, within Jewish religious doctrine, creation is conceived largely in this spirit of rationalism. The very first word of the creation story, with which the Bible opens, was not interpreted as meaning simply "beginning" but rather as in the derived sense of "perfection" or "excellence" or "merit." For the idea of a beginning still belongs to the conceptual world of cosmogony.

But even the very concept of "creation at the beginning" was not maintained as the decisive one, but another one was placed by its side, namely that of "the renewal of the world." This idea was taken up and absorbed into the daily prayers where God is referred to as "He who each day continually renews, in His goodness, the work of creation." Thus this idea of the *continuousness of renewal* was made into a cardinal doctrine, whereas the older doctrine of creation at the beginning receded in importance. Every day is a new beginning. The mystery of the initial creation is assimilated into the daily miracle of renewal, and consequently, into that of the *maintenance* of the world. The Creator becomes the Maintainer. The uniqueness of God fulfills itself in *divine Providence.*

With this shift a tremendous transformation takes place in the entire range of religious thought. By this change religion is separated from mythology and is brought to its true originality. Henceforth creation out of nothing or out of some primal material is no longer the basic question for religion. Indeed the primeval nothingness disappears or becomes dissolved in the source or *origination* (*Ursprung*) of the unique being of God. No longer does nothingness constitute the terrifying spector of knowledge. Now the uniqueness of God has become the ground of the origination and existence of nature.

This origination gives creation its significance, in contrast to the desperation which arises when God is identified with nature. Nature is not identical with God. Rather is it His creation; and this creation is a result of the factor of origination in the unique being of God.

Creation is, however, renewal and as such is an enduring process, which, in logic, is termed continuity. The shift from creation to renewal does not remain, however, at this point of the logical significance of renewal as the process of creation becomes transformed into Providence. But in Providence the logical meaning of the God idea becomes transformed into an *ethical* meaning, in which the truly elemental power of the unique God comes to its fullest expression.

27. Revelation

A s in the case of creation, revelation need not constitute a mystery nor present any contradiction to the firm and clear concept of the uniqueness of God. Rather revelation may appear as a consequence of both this idea and of creation. For just as the uniqueness of God as the source (*Ursprung*) is the necessary basis for the existence of the world, it must also be the necessary foundation for the concept of man, insofar as he is distinguished from all of creation as the rational being. Moreover this capacity for reason denotes not only the capacity of man's mind to theorize, but also his propensity to create and maintain ethical values. Revelation must proceed from the unique God as the source of a unique ethics for the world of men.

The rationalism of the Jewish doctrine of God is distinctively formulated in the terms dictated by the revelation at Sinai. This purely literary fact already provides material for thought. Is not the entire Torah the revealed doctrine? How then can the revelation be limited to the Decalogue alone? The contents of the Decalogue form the basis of all human ethics, by virtue of their being grounded in a unique, imageless and spiritual God. Moreover this ethics penetrates into the deepest inwardness of man, his inclinations and desires, as well as into the collective form of his political organization. For this reason the Sabbath, with its liberation of the slaves and the hirelings from incessant toil, stands at the very center of the summary of morality that is the Decalogue.

Indeed even the term used to designate revelation definitely rejects, with a certain naive sureness, any appearance of unveiling or disclosure, for it is referred to as the "giving of the Torah" (*matan torah*). Now the decisive Hebrew word in this phrase is not correctly translated as "gift," because this would denote an object that may be given. The Hebrew word *matan* is not the same as *matanah* which means gift, but it connotes rather the act of giving or offering.

Thus the feeling of the Hebrew idiom suggests sharing, and refers to God giving of Himself, which is what He does in everything that emanates from Him. The religious spirit of monotheism is not overly concerned with the nature of this process of self-sharing by God, possibly because it zealously endeavors to remove from the notion of the divine self-sharing by the unique God everything corporeal and material. God creates man's spirit, and this He creates as a holy spirit, or more correctly, as the spirit of holiness. This is the only view of creation that solves the various riddles one may find in the process of God's sharing Himself with men.

Yet the Mosaic doctrine is not just theory, for it is at the same time the representation of Israel's history. The people of Israel had from the outset to be admonished about their history and genesis, in order that the national consciousness might be suffused by a sense of its spiritual responsibility; and that the latter might find fulfillment through proper awareness and zeal in the soul of the nation.

The Significance of Moses in the History of Judaism

In the luminous figure of Moses this inner history of Israel reaches its summit. It was not necessary for him to become a hero nor a demigod, much less a divine being of some sort. Yet it was inevitable that the revelation should be mediated by him, that the two tablets of the law should be brought down by him. Such a luminous figure had to break through if the darkness of myth were to be pierced, if the way were to be found, through the historical sense, to the spirit of the unique God. It is characteristic that Moses is deeply etched in the Jewish psyche as "our teacher Moses." That is, he is not our redeemer but only our teacher. The intermediation which he undertook to effect between God and the people is interpreted simply as teaching. All spiritual intermediation is instruction.

It corresponds to the primitive tone of the Biblical narratives that the distinctive character of Moses is represented by similes which extend to the farthest limits of spirituality. Thus the Bible does not hesitate to use the expression that God spoke to Moses "mouth to mouth." Of course God has no mouth and so He is unable to speak to the mouth of Moses. Ibn Ezra supplies a succinct explanation of the correct meaning of this expression by interpreting it in his commentary as "without intermediaries." The entire problem of the transmission of revelation is illuminated and settled by this phrase of the commentator.

Yet the Biblical account in its almost epic naivete works through to the logical consequence of this approach: "Face to face did the Eternal speak to you at the mountain out of the fire." That is, God spoke to the entire people face to face or even mouth to mouth. The preferential position of Moses disappears or rather he shares it with the entire people. This summons of the entire nation to equality with Moses at the reception of the revelation also has the tendency to stimulate the national consciousness that had to be aroused in order for the people to understand its mission.

Yet in the account of the theophancy there always remains a suspicion of materialization on the part of the divine spirit. Hence it is, one might say, a literary marvel in this entire process of national self-spiritualization when Deuteronomy teaches: "Not with your fathers alone did the Eternal conclude His covenant but with us also—with all of us who are alive here today." The multiplication of modifying words toward the end of this quotation serves the purpose of directing attention away from the past and placing the theater of revelation in the present. In this fashion there is prepared that great thought with which Deuteronomy deflects the origination of the Torah from the external world and bases it completely on the spirit of man alone.

In that great address on the plains of Moab, *which I do not hesitate to term the greatest work of art in the entire literature of rhetoric,* this apparent mystery of revelation is solved simply and effectively: "For this doctrine is not wonderously concealed and remote from Thee that Thou mayest say 'whom shall I send into the heavens and fetch it for us?' Rather is it in Thy mouth and in Thy heart that Thou mayest fulfill it." Now the last shadow has been brushed away from the utterly pure spirituality of revelation. The doctrine is not in Heaven but it is in the mouth of man, in his capacity for speech and in his heart, and hence in his mind. It has not come to man from without but rather it wells up from his inmost parts. It is rooted in man's mind which God, the Unique One, has implanted in him as the spirit of holiness; and this is the spirit of morality.

Is revelation still a riddle? Is it not rather the precise consequence of the concept of the Unique God?

Only the Unique God can reveal the unique morality. This is a morality which may not be fragmentized and diversified according to individual men or particular nations, rather must it be one unique system of ethics in the infinite history of the human race.

Now this unique holiness has its adequate ground in the heart of man. This derivation of morality from man is no contradiction of the revelation of God which occurs among mankind not just in Moses alone but in the entire people. Indeed this origination of instruction in the heart and spirit of man is identical with the revelation of God, for God has sent his spirit into man. "He forms the spirit of man in his inward parts." Consequently the holy spirit, the spirit of holiness, is an inalienable possession of man, and it is not lost even in sin.

One other consequence follows from the fact that revelation is an emanation of the uniqueness of God. As God is unique, so also is morality a uniform law for all men and all peoples. This uniformity must be distinguished from all the variations and oscillations of ethical ideas and prescriptions in the life of nations. This uniform morality is the eternal element in the human spirit.

In logic and ethics and indeed in a systematic scientific philosophy, anything so eternal and original is termed *a priori* and implies a contrast to all ideas of psychological development. So, too, revelation in an aprioristic sense must necessarily be distinguished from all phenomenal forms thereof of the history of religion. Revelation is the eternal element and as such it constitutes the divine factor in the spirit of mankind.

28. The Sabbath

The Jewish Sabbath as the Fundamental Law of Social Ethics in Western Culture

M o r e than by any other specific Hebrew legislation which, starting from the protection of the poor also extended to all other ethical and legal relationships among men, monotheism expressed God's love for man by one great law that has become the fundamental social law of European nations. Christianity retained this law but changed its significance in order to mark off the separation from its social roots in Judaism; and it divested the law itself of its socio-ethical significance. Yet the law of the *Sabbath* must be regarded as the quintessence of the monotheistic ethic.

The controversy centering around the problem of the relationship of the Bible to Babylonian culture (the so-called *Babel-Bibelstreit*) has revealed anew that the significance of this Hebraic law enjoining the Sabbath is not really alive in the spirit and mood of modern man. This is the less understandable since all modern social policy reveals this significance. What is more, the strengthening of the law concerning rest on Sunday has again brought this meaning to general attention. Yet the Jewish Sabbath is interpreted as relating only to the division of the week; and the originality of this Jewish institution is believed to be impugned by the fact that in Babylonia also there was such a thing as a week and that this Babylonian seven day period also contained such a festive day, albeit a movable one. It should be recalled that the investigations of Movers and the treatise of Chr. Baur (concerning the Sabbath and festive days) leave no doubt that any calendrical arrangement according to the seven planets was not a Jewish invention. But even if it were such, it would not yet be a monotheistic one. It became such only by virtue of the fact that the Babylonian division of the week which was taken over was employed by the prophets in their construction of a social ethics. For this ethical structure the keystone was the Sabbath.

Both of the formulations of the law of the Sabbath contained in the Decalogue provide strong testimony regarding the fundamental importance of this day, to which attention has already been drawn. In Exodus (Ex. 20:11) the formulation is: "Remember the Sabbath day to keep it holy. Six days shalt thou labor and do all thy work; but the seventh day is a Sabbath unto the Lord thy God. In it thou shalt not do any manner of work, thou nor thy son, nor thy daughter, nor thy man-servant, nor thy maid-servant, nor thy cattle, nor thy stranger that is within thy gates. For in six days the Lord made heaven and earth, the sea and all that in them is, and rested on the seventh day. Wherefore the Lord blessed the seventh day and hallowed it." Here rest on the Sabbath is enjoined for servants of both sexes, but the basis assigned for the law is the fact of God's having rested from the labor of creation as narrated in the first two chapters of the Book of Genesis. Consequently the Sabbath is here regarded as the completion of the work of creation. God's rest unquestionably signified nothing else other than the completion of His work.

On the other hand the formulation of the law regarding the Sabbath in the Book of Deuteronomy shows a distinctive socioethical and reformist character. In the Deuteronomic version of the Decalogue, the only change from the formulation in the book of Exodus, apart from the prohibition of covetousness, is in the law regarding the Sabbath. The enumeration of the persons and animals who must rest thereon is followed by this dictum (Deut. 5:14): ". . . That thy man-servant and thy maid-servant may rest as well as thou. And thou shalt remember that thou wast a servant in the land of Egypt, and the Lord thy God brought thee

out thence by a mighty hand and by an outstretched arm; therefore the Lord thy God commanded thee to keep the Sabbath
Day." Even the initial word of the injunction regarding the observance of the Sabbath is changed, seeing that in Exodus it is
"remember" whereas here it is "observe" (*shamor*). Moreover
while in the Exodus formulation the root of the Sabbath suggested by the statement, "Wherefore (*al cayn*) the Lord blessed
the Sabbath Day," is related to God's six days of creation and
His rest on the Sabbath. In the Deuteronomic version this clause
is applied to divine injunction, "That thy man-servant and thy
maid-servant may rest as well as thou," which manifestly indicates the purpose of the Sabbath, as concerned predominantly
with the humane provisions of rest for servants, strangers, and
farm animals, and as a symbol and reminder of God's liberation
of Israel from Egypt. It is noteworthy that the Hebrew word
Kamocha, meaning "as well as thou," is the same word that is
employed in the injunction to love one's neighbor as oneself.

From this inspection of the source material derived from the
two versions of the Decalogue and the motivations behind the
changes, there can be no question that the Sabbath aims to secure
the equalization of human beings irrespective of their diverse
social positions. This indubitably clear significance of the Sabbath provides excellent documentation of the basic ethical orientation of monotheism and its moral originality.

The Sabbath and Monotheism

Genuine originality in social institutions is extremely rare but
in the case of the Hebrew Sabbath there can be no question about
its presence, and all attempts to impugn it have foundered. The
Mosaic injunction regarding the sabbath derives from a distinctive national spirit which produced a concept of God that is
equally unique in history. The Sabbath is the clear and luminous
confirmation of the ethical significance of monotheism. In order
to clarify this matter, we must take up our position at the point
of God's love for man. The complete scope of this divine love
may be recognized and known in the Sabbath. This institution
was first given to Israel but the world has taken it over, even
though a new dogmatic reason has been assigned for it, one that

is to be sure, different from that of God's resting subsequent to the process of creation. In any case the institution of the Sabbath has become a universal law, at least for European nations. In the Sabbath all forms of God's love for man are brought together and unified.

It is understandable therefore, that for the prophets the Sabbath becomes the simple and complete expression of morality. Thus Isaiah (Is. 56:2) refers to the person "that keepeth the Sabbath from profaning it and keepeth his hand from doing any evil" a parallelism suggesting that for Isaiah the observance of the Sabbath was equivalent to the total practice of ethical living; and in another context he appears to regard "calling the Sabbath a delight," as parallel with religious faithfulness. It is as though the prophet were saying: the Sabbath must not be regarded only as a regulation of social life but must rather be thought of as the summit of religious inwardness. Again, Jeremiah referring to the Sabbath, says (Jer. 17:27): "But if ye will not hearken unto me to hallow the Sabbath day, and not to bear a burden and enter into the gates of Jerusalem on the Sabbath day, then I will kindle a fire in the gates thereof," etc. The love of God for mankind comes to expression in His having instituted the Sabbath out of His pity for man who has been expelled from Paradise and condemned to labor. Basically the Sabbath eliminates the distinction among human beings which comes to expression in their various forms of work. On this day the manual laborer becomes his own master. The weekly rest on a particular day renders the worker equal to his employer.

The Sabbath became the most effective guardian of the Jewish people. Throughout the long medieval period they lived almost like slaves—a condition which is not yet completely ended. But the Jews of the Ghetto shed all the troubles of their every-day life when the Sabbath candles were kindled. All sordidness was shaken off. The love of God which brought the Jew the Sabbath anew every seventh day, restored to him in his humble hovel, his honor and his human rights.

Scholars still engage in fierce debate about the factors which ultimately made possible the survival of the Jews, but despite everything they remain ignorant of the causes. They are unwilling to recognize that the ultimate ground must be sought in the truth of the Unique God, and they prefer to attribute the survival to the Jewish law which they insist on interpreting disrespectfully as equivalent to legalistic formality and as lacking in all inner feeling.

Yet the Sabbath is the most authentic and the most intimate exemplification of the Jewish law. It was this Day of Rest, with its law expressive of the Unique God who loves mankind, that preserved both Judaism and the Jews. Both were sustained by the mission of diffusing monotheism over all the earth, and of continually deepening its meaning and spirit, and thereby establishing true love for man among all the peoples of the earth. It is in the Sabbath that the God of love showed Himself to be the Unique God of Love for all mankind.

We have asked what is the meaning of the love of God. The answer has now been found. It is sympathy with the poor such as God has awakened within us by means of his precepts and this has become for us the intelligible foundation of the meaning of God's love. The Sabbath has removed from mankind every miserable appearance of enslavement and inequality. As God has established within us human pity because of the dregs of poverty, so has He disclosed His love for mankind in this social insight. This divine love is the guiding star of world history, whose significance no one may doubt, for it is both present and past. "A thousand years are in Thy sight as yesterday when it is past." (Ps. 90:4).

This world history has scarcely begun. Not quite three thousand years have elapsed since Moses and the prophets. Thus monotheism has really only begun to traverse its path in world history. Monotheism is the veritable consolation of history.

From the social love of God for man there also develops the universal love of God in Messianism.

29. Atonement

. . . I T is understandable that in Judaism atonement becomes the center of the entire ritual of worship and that a special holiday is allocated to it. On this day it is intended that both the individual and the community reach and confirm the high point of the religious life. . . .

Moreover, it is also a very valuable symptom of the inwardness of the mood animating the worship ritual instituted for the Day of Atonement that the catalogue of specific sins recited in this confession explicitly itemizes only purely ethical infractions between man and man. . . . In this selection of, and concentration upon, purely ethical transgressions we are bound to see a great monotheistic achievement of Rabbinical Judaism. For we are not dealing here with some peripheral matter, as this itemization of sins forms a long register with a precise listing of moral delinquencies. Indeed, there comes to expression in this list a psychology and a pathology of human passions. The authors of these confessional prayers must have found it difficult to refrain from including ritual trespasses, yet they managed to do so. That they succeeded in this must not be attributed only to their own merit, which was a consequence of their ethical maturity and their inner freedom from the chains that in a measure they had placed upon themselves through the ritual laws. The concentration upon ethical infractions in the Day of Atonement confessional is also and indeed primarily the direct result of the rabbis conception of sin as involuntary wrong-doing (*shegaga*) and of their trust in God who as the source of all goodness would forgive the sins of mankind.

. . . The closing prayer of the day has an equally illuminating and moving significance. One cannot praise too highly the chief section (the *Shemone Esre*) of the final prayer (*Neilah*) "Thou extendest Thy hand to sinners and Thy right hand is outstretched to receive the penitent; and Thou, O Eternal our God, has taught us to confess all our sins unto Thee so that we may withdraw from the violence of our hands and Thou mayest receive us in utter repentance before Thee." The closing verses constitute a confession that has entered into the daily morning prayer: "What are we? What is our life? What our righteousness? What our justice? What our virtue? What our power? What our heroism? . . ." The superiority of man over beasts is as naught for all is vanity. Yet the prayer does not remain at this point of skepticism as Ecclesiastes does. Indeed the very next verse provides the correction: "From the beginning Thou hast distinguished man and hast recognized him so that he may stand before Thee." Thus despite all, man has been singled out from the animals, and all is not vanity by any means, for man has been set apart, distinguished, and appointed to stand before God. This last phrase is one of the technical expressions for worship in Hebrew. Man stands before God. In this fashion there is asserted the independence of man in his correlation with God; it is in this upright posture before God that the individual achieves his self-sanctification.

It is characteristic that in the confession of sins the otherwise customary expression of self-prostration is not employed. This worshipful posture and genuflection which are typical in worship, may be used in prayer and in a solemn affirmation of God. But when a man avows his sins and in a related act expresses his confidence that the good God will forgive them, the appropriate posture is not self-prostration but much rather standing upright before God. Otherwise, the distinction of man from the beasts would not be complete, for this distinction entails an upright stance. Thus the proper position for man as he is redeemed from his sins is a humble yet still upright posture before God.

. . . It must also be realized, however, that in their development of the Day of Atonement the rabbis lost no time in making the atonement of man with God dependent on atonement between man and man. This is no mystical atonement which spreads a veil over all the transgressions of everyday life so that only the intimate human aspects may be freed from bleak anxiety and melancholy. "The Day of Atonement brings forgiveness only in regard to sins committed between God and man; but for sins committed against other men, the Day of Atonement will provide forgiveness only after the guilty person has made restitution to those whom he has offended." This law is primary. Thus atonement with God becomes at the same time a summons to atonement with man.

Still all the ethical endeavors of men remain imperfect and the idea of man remains something that can be approached only approximately. The practical outcome of the veneration of God is the recognition of the sinfulness of man when contrasted with the paradigm of morality in God. It is by virtue of this central thought that the institution of the Day of Atonement achieved monotheistic maturity, but not as some sort of a mythical device to facilitate or even thwart ethical responsibilities to his fellow man.

The Day of Atonement is the summit and consummation of the religious consciousness that comes to expression in it. At the same time it is an example of the principle of evolution which directs and regulates all religious ideas and institutions. Out of the connection of the primitive sacrifice with the primitive festival that everywhere accompanied the great sacrificial feasts, this unique day, which is certainly unparalleled in all the chronicles of religious communities, developed to such a degree of purity that only the most intimate questions of faith between God and man were dealt with that elsewhere fell into the domain of tragedy. For on this day life and death, the basic themes of tragedy, were not separated from questions of sin and its effects. On this day the simple human heart was to undertake with profound honesty the deepest inspection of all of human life and its value, as one of the Day's prayers suggests: "Thou knowest the secrets of eternity and the concealed mysteries of all living things." On the Day of Atonement the Jew subjects the destiny and the significance of life to the most searching inquiry.

. . . There is deep significance in the observation concerning the Day of Atonement attributed to Rabbi Akiba, the great Mishnaic teacher and illustrious martyr: "Happy are ye, O Israel! For who purifies you and before whom do you purify yourselves? It is your Father in heaven." The father of all mankind, who, according to the Biblical imagery, is set apart from terrestrial beings by the heavens, becomes manifest in this purification of mankind. But Akiba was not content to remain at this point, and in his praise of Israel he moves forward to draw attention to the fact that it purifies itself. It is not God that purifies, nor is it God alone who forgives. Scripture admonishes, "Before the Eternal shall ye be pure," but it also enjoins, "Ye shall sanctify yourselves and ye shall be holy." From this Akiba drew the correct inference that Israel has to purify itself and become pure before their Father in heaven. What Akiba was teaching was that no man can purify Israel nor any man who purports to be also a divinity; no son of God will purify Israel but only the Father himself. Moreover, Akiba's doctrine implies that Israel is not to purify itself before any intermediate being, and that only when God alone is the goal of its self-purification can the process of atonement be accomplished. In this formula of Akiba all of monotheism is contained. The question as to the deepest meaning of the unity of God may be answered thus: God is the Unique One because only before Him can man purify himself. Were any other being to be combined with the Unique One, or with any other concept, this would result in the loss of man's possibility of achieving self-sanctification. Truly the Day of Atonement is the day of monotheism. Even now we have not yet exhausted the entire significance of the Day of Atonement. Truly there is no more noble transfiguration of mankind than that provided by its self-purification. Hence to the mind of the Jew the Day of Atonement is just the symbol of his trust in God, in conjunction with the power of his contrition.

The Talmud has expressed this reliance upon contrition in the following memorable statement: "If a man has committed a sin during the day, let him not agonize over it at night, for in all likelihood he has already done penitence for it." From this it may be inferred that the practice of repentance was the most common aspect of Jewish piety. "Repent one day before Thy death" runs the admonition in *Abot*, 2, and in this enigmatic fashion the Mishnah made repentance an obligation for every day of life.

It is the most unfounded defamation in the world that Jewish piety is nothing more than accumulation of good works alone or that its rigorous obedience to law engendered such a consequence. For obviously the punctilious practice of Jewish law which covered and controlled all of life and practically every hour of it, could never render repentance unnecessary. On the contrary, the totality of all the laws and the fulfillment of them constituted only an introduction to penitence, and a turning toward and a contemplation of correlation with God.

30. The Nature of Hebrew Prophecy

Hebrew Prophecy and Social Religion

F R O M the point of view of social awareness, the purest spring of religion is to be found in Hebrew prophecy. . . . By virtue of the fact that the prophets separated the love of God from mysticism and, without following the path of science still endeavored to prepare a way for knowledge within the domain of love, they became the *founders of social religion* and therein of the social conscience as such. How were they able to accomplish this? Had the prophets halted at God, this development of the social conscience would not have been possible. They did not concentrate on God alone, however, but rather set Him into relationship, connection, and interaction with man. Consequently the problem of love arose for them not with God but rather in connection with man. It was man that the prophets aimed to understand—only not on the basis of a science of man. Indeed such an understanding of man, on this basis, was impossible even for Plato; and he sought assistance in his endeavor from his Idea. In their effort to understand man the prophets sought assistance from their concept of God.

It would, of course, be unthinkable that the Hebrew prophets, alone among the seers of mankind should have excogitated the notion of the Unique God without any stimulus from speculation. Only their reflection concerning God as the Unique

Being remained without the support of science. This is decisive, since it was responsible for the transfer of the center of gravity from the entire domain of metaphysics to the problem of morality exclusively. Not only were questions concerning God approached in this manner, but also those relating to man and indeed to an even greater degree. Thus it was that for the prophetic mind the God deriving from Babylonia, as the author of heaven and earth, became transformed at the outset into a God of human beings, the Creator of mankind.

Presently the prophets were to hail even God to judgment before the legal tribunal of human justice. Yet for them man was not ideally the son of God, the demigod, the hero; for them it was rather man in all his weakness who was the paradigm. This weakness was primarily moral, and so it man's sinfulness that determined the primal image of him. But just as the philosophy of morality remained alien to the prophets, so also did tragedy. Hence they did not stop with either guilt or punishment—the two sides of fate which form the poetic background of all human existence, but rather they tore away the wrappings of dignity that had become attached to this duality of guilt and punishment. They interpreted suffering not as the fate of man, but as a stage in the evolution of the concept of his human condition. By eliminating this basic tragic concept, they did away with the primeval mythical idea of the envy of the gods. In the prophetic interpretation God is the Good Being, not goodness as such. If suffering also derives from Him, it is not an evil, but it must be placed in context in the development of the good, for which the Good God is responsible.

That henceforth suffering was set apart from guilt and was not identified with punishment is one of the most significant consequences of monotheism, and one of the deepest clarifications of the social problem. For suffering constitutes the most difficult indictment against the goodness of God. Yet if this problem is thought of primarily in connection with death, myth remains in sole control of the field. Death is an image of the fate that controls gods and men; of this fate, as far as human beings are concerned, death is a manifestation, and inevitably befalls all men. Wherever thought takes this line, nothing remains for human morality to accomplish, and so it remains necessarily estopped at the level of mysticism. If there is to be any evocation of ethical activity against suffering, attention had to be averted from the common human fate of sickness and death. Henceforth the quest would have to be not for the biological causes of human misery but rather for the sociological ones. Accordingly, for the Hebrew prophet, the *pauper* became the symbol of man.

With this fundamental idea as a guide, we may follow the entire evolution of the prophetic movement. God was not interpreted as the Father of heroes, and such worthies were not represented as being His favorites; rather was it held to be true that God loves the stranger. In polytheism the stranger, apart from the fact that he may be shown hospitality, was regarded as the opposite of the ideal man, who must necessarily be a member of the in-group. Indeed the stranger is represented as a barbarian. But once the God of the group is represented as loving the barbarians, and regards hostile nations as his own quite like his own people of Israel, the horizon of mankind becomes luminous. The Messianic movement advances and accelerates this evolution, which culminates in internationalism.

We must now turn to another consequence of the prophetic attitude—the one leading in the direction of socialism. Even as God loves the stranger, so too He is practically always represented as loving the widow and the orphan, for all of them are subject to social oppression, from which the justice of God will liberate them.

Yet no matter how consistently the prophets invoked law and justice, and proclaimed their God to be the God of justice, they did not remain content with this abstraction, which constituted a sort of knowledge. They directed their attention to the heart of man, which they regarded as the only treasure trove of his spirit, and in this manner they evoked sympathy as the form of awareness corresponding to suffering. In the Hebrew language there is an original term for sympathy or pity, one that is derived from the word for womb (*rechem*). This is the feeling that God feels for the pauper; this is the feeling whereby a man should discover for himself the common human being behind the poor.

Accordingly, sympathy is not a passion, nor a physiological effect which man has in common with animals. Rather is it a spiritual factor or perhaps one might say, a surrogate of the spirit. In it one may observe how the entire power of a philosophy of life struggles to achieve awareness. Indeed one would have to doubt the justice of God, as well as His goodness and providence, did not such sympathy become one of the powers of the human consciousness, which may overcome the scepticism that emanates from the so-called human mind.

Of all the human sufferings, poverty alone holds the greatest interest for me, as representing the heaviest fetter of man's burden of pain. Man might even conquer death itself but poverty would remain his indelible mark. It is one of the most fateful deceptions that poverty should have come to be regarded as the retribution for man's guilt. Actually on such a fallacious view, it is impossible to arrive at the truth of God and little at the truth of man, and indeed not even at the first discovery of man. It is sympathy that first makes possible the discernment of the common humanity in mankind. In sympathy the suffering of another becomes one's own, and thereby the other man becomes a fellow-man.

It is significant that Plato had not yet developed an idea of man. It is equally significant that this step forward in the doctrine of ideas was achieved by Philo, the Jew. To his mind man needed this distinctive aspect of the value of knowledge, as much as he did the mathematical ideas of nature. Nor was Philo satisfied with just the idea of the good. To be sure, Plato himself had already advanced the idea of God as the Good, but this idea had remained one-sided and incomplete as long as man did not attain a personal share in the Good.

It was the Hebrew prophets who discovered this unique human value, and this discovery derived from their social consciousness. *They equated the poor with the righteous.* This equation of the categories is the decisive climax in the evolution of Messianism. As a consequence of this development the Messiah himself became the standard-bearer of poverty. He takes upon himself all the guilt of mankind because he has shouldered all the suffering, quite without the charm of heroic strength or superhuman beauty. He eschews all participation in the aesthetic attractions of the world, and in his social misery he represents only the collective misery of mankind.

It was in this wise that the Faust poem of the ancient Bible, the Book of Job, enters into the sphere of messianism. Once the prophets had expounded to the people the view that a man does not sin or suffer because of his ancestors, people were bound to ask what then was the source of evil in man? Instead of raising this metaphysical question, the prophets felt that it was necessary for the people to learn to ask what is the source of suffering among men, and that means, what is the significance of poverty. First it was necessary for men to realize the fallacy of attributing this to some guilt in the sufferer; and on the positive side they had to develop the insight that the poor man had to be regarded as the thoroughly good man. This insight was not to be shaken by any concept of God or of man, or by an experience of the world. God is the God of righteousness, and He would help the man beset by poverty. He is the God of world history, and He would make good for humanity what the individual has to suffer. As the God of goodness He can impose the suffering of poverty upon man only out of the light of goodness.

Finally, the knowledge of His goodness brings me to the insight that the poor man is the pious and God-fearing one, and indeed the favorite of God. Obviously this conclusion does not result from any science; and hence it is not an idea of the Good either. Nor is it an idea of some abstract good that may be applied to things. Rather is it something that becomes concrete and personal in man. And it is in regard to man that there is first enkindled love for God. . . .

31. Views on Education

Retention of Hebrew in Divine Services

I N other educated circles (i.e., among various Christian groups)
in our country, religious education is pursued with wise insight and religious fervor. Indeed many of our own young
people are attracted by this alien fascination and seduced by it
into conversion.

It is impossible to hope that simply by our modern abbre-
viation of religious services we can succeed in nurturing, maintaining, and developing a vital, sturdy, and self-assertive religion. There is no escaping the obligation to increase and deepen
the educational level and religious knowledge of all strata of
our liberal Judaism. For an enduring liberal religion the knowledge of religious literature is the indispensable prerequisite.

Here the prejudice of the times presents a difficult barrier.
The decline of our education, which is gradually becoming
amply evident, has led to the view that translations of foreign
languages constitute an equivalent vehicle for intellectual training. In all cases this is a great error but in the case of religion it is
absolutely fateful. Without an anthology of basic passages in
the Hebrew original, the full force and emotional power of
Hebrew prayer cannot come to expression. But apart from this
ritual question, the spiritual power of the religious emotion cannot be comprehended without the reception of the original

Jewish religious genius in the pristine force of the Hebrew tongue.

. . . I do not wish to miss the opportunity of expressing my view, which is one relating to religious practice, as well as a literary and esthetic judgment fortified by considerations of the psychology of language. In our Lodges we must somehow reach the understanding that despite the difficulties of our contemporary situation, we should endeavor to acquire and maintain in vital fashion the basic ideas of our religion in the original spirit of the language. If we pursue this goal ever more consciously in our religious education and correspondingly in the conduct of our services, the strife of parties in our midst will almost automatically be mitigated, and the awareness of unity will rise to ascendancy.

32. The Scientific Study of Judaism

. . . O U R survival depends on the spiritual, intellectual and moral power of our stock. But all of these have their root in our religion. And even though modern culture must fructify our spiritual-intellectual nature, yet our ethical power is primarily rooted in our religious folkways and education.

Without religious education, without a living knowledge of our ideas, literature, and history, religious training remains without fulcrum and content. In the absence of solid knowledge no complex of feelings can be cohesively maintained. It must be realized that the entire intellectual training of today stands in opposition to the foundations of our distinctive religious position. Hence, even the needs of defense make it imperative that we do not neglect our specialized Jewish education in favor of general education. Actually, however, the cause itself makes a certain measure of religious knowledge an indispensable prerequisite of any religious feeling. Clearly, I must know what ethical content the ideas of my religion contain if I am to develop any feeling and enthusiasm for such ideas, and if I am to perpetuate them.

Now we have all had the experience that regrettably the upper classes of society are constantly succumbing to temptation. The course of social history would seem to entail the following process: as ascent from the lower classes to the higher, and thereafter generally a decline into "higher types" of evil and degeneration. Everywhere it has to be the lower classes by whom historical life is rejuvenated, and ethical and spiritual power revitalized. It is for this reason that our ancestors admonished us: "Be heedful of the needs of the children of the poor, for out of them does the Torah come forth." The more the defection of the higher classes brings us painful losses, the more diligently and deeply must we be concerned to secure for ourselves the lower classes; and we have in mind here not only their intellectual training but also their religious education. . . .

Accordingly the secondary purpose for establishing our institution for children in Marburg was to train a group of young people who would be accumulating a creditable measure of religious knowledge so that they might be protected against the seductions of the age. Knowledge remains the most secure ground for developing the nobler sentiments. In addition, this religious knowledge sharpens the intellect's potentiality for general knowledge. We would never have been able to penetrate so fast and so variously into general culture had we not carried in our heads this intellectual capital drawn from our religious learning. Moreover, it must be noted that religious reflection and knowledge is the source of the entire spiritual essence of our tribe. Were it ever to come about that the power of religious thought among us would become paralyzed, our spiritual survival would become altogether questionable. . . .

The second suggestion which I wish to share with my brethren on this festive occasion goes even deeper. Actually it is related to the first and may possibly be regarded as an extension thereof.

. . . If we desire to secure our survival, we must take such action for the sake of our religion. This must survive and its continuation must be assured. Now we must be concerned to strengthen religious knowledge in the education of our youth; but we have also to be more concerned generally with maintaining the scientific study of our religion and with planning for its development from the point of view just formulated. It might appear as though in regard to this matter the Christian world does not propose to wreak destruction upon Judaism, inasmuch as by so doing it would be burying its own foundation. Nevertheless, we have recently had a terrifying example of how hatred corrupts insight. In general, a healthy development of the scientific study of Judaism is hindered by the view on the basis of which the science of Judaism is cultivated in the universities and literature, namely, that Judaism is merely a *precursor* of Christianity. Of course, where there is operative the central political goal of the extinction of Judaism, the general prejudice becomes ever more obdurate. The case of Professor Noeldeke is a perfect example which may serve as a warning. This man is famous for erudition, personal goodwill, and considerable freedom from theological prejudices. Nevertheless, he has denied Judaism any right to continue to exist. Such is the opinion of a professor of Semitic languages and literatures, who has trained several generations of Semitic scholars. We can well imagine that even among Jewish students many a germ of religious vitality has been asphyxiated by this most dangerous of all missionaries.

Yet we must be concerned not only or exclusively with the sources of the scientific study of our religion but also with their relationship to general knowledge. The philosophers, philologists, historians, jurists, and political economists, to mention only the representatives of the so-called humanistic disciplines, must obtain a far better knowledge of the essence of our religion, if it is to achieve an enhanced influence in history. Indeed, from such a process of cultural interchange even a natural scientist might be influenced to a more correct evaluation of the nature of Judaism. What Zunz wrote remains true: "the achievement by the Jews of equal status in morality and life will follow from the equalization of the scientific study of Judaism with other academic disciplines." Indeed, the attainment by the scientific study of Judaism of a position of equality with other academic disciplines is an indispensable prerequisite of any genuine and effectively implemented social emancipation. Now in Germany, at least, the achievement of such equal status by the scientific study of Judaism, can be expected only in the universities; and, as I know the circumstances, the same condition seems to obtain in the United States. In Germany the sciences have developed primarily at the universities. Hence, only the knowledge which is propagated there has any chance for enduring success, as contrasted with the sensational vogue of the moment. Only such science continues to have the validity of a mature and objective conviction or doctrine, notwithstanding many weaknesses and interruptions. Whatever we may achieve in the way of establishing our own institutions of higher learning for advancing the scientific study of Judaism will certainly redound to our benefit in many ways, and hopefully may exert some influence upon the general world of learning. Yet it remains true that this influence remains impeded and stopped because it is concealed and diverted by the prejudice against the Ghetto.

It must therefore be our aim to establish and domesticate the scientific study of Judaism at the universities. We know that the state in its present condition will not undertake to acceed to our request. There would be even less likelihood of such a development were we to insist that only Jews be the professors of the scientific study of Judaism. For Judaism is our living religion and not just an area of the scientific study of antiquity. Nor is it simply an aspect of Christian theology or of the history of religion or the philosophy of religion, insofar as these disciplines treat Judaism as a preliminary to Christianity, which happens even at meetings of Orientalists and at congresses of religion. It is impossible for one of another faith to profess the scientific study of a living religion, in this case of our religion. A living religion can be represented scientifically only by one who belongs to it by an *inner religious attachment.* Such a presentation must be distinguished from denominational partisanship by its scientific approach and temper, and by the various controls appropriate to science. Still, one cannot scientifically set forth the essence of religion if one has another religion in his heart. The time will come when the state will regard itself as compelled to recognize its responsibility in providing for the scholarly exposition of our religion, whether primarily in the interests of its Jewish citizens or as part of its obligation to scientific truth. How near or far this time may be, we cannot here estimate. At the moment, however, we must reckon rather with the intention to exterminate Judaism.

Moreover it is also a matter of experience that the number of those dedicating themselves to the scientific study of Judaism is progressively dwindling. At an earlier period it was expected that the rabbis would be the depositories and developers of Jewish learning, and in the majority of cases one could rely on this expectation. Nowadays, however, the practical demands upon the rabbi are so numerous, and pastoral duties have become so manifold and urgent, that there is a danger that the rabbis themselves may lose religious depth and power. For this reason we must give more and more attention to insuring the furtherance of Jewish learning at the hands of scholars outside of the rabbinical calling. This entire matter provides yet another argument for our proposal to find a proper refuge for the scientific study of Judaism at the universities.

The upshot of my second proposal therefore is that, following the example of patrons of learning in the United States of America, many of whom are our own noble co-religionists and who indeed as such have wrought imperishable deeds in our great Order of B'nai B'rith, there be established foundations for the subvention of such scholars of Judaic studies. These professors would be equipped to teach our discipline, namely, the study of the living religion of Judaism at the universities and would be animated by the desire to do so.

Some may raise the objection that this might lead to the exertion of denominational influence on the philosophical faculties in much the same way as theological and political or economic interferences with academic freedom have lately been attempted. But this analogy rests on a purely superficial consideration, for in the other endeavors the state was to be compelled to exert pressure upon the faculties. Our plan excludes any such interference. The faculty remains sovereign with respect to the Jewish scholar who applies to it for admission to its ranks.* The Jewish scholar need have no connection with the authorities who administer the required capital. It is sufficient for him to know that authorities exist who administer the necessary funds, and such knowledge provides his support. He knows that if he continues with his teaching and scholarly activity his remuneration will be assured, even though the state declines to carry this responsibility. We do not seek for these Jewish scholars at the universities either formal invitation or official appointment to any particular level of the academic echelon. It is our concern only that the Jewish scholar who makes it his life's work to represent and profess the scientific study of Judaism at the university receive an income which corresponds to that of the official professors. His religious idealism will help him to do without

---

* Literally, "for seeking the *venia legendi*"—the Latin term for official license to lecture in the German university.

the official honors which the state may or does deny him, insofar as this may be the case. The young Jewish scholar who feels that it is his vocation to represent our cause at the university must be shielded from the worry that he is undertaking something which will prevent him from earning a livelihood.

I close by recalling a verse from our Hallel prayer, "Thou didst thrust sore at me that I might fall; but the Lord helped me." (Psalm 118:13)

33. The Importance of Jewish Unity

". . . ULTIMATELY the controversies which are agitating
our communal life today must be interpreted rather as significant
symptoms of the inner life of our religion. A modern religion
can never regard itself anywhere as firmly fixed and anchored.
Rather must it create anew, by independent effort, the bases and
the warranties of its faith. In this process errors and deviations
are inevitable, as are also frictions and attacks. It does no good
at all to register complaints on this score or to make lamentations over it for such is the course of human affairs. There is
no life without struggle and no religion without evolution.

Yet truly the goal of religion is not just the security of the
individual in his own personal faith but surely also the protection and renewed establishment and fortification of the religion
itself for the sake of the community, in the unity of which the
individual himself first achieves religious unity. As one who
professes a liberal type of religion (*freie Religiosität*), I must
always bear in mind, therefore, that I am dependent on a traditional and historical background of doctrines and teachings,
with which I must never lose relationship, even as I must bear
in mind that I am connected with a community with which I
must and will remain associated. Even though I regard it as my
religious obligation constantly to revitalize for myself this background and hence to make certain changes in some of its individual components, which is inevitable in every intellectual

effort in regard to their value and in their practical effectiveness, I nevertheless remain linked with the ideal unity of this background.

Hence, for all my religious freedom I have a relationship to the community as the indestructible and indeed inexhaustible background of a fellowship in which I find the focus of my own religion. Indeed, this is a principle that I must continue to bear in mind. There is a dictum of Talmudic wisdom which cannot be admired too highly: "Whoever proclaims the *Shema*, is termed a Jew." What is noteworthy in this remark is that in the mind of this sage it is not the six hundred and thirteen commandments, positive and negative, that occupy the forefront of his historical consciousness, and certainly not the various other supernumerary elements that have accumulated in the tradition of Judaism. The only element that ties together into a unity all members of the house of Israel is the *unity of God*.

This proposition holds true in two directions. I am entitled to demand of the orthodox Jew that he recognize me as a Jew and that he do so without reservation though not in any explicit dogmatic assertion; and that in all his controversies with me he remain ever mindful of this background unity which unites us inseparably. On the other hand, in formulating my own point of view and my differences from the traditional position, I must also retain a very lively memory of this unity which subsists indestructibly among us and for out sake. My own standpoint becomes one-sided or partial unless I complete it with this supplemental position. Nor does it suffice to practice this considerateness in dry, stiff abstraction like some forced act of sufferance. Rather must I endow this political logic of my religious communal life with the warmth of emotion and with the sympathetic perceptiveness that it is with a brother in the faith with whom I must engage in controversy, but only in order to achieve victory together with him; for alone, and without him, I cannot be victorious, nor do I wish to do so.

Our B'nai B'rith Lodge is the natural refuge for such education and training in our communal and religious politics. The orthodox person sits by my side and despite his energetic and deeply rooted preference for the traditional protective life of our religion, he recognizes me as a co-religionist, and this is all that I am entitled to demand of him. In this regard he is reflecting the broad-minded position of the Talmud, which is the basis of all religious toleration. What then in return do I owe him?

As I have grown older, I have more and more come to the conviction that we liberal Jews should meet our traditional co-religionists half way at *one* point. Fortunately, in this regard, we need only follow a certain basic trend of our contemporary culture. What is this essential trend? To foster education, without regard to any difference of opinion, to advance education generally, are goals to be striven for in all questions of culture. Among us, too, education is generally fostered in most respects. Yet we reject this position only when it comes to religion, in regard to which the attitude seems to be that we should content ourselves with the crumbs which are very sparingly thrown to us by the Jewish journals and sermons. In regard to this matter alone we do not wish our children to be burdened with new knowledge, as though there could be any training without a foundation of knowledge. Scholarship has been lost to the broad masses of our community. I refer to the loss of that general diffusion of Jewish learning in the past by virtue of which there was no such thing in the Jewish community as a difference between faith and knowledge.

34. Peace and Death

I F there had to be one word to characterize the essence of the
Jewish spirit, this word is peace. To be sure only he is able to
comprehend the unity of the Jewish spirit, who is able to penetrate to its deepest religious levels. To any external view hatred
and revenge might appear to dominate the spirit of the Jew,
seeing that he has been hated and persecuted by the whole
world. Would it not be remarkable if he did not harbor venge-
ful resentment in his soul? Indeed it would, were it not controlled by the greater marvel of the Jewish doctrine and the
religious life in accordance therewith. The life of religious obligation lived under the yoke of the law implanted such freedom
and peace in the heart of the Jew that hatred and the desire for
vengeance could not take root therein. For the yoke of the law
was for the Jew—the yoke of the kingdom of God and the
latter was the kingdom of peace for all the people of a unified
mankind. How could hatred become domiciled in a type of spirit
which believed in peace among men with all the power of religious faith and all the sense of obligation imposed by such a
faith?

Messianism is and remains the basic power of the Jewish spirit
and the Messiah is the Prince of Peace. Indeed Canticles celebrates peace even in regard to the very name of the heroine of
love, namely Sulamith, the maiden of peace (etymologically related to the root of the word for peace). Similarly the poetry of

the Psalms is not pastoral poetry but the heroic poetry of peace
for man and within man.

What is the summation of all of human life in the spirit of
the Bible? It is peace which comprises all the significance and
value of life. It is tantamount to the unity of all its vital potentialities of life, its balance, and the resolution of all its contradictions. Peace is the crown of life.

Human life has its terminus in death, yet death is not the end
but only a termination and a new beginning. It is significant that
in the Jewish view death is designated as peace. "May peace be
upon him" or "may peace be over him," is the phrase customar-
ily used among Jews when referring to a deceased person. Thus
peace takes the sting from death and also provides a solution for
its mystery. The person who has been removed from life has
not been taken further away from peace but rather has been
brought closer to it. Now he stands directly under the peace of
God. Consequently the memorial dedicated to the deceased is
not the product of concern for his soul's welfare, much less a
supplication for the liberation of the deceased from the terrors of
purgatorial punishments. The man has died with the confession
of sins upon his lips; he has accomplished his repentance in his
self-purification. Consequently, his salvation is recommended
to the grace of the forgiving God. Over him there is peace—
this is the best and indeed the only thing one can say about the
cessation of his existence now that he is no more. Hence, for
those who survive the remembrance of him comes to expression
in an ineradicable feeling of gratitude and in a consequent admonition to follow the responsibilities and obligations of love
and to be faithfully obedient even as the ancestors have done. If
there could be any doubt at all whether peace is one of the
primary sources for the power of the Jewish virtues, the Jewish conception of death alone ought to allay it. For death is the
world of peace.

No greater praise can be attributed to death than to describe
it as peace achieved beyond the world of struggle and beyond
the life of error and conflict. Life must seek peace; it finds it in
death. Hence death is not the real end of human life but rather
the goal and the victorious prize of life in all its efforts. Who-
soever loves peace cannot fear death. "The Lord is my shepherd,
I shall not want . . . Though I walk through the valley of the

shadow of death I shall fear no evil for Thou art with me"
(Psalm 23:4). The unique God is at the side of man also in
death. This is the high point in Judaism's thinking and in its
attitude toward peace. . . . It is characteristic of the psychology of the Jew that he does not fear death. This unique feature
may be explained only by the complete absence of the fear of
purgatorial punishment. Such is the strength of the peace of God
in the Jewish spirit that it is unable to envisage God as the Judge
of hell. To the Jew, God is only the God of forgiveness, and
when he acts as Judge it is only in the process of atonement.
Consequently there is no fear of death in the Jewish attitude.
For this reason also the remembrance of the dead is not concerned with the welfare of the souls of the dead in the sense
that these must be protected from punishment. By the prayers
of their survivors, we observe the memory of our dead in the pious hope that their souls will have been united with those of
our patriarchs and matriarchs. In the memorial of the dead as
we celebrate it, this unification with the history of our religious
people is our only concern. Just as the patriarchs were gathered
unto their fathers and their people at their death, so every Jew
to this day dies with the hope of such an historical survival in
a unification with the ancestors of his group. Thus death becomes an historical survival; and in this survival the dominant
factor is peace which has transcended all terrestrial struggle.

Thus in this higher sense, peace is also a way of virtue because
it is a path leading to eternal life. On the road to peace there can
be no fear of death, for peace as denoting the condition of
eternal life becomes itself eternal peace, the status of eternity.
But the meaning, goal, and purpose of all of human life is eternity. Everything in the world of time leads to eternity if it is
following the right path. Now this correct road is that of
peace—the virtue of eternity.

It is characteristic of the Jewish feeling for language that it
employs the same word *olam* to denote both the world and
eternity. "He hath set the world in their heart" (Ecc. 3:11).
This world is eternity, so that one can speak of God's having set
eternity in the heart of man. It is peace that explains the apparent
contradiction of these two concepts. Clearly the world about us
certainly cannot be equated with eternity, as it is only transitory.
Nor could the myth of the decline and renewal of the world
find any reception in a religious consciousness which envisaged

God as the creator of the world for the very reason that He had to be the creator of man and of his holy spirit. Yet for such a religious consciousness, that regards the world as the creation and the revelation of God, neither the world nor man could be regarded as just ephemeral. The intimation of man's immortality and the world's eternity comes to expression in this profound word of the Hebrew language.

Later linguistic usage still retained this intimation by designating the cemetery (or God's acre as the German idiom has it) as "the house of eternity" (*Bet Olam*). Death is peace, and the grave is the house of eternity, which is the true end and goal of the terrestrial world. The virtuous path of peace leads to this eternity, which is, however, only a continuation of terrestrial life. The same root word covers both sides of existence, so that the peace which leads to eternity is also the guide for terrestrial life, to the beginning which is contained within it for all historical survival. Thus, peace is the symbol of eternity and at the same time the guide of human life both in its individual unfoldment and in the eternity of its historical vocation. In this historical eternity there comes to fulfillment the peace-bringing mission of messianic mankind.

FOR FURTHER READING

Books by Hermann Cohen

Religion of Reason Out of the Sources of Judaism (New York: Ungar, 1972). A translation of Cohen's best known work.

Books about Hermann Cohen

BOROWITZ, Eugene B., *Choices in Modern Jewish Thought* (New York: Behrman House, 1983). Pages 29–52 contain Cohen's essay: "Neo-Kantianism."

"Hermann Cohen" in *Encyclopedia Judaica*, Volume 5: pp. 673–676 (Jerusalem: 1972). Includes a biography and overview of his philosophy.

GLATZER, Nahum N., editor, *Modern Jewish Thought: A Source Reader* (New York: Schocken, 1977). Pages 46–54 contain a brief introduction and a translation of an address given by Cohen in 1907.

LEO BAECK
(1873–1956)

EDITOR'S NOTE

After the death of Hermann Cohen, Rabbi Leo Baeck emerged as the leading exponent of liberal Judaism in Germany. Scholar, preacher, community leader and teacher of a generation of rabbis, Baeck was the last representative figure of German Jewry during the Hitler era. To German Jewry, he was the heroic symbol of courage and spiritual resistance in the face of Nazi tyranny.

Baeck was born in 1873 in Lissa, Prussia, where his father served as rabbi. He studied at the Jewish Theological Seminary in Breslau and in 1897 received his rabbinic diploma from the *Hochschule für die Wissenschaft des Judentums*. For ten years he held the position of rabbi in the Silesian city of Oppeln and for another five years he was rabbi in Düsseldorf. In 1912, the same year that Hermann Cohen came to lecture at the Hochschule, Baeck began his career as rabbi of the Berlin Jewish community, where he soon emerged as one of the leaders of German Jewry. During the 1920's he taught at the *Hochschule* and served as head of several German Jewish organizations, including the General Rabbinical Assembly and the B'nai B'rith. When Hitler came to power Baeck was elected president of the Representative Council of German Jews. As conditions in Germany grew worse, Baeck was urged by friends in many countries to emigrate, but he refused, insisting that he could not desert his persecuted brethren. In 1943 he was sent to the concentration camp of Theresienstadt in Czechoslovakia where his teaching and religious activities set an example of hope and spiritual courage. After the war he went to live with his daughter in London and also lectured for several years at the Hebrew Union College in the United States.

In 1905 Baeck published *The Essence of Judaism* in answer to the German theologian Adolf von Harnack, whose classic work *The Essence of Christianity* asserted that the Christian faith was the absolute religion to which Judaism was plainly inferior. In reply, Baeck set out to prove Judaism's superiority by describing "the main road" rather than the "bypaths" which Judaism has taken, the "fundamental ideas which may be traced in all periods of its existence." After the war the book was rewritten and enlarged. In 1927 he published his volume on the *Pharisees* which created much discussion in Christian theological circles. His last book was entitled *Dieses Volk: Jüdische Existenz (This People: Jewish Existence)*. It was written on occasional scraps of paper in the concentration camp and completed together with a sequel just before his death in 1956. While most of his books have been translated, these last volumes have not as yet appeared in English.

Baeck's writings are neither as complex nor as philosophical as those of Hermann Cohen. However, their heaviness of style and frequent personal idioms do not make them easy reading. But they are rich in historical associations. The manner in which he contrasts Judaism with Christianity, Buddhism and the Greek philosophies lends depth to his analysis. We have selected several passages from the *Essence of Judaism*, the book for which he is best known, and two of his essays *Mystery and Commandment* and *Romantic Religion* in which he contrasts Judaism and Christianity, a subject that interested him throughout his life.

Judaism to Baeck was characterized by its emphasis on deeds rather than on dogma. Its essence lies in its ethical affirmations, in the divine command to redeem mankind from evil and, in contrast to other religions, in its essential optimism.

In our first selection, Baeck describes the unique quality of Judaism's optimism and its refusal to succumb to indifference or resignation in spite of its recognition of the presence of evil in the world. The Jew evolves a threefold relationship based on belief in God: a belief in himself, his neighbor and in mankind.

The two selections which follow deal with his concept of monotheism whose uniqueness, to Baeck as to Hermann Cohen, lies not in God's "numerical unity" but in His difference and incomparability. For Baeck, God is not a philosophical idea, but a living and commanding God who is a vital fact of personal experience. It is important that we have a relationship with Him, that we have, as he puts it, a "consciousness of being created." The ethical emphasis in Baeck's monotheism can also be seen in his discussion on prayer and in the Sabbath and holidays when the meaning of life becomes visible to us.

Baeck does not give any great prominence to *Halakhah*. The ceremonies and rituals of Judaism are a "fence around the law," a protection to insure the existence of the religious idea, but do not serve the religious idea itself. They are not to be regarded as "good deeds." According to Baeck, this characteristic of Judaism has been misunderstood by the Christian thinkers who criticize Judaism as overly legalistic.

In *Mystery and Commandment*, originally written in 1922 as a scholarly article, we are introduced to one of Baeck's best essays. His characterization of the religious experiences of "mystery" by which he meant an awareness of God and reality and "commandment"—the ethical obligation of man and the tasks he is to realize, is typical of the vivid contrasts he tries to establish in his writings. In Jewish existence, Baeck points out, "the mystery and the commandment are woven into one. Every mystery spells a commandment and every commandment means a mystery."

Our final selection is taken from his lengthy essay *Romantic Religion* in which he contrasts the types of piety to be found in Judaism and Christianity. It was originally published in a shorter version in 1922 and was later revised and expanded for a book which the Nazis confiscated before it was published. It is characterized by profound scholarship and penetrating insights into religious phenomena. Baeck wrote a number of articles on various aspects of Christianity; but this is probably his most important effort on that subject. Though strongly critical of Christianity with its romantic emphasis on feeling, imagination and the miraculous, he does not hesitate to point out that there are also aspects of "romanticism" in modern Judaism.

35. The Optimism of Judaism

. . . T H E distinctiveness of Judaism, which it has passed on to the rest of mankind, is its ethical affirmation of the world: Judaism is the religion of ethical optimism. Of course this optimism is completely foreign to the complacent indifference of the man who declares the world to be good simply because he is well-off in it or that dilettantism which denies suffering and praises this as the best of all possible worlds—*la rage de soutenir que tout est bien quand on est mal*. Judaism rejects this superficial optimism. Israel knows too much about life to speak of want and suffering as anything but what they really are. More frequent and more moving than the paean to life's joys is Israel's lament that this world is a place of misery and affliction. "The days of our years are three score years and ten, or even, by reason of strength, four score years; yet is their pride but labor and sorrow." So reads the prayer of Moses, the man of God, of which echoes may be heard throughout the Bible: it is a book of sighs and tears, sorrow and affliction, spiritual oppression and anguish of conscience. The same tones can be found in the songs which Judaism sang through the centuries. Distinctly audible in the voice of Judaism is a note of contempt for the world—a pessimistic and serious note that vibrates as a dark undertone of Israel's fundamental optimism.

This undertone resounds with especial volume in the emotion of the soul which experiences the depths of baseness and depravity. It resounds in the feeling of those wounded by earthly power and of those who would turn away from all the low and evil things that fill the lands of the earth. This cry of denial— the denial of power and prestige—comes from the deepest need for affirmation; it despises and rejects in order to be certain of what is lofty and true. An optimism aware of the ideal will view the facts with pessimism. There is no persistent goodness without the power of disdain, no true love of man without this faculty of contempt for man. But the unique quality of Judaism's optimism is that despite the prevalence of wickedness in this world, it does not succumb to mere indifference to, or resignation in, this world. Its ideal is not that of the sage of antiquity who, satisfied with his own wisdom and peace of mind, is no longer moved by the struggles of man. In this respect Judaism differs radically from the thought of Greece and India. It faces the world with the will to change it and with the commandment to realize the good in it. The sage of antiquity knows only the satisfaction of his own contentment. Judaism never abandons the goal of the world since it has no doubt in the God who has bid men to march to that goal. Its optimism is the strength of the moral will; its call is "Prepare the way!" (Isaiah 40:3).

. . . The optimism of Judaism consists of the belief in God, and consequently also a belief in man, who is able to realize in himself the good which first finds its reality in God. From the optimism all the ideas of Judaism can be derived. Thereby a threefold relationship is established. First, the belief in oneself: one's soul is created in the image of God and is therefore capable of purity and freedom; the soul is the arena in which reconciliation with God is always possible. Secondly, the belief in one's neighbor: every human being has the same individuality that I have; his soul with its possible purity and freedom also derives from God; and he is at bottom akin to me and is therefore my neighbor and my brother. Thirdly, the belief in mankind: all men are children of God; hence they are welded together by a common task. To know the spiritual reality of one's own life, of the life of our neighbors and of the life of humanity as a whole as they are grounded in the common reality of God—this is the expression of Jewish optimism.

These three aspects of the belief in the good cannot be separated in the demands they impose on us any more than they can be detached from their mutual foundation: the One God. Only the knowledge of our own soul, of its personal character and the depth of its being, gives certainty and freedom to the spiritual relationship with the life around us. Conversely, only in the knowledge of the soul of our fellow, and in the consciousness that that which we call our own is also possessed by him, does our own individuality find its duty and expression. Faith in others necessitates faith in ourselves; faith in ourselves necessitates faith in others. And, finally, only from the idea that all human life has unity, does one's own self and the self of one's fellow derive inter-relatedness. These strands of belief are rooted in the certainty that the path of this life comes from God and leads back to God. From faith in God we come to discover the value of our own soul, of our fellow man, and of all mankind. . . .

36. The Religious Value of Monotheism

. . . T H E difference between the many gods and the One God is not a mere difference in number—there could be no grosser misunderstanding—but a difference in essence. The demarcation is not arithmetical; it is religious and ethical. In many of the pagan religions, especially the Greek, the plurality of gods coalesced from time to time into a sort of unity, a so-called henotheism. It came into existence either when a general divine principle was accepted as acting through many gods, or when one special God, endowed with an unusual effectiveness, was temporarily worshipped in place of the others. But there is no basic equivalence between this phenomenon and Israel's monotheism. This is true quite apart from the fact that in the Greek view, as Xenophon says, besides that "one God who is greatest among gods and men," all the other gods must be recognized and worshipped as gods. What is decisive is that even this "greatest god" and that universal divine element are not to be compared with the One God of Israel, for they are not what the Holy One is; their basic nature and demand to men are not ethical and not the essence of the revelation of their divinity. Resultantly moral action is not demanded in the Greek view as the true worship which man offers to God.

The religious value of monotheism consists not in its numerical unity, but in the reason for its unity: the content of its idea of

God. The God of Israel is not One merely because he alone can accomplish what all the gods of polytheism can together accomplish. He is different from them all, he acts differently from them all. Not only is he more exalted than they; he really cannot be compared with them. For he alone is the creating and commanding God whose nature it is that he can be served by man only by the fulfilment of moral demands. Hence monotheism was not a mere development from previous beliefs; it was rather their great contradictory, the revelation of the other principle: "Thus saith the Lord, the King of Israel and its redeemer, the Lord of Hosts: I am the first, and I am the last, and besides me there is no God" (Isaiah 44:6).

Certain thinkers have paradoxically maintained that the idea of God is in itself no more religious than, say, the idea of gravitation. There is a certain truth in this view. For it is possible to accept the existence of a God on philosophical grounds to explain the cosmic order by establishing a first cause in the process of nature. Toward that concept of God, the paradox is justified. The philosophical formula of God as the first mover is in itself not really richer in religious significance than any other philosophical idea. In this idea faith can find neither its basis nor strength. The gift of religious certainty is conveyed solely by that which God means to our existence and our soul, by the inner consistency which our life thus gains, by our resultant moral power, by the satisfaction of finding answers to our questions and demands, and by our discovery of the relationship between our spiritual nature and the Divine—that feeling which realizes the call from God to us each day of our lives: "Where art thou?" (Genesis 3:9).

For Judaism, religion does not consist simply in the recognition of God's existence. We possess religion only when we know that our life is bound up with something eternal, when we feel that we are linked with God and that he is our God. And he is our God, as the phrase has it, if we love him, if we find through him our trust and humility, our courage and our peace, if we lay ourselves open in our innermost being to his revelation and commandment. Our attempts to grasp and express this inner connection are always only in the form of a simile—an expression of the human soul. Our praise of God, with its use of "I" and "Thou," shapes the features of ourselves, and our meditations about God, with the use of the word "He," forms our idea of him. But whether we approach God with devout words of intimacy or we desire to approach God by pure thought, the result is essentially the same so long as we feel that he is our God. Of our God our minds may form their own conceptions and ideas and our hearts may concurrently pray to him: "Thou, O Lord, art our Father, our Redeemer; thy name is from everlasting" (Isaiah 63:16). "Whom have I in heaven but Thee? And there is none upon earth that I desire beside Thee. My flesh and my heart faileth: but God is the strength of my heart, and my portion forever" (Psalms 73:25f). That is why Judaism speaks so little of religious doctrine and confessions of faith, but speaks rather of the living God, who is God to every man. Only thus does the idea of God become a religious one, only thus does it gain in religious strength. To know of this One God, in whom all things find meaning, to bear witness to him, to trust in him, to find shelter in him, to believe in him—that is what Israel taught mankind and that constitutes the monotheism which its prophets gave to the world.

The characteristic feature of Judaism is thus the relation of man to God. Essential to it is the consciousness of being created. This conception is uniquely Jewish, peculiar to the belief in the One God. When man faces fate and nature and their gods, he feels himself dependent upon them in both the accidents and occurrences of his life; he is compelled and driven by neutral forces, wholly elect or wholly rejected. But when he faced the One God, the Israelite felt quite differently: for he knew himself to have been created by God, created just as everything else had been created. His life, and the lives of all others, thus became for him the revelation of the One God; in the religious sense, revelation and creation are the same. Israel was filled with the consciousness of being united with the One who is different from everything else, of being embraced and sustained by him, of knowing that in him lies the answer to the secret of man's origin and of all that exists. And thereby man experiences in himself the meaning of the entire world. Man and the world are linked in one certainty of life, a conviction that all life was bestowed, is upheld and will be maintained in safety forever. The One God is the God of the beginning and the end; he is *my* God. "The earth is the Lord's and the fullness thereof, the world and they that dwell therein" (Psalms 24:1). In place of the mythological legends of formation and annihilation there is here the idea of creation, the spiritual experience of the relation of all things human, all the world and all time with the one living God. In place of fatalism, which shows only the abysses of the inevitable, there is the idea of God in his creation. The mystery of growth becomes the certainty of origin and life. Not contingent events, but creation and divine action characterize the principle of the world. . . .

37. Prayer and Holidays

. . . O N L Y when man cries out for his God is he able to invoke him. That is why mysticism, which unifies man with God, knows no prayer, but only absorption and contemplation. Prayer to the One God can arise only on the basis of tension and yearning with their fear and knowledge and trust. In prayer man turns toward the exalted God "who dwells on high" but whom he knows to be near. He is the God of the farthest remoteness and yet is the One who is with man—the God to whom man may cry: "Hear my prayer!" "The Lord is nigh unto all of them that call upon him, to all that call upon him in truth" (Psalms 145:18). "Seek ye the Lord while he may be found, call ye upon him while he is near" (Isaiah 55:6). This note of certainty is coupled with a note of anxiety: "Be not far from me" (Psalms 22:12). And Judaism also knows the sorrowful and almost despairing cry: "My God, my God, why hast thou forsaken me?" (Psalms 22:2). But here too, even in this cry of doubt and despair, there yet remains the sense of filiation: "*my* God." Whatever Judaism expresses in prayer—be it the longing to elevate one's soul to God; be it the desire for deliverance from danger and affliction or for redemption from sin and guilt; be it the desire for the gifts of life and the road to the blessing—it is always this tension between the sense of God's exaltedness and the sense of his proximity from which there rises the feeling of him who prays to God. There is thus always in it a wonderful intermingling of mystery and certainty: it is as if heaven and earth touched each other and the far God thereby became the near God. In prayer the life-impulse of the man who knows that God has created him turns toward the foundation of its existence. To the living God there turns the living man whose innermost being craves for the elevation and fulfilment of transcending the limitations of mortality. To speak of the expansion of life is thus a true word of prayer. "Out of straitness I called upon the Lord: the Lord answered me, and led me into enlargement" (Psalms 118:5). . . .

One of the gifts with which Judaism has enriched mankind is the custom of setting aside certain fixed hours for reverential worship, hours in which the public conscience is voiced and the divine will speaks to men's souls. At such occasions the ethical demand is linked with the divine service and through the sermon we again learn what we are meant to be. What we should perhaps not say to one another—since we are all only human—may and must be pointed out to everyone by the word of God. We may be lenient, but the word of God has the right to be severe. With its powerful zeal for the right and true and with its flaming wrath against baseness, God's word may rightly oppose the measured feelings of everyday life as they are compressed within the boundaries of conventionality. The hard and unyielding bluntness of the Bible is needed to shatter that weak conventionality which is so easily satisfied with compromise and that smooth sagacity which merely disguises lack of character. In contrast to the standards which govern and judge us in the outside world, we need constantly to reawaken the consciousness that "the Lord is our Judge, the Lord is our Lawgiver, the Lord is our King" (Isaiah 33:22).

Together with its Sabbath days Judaism has created the solemn seasons which twine themselves round the year like a holy bond. By pointing to the true meaning of existence, these holidays help to hold our life together so that it does not disintegrate into a mere succession of days. We must find occasions during our life, intervals between work and pauses in our path, when the meaning of life can once again become visible to us. No later religion or historical period has been able to add anything to the essence of the Jewish holy days. An external or artistic development took place, but nothing that raised the conception of the holy days. Here too the creative power of Israel revealed its lasting strength. . . .

38. The World Beyond

. . . THOUGH belief in the continuation of life after death is inherent in the nature of prophetic religion, the Bible, while not denying or repudiating this belief, says little about it. There is a special reason for this biblical reserve on the subject of immortality. It is a silent rejection of all the excessive and unbridled fancies in which the "nature" religions surrounding Israel decked out the world beyond. It was a significant, eloquent silence. The prohibition, "Thou shalt not make unto thee any graven image, or any likeness of anything," was interpreted, consciously or unconsciously, as a command that no images of the realm of death should enter the spiritual life of Judaism. In true conformity with the second commandment, this was essentially a rejection of paganism with its cult of images.

Once idolatry, however, had been overcome in Judaism, it became possible to speak of eternal life in a freer, and more definite fashion. To the hopeful mind eternal life is as a spiritual kingdom, a life of the soul in a purity which is denied to man in this world; it is a "purified world" which "enables him to enjoy the glory of God." The reward of piety of which the Holy Scriptures speak is now transferred to a world beyond. The "length of the days" which it promises now appears as "eternal life," and the message of happiness which it brings is interpreted to mean "eternal bliss." Thus the reward becomes spiritualized; the spirit comes from God and returns to him again. It unites man with God; God is spirit and spirit is in man; God is "the God of the spirits of all flesh" (Numbers 16:22). The conception of a spiritual vocation is now developed—a higher life which is to begin in this world and attain completion in the world of eternity. Here again the distinctively Jewish view is that this spiritual element is bound up with the ethical. The spiritual is the power of the good, the faculty of religious action. A solemn sentence in an old rabbinic writing says: "I call heaven and earth to bear witness: whether it be heathen or Israelite, whether it be man or woman, man-servant or maid-servant, all according to his deeds does the Holy Spirit rest upon a man." . . .

39. The Fence Around the Law

... T H E difference between the two religions [Judaism and Christianity] is indeed essential. In Judaism—this is its innermost being—anxiety for the preservation of the holy community is expressed as a demand for definite deeds. The individual is considered as a religious personality to whom the commandment is directed; the individual must join in the creation of the community and in the strengthening of the bond which preserves it; he maintains the community. To the tasks set by Judaism's faith in God and in man are added the duties based upon the commandment for the continued existence of the religious community, which are to be fulfilled by action. In accordance with the severity and duration of the struggle which Judaism had to conduct, these duties were exceedingly numerous. They include the manifold statutes, forms, customs, and institutions—e.g., the dietary laws and Sabbath rules, elaborated in the Talmud and usually given the erroneous name of the ritual Law. These serve not the religious idea itself but mainly the protection it needs—a security for its existence through the existence of the religious community. This, and only this, is the primary measure of their value.

Their significance is characteristically expressed in the talmudic phrase, "The fence around the law." They are a barricade for, rather than the doctrine of, Judaism. Historically, this distinction has been maintained: the religion was not confused with or put on the same level as these statutes. One item of evidence makes this distinction sufficiently clear and definite: the performance of a ritual statute is never regarded as a "good deed"; only religious and ethical action is so viewed. But that is not the only evidence. The great confession of sins on the Day of Atonement concerns only the ethical conduct of life and all of its ramifications. Though the boundaries of this confession reach far and deep, trying to include all human failings, they do not take into their fold violations of ritual and ceremonial statutes; only the transgression of ethical law appears as a sin.

But the strongest proof of all is, perhaps, that the Talmud openly declares that one day all these customs and institutions will lose their binding force and become superfluous. In the days of the Messiah—that is, when the struggle for the preservation will have been consummated in its goal of peace—these customs will have reached the limits of their relevance and will be allowed to lapse. No sharper distinction can be drawn between the true duties of religion and those which serve only to preserve it.

That the peculiar quality of this "fence" of custom can all too often be misinterpreted or misunderstood, especially in the interests of a Christian construction of history, is partly due to the misunderstanding caused by the old translation and to the misleading effect of old polemics. The Greek translation of the Bible, the Septuagint, renders the word Torah, "teaching," by the word *nomos*, "law." A literal translation would have been unsatisfactory since the two conceptions do not convey quite the same meaning in the two languages. To the Greeks the word "law," suggesting a note of religious solemnity and authority, seemed more adequate. It suggested to the Hellenic mind the conception of divine teaching as contrasted with human teaching. But afterward this word *nomos* or law became susceptible to misunderstanding since it seemed to imply the idea of bondage, compulsion, and even despotism. The polemic of Paul's epistles makes special use of this implication. He opposes the new covenant of Faith to the old covenant of Law, and suggests that the law is something lesser and lower, something temporary, now to be supplanted by Faith. Judaism, the religion of law, is superseded by the religion of grace, which tells of the all-significant miracle that can happen to man and for which he needs but wait. Compared to this miracle, all human action vanishes and is valueless for the relationship between God and man.

When in contrast to this Christian conception, Judaism is called a religion of law, that is not an inaccurate statement; for it is the religion which tells man what is required of him but leaves the decision with him. In the epistles of Paul law is, in fact, first and foremost this domain of religious and ethical commandment—the categorical "thou shalt" which man has to choose. "Honor thy father and thy mother," "strive after righteousness," "love thy neighbor as thyself"—all these are here "law." Paul also accepts as "law" in the same sense all that comprises, in the eyes of Judaism, the fence around the Teaching. Both are here combined in a single conception; the moral and the ritual are on one level; both are equally inferior to faith, and both, compared to faith, are of no significance for the covenant between God and man.

In polemics against Judaism this fact was frequently misunderstood or completely forgotten, especially during those later periods when the followers of Christianity became uncertain in their faith and therefore sought all the more arduously to discover its special and novel feature. Judaism had to be deprecated by representing it as the religion of the Law, a religion characterized by legalism and rigid formalism. It thereby became increasingly difficult to regard the commandments about justice and love, which to Paul are also Law, as law in a disapproving sense. The so-called "ritual" commandments were then assigned the blame and until this day they serve as grounds for reproaching Judaism with being a religion of law. And since Judaism had to be represented as essentially a religion of law, there remained no alternative but to regard these ritual statutes as its most important part. In the eyes of the polemists against Judaism, they stand on a level of complete equality with the commandments of love and justice, if indeed they do not supersede them. In this way the doctrine of Paul, which had put morality side by side with ritual, was foisted upon Judaism. And accordingly this Jewish law, in the interpretation of the Church, was described as mere outward service, something which had significance and value in its mere routine performance, a kind of sacramental act. Only by disparaging the opponent did the conception of their own superiority appear tenable. . . .

40. Mystery and Commandment

THERE are two experiences of the human soul in which the meaning of his life takes on for a man a vital significance: the experience of mystery and the experience of commandment; or, as we may also put it, the knowledge of what is real and the knowledge of what is to be realized.

When man wants to be certain of his existence, when he therefore listens intently for the meaning of his life and life in general, and when he thus feels the presence of something lasting, of some reality beneath the surface, then he experiences the mystery: he becomes conscious that he was created, brought into being—conscious of an undetectable and, at the same time, protective power. He experiences that which embraces him and all else. He experiences, in the words of the ancient metaphor on the Blessing of Moses, "the arms of eternity."

And when man looks beyond the present day, when he wishes to give his life direction and lead it toward a goal, when he thus grasps that which defines his life and is clear about it, then he is always confronted with the commandment, the task, that which he is to realize. The foundation of life is the mystery; the way of life is the revealed. The one is from God; the other to be achieved by man. To cite another thought from the Bible: "That which is concealed belongs unto the Lord our God, but that which is revealed belongs unto us and unto our children forever, that we may do all the words of this Torah." And both, mystery as well as commandment, represent certainty—the certainty of life, the certainty of the self.

This twofold experience could also be called humility and reverence. The humility of man is his recognition that his life is framed by infinity and eternity, by that which transcends all human knowledge and apprehension, and surpasses all that is natural and existent; that his life is absolutely dependent; that the unknowable and unnamable, the unfathomable and unthinkable enters into his life. Humility is the feeling for that deep and mysterious sphere in which man is rooted; the feeling, in other words, for that which remains in being and is real—the great quiet, the great devotion in all philosophy and all wisdom. And reverence is man's feeling that something higher confronts him; and whatever is higher is ethically superior and therefore makes demands and directs, speaks to man and requires his reply, his decision. It can reveal itself in the small and weak no less than in the sublime; it can manifest itself in the other as well as in oneself. Reverence is thus the recognition of the holy, that which is infinitely and eternally commanding, that which man is to accept into his life and realize through his life—the great impelling force, the active aspect of wisdom.

This twofold experience can also be intimated in this way: the consciousness that we have been created versus the consciousness that we are expected to create. The former is our certainty of that through which all that lives has life; our certainty that, at heart and in truth, we are related to the oneness of all life; our certainty of that which is omnipresent and enduring. It is the capacity of the soul for grasping the invisible in the visible, the lasting in the momentary, the eternal in the transitory, and the infinite in the earthly and limited. It is this faith which ever and again grasps that which has reality and which is the principle and source of life. The latter, on the other hand, is the capacity to be aware of the demand and determination of the hour; it is the certainty of the task, of that which admonishes, points ahead, and directs our life; the certainty that every man's life can do its share and accomplish its function; that man has some quality that lifts him out of the universe which has been created even as he himself has been created—a quality which gives man a quite personal aspect, a quite individual place and a unique direction and freedom, a capacity for decision by virtue of which man comprehends again and again what he is supposed to fulfill.

These are the two experiences of the meaning of life. And what is peculiar to Judaism is that these two experiences have here become one, and are experienced as one, in a perfect unity. And it is thus that the soul becomes conscious of its own unity and totality; it is thus that piety springs up in the soul. From the one God come both mystery and commandment, as one from the One, and the soul experiences both as one. Every mystery means and suggests also a commandment; and every commandment means and suggests also a mystery. All humility also means and suggests reverence, and all reverence, humility; all faith, the law, and all law, faith. All consciousness that we have been created means and suggests the demand to create, and every demand to create means and suggests the consciousness that we have been created. What is evident is here rooted in that which is concealed, and what is concealed always has its evident aspect for man. The profundity of life cannot be grasped without its also speaking to us of duty in life; and not a single duty of life is perceived truly without at the same time proclaiming the profundity of life. We cannot have knowledge of the foundation of our life without at the same time beholding our way, and we cannot understand this way without penetrating to the foundation of our life. We cannot fully take to heart that we are the creatures of God without apprehending also that we ought to be the creators of our own lives; and we cannot be in full possession of this commandment to create unless we remain aware that we ourselves have been created—created by God that we ourselves may create, and creating because we have been created by God. This unity of both experiences in the human soul constitutes Jewish piety and Jewish wisdom; the meaning of life reveals itself here in this form.

Therefore Judaism is not marred by the split which is introduced by other conceptions of God. Judaism lacks any foundation for the conflict between transcendence and immanence. Jewish piety lives in the paradox, in the polarity with all its tension and compactness. That which is a contradiction in the abstract world of mere theory is made a unity and a whole in the religious consciousness. For this consciousness there is no such thing as this world without any beyond, nor a beyond without this world; no world to come without the present world, and no human world without that which transcends it. Whatever is on this side is rooted in the beyond, and whatever is beyond demands completion on this side by man. The infinite appears in the finite, and whatever is finite bears witness to the infinite. The life of man leads from God to man and from man to God. God is He in whom is all being, and God is also He that is positively different. God gives man life, and God demands man's life from him. Our soul is what is divine in us, it is our mystery and shares the mystery of all souls; and yet it shows also our individual stamp, that which is unique within us, our very self, that which belongs to it alone. The human dwells in the divine, and the divine demands of every man his humanity. This unity of both, the meaning which emerges from this opposition, alone is truth and pregnant with thoroughgoing certainty.

Hence any opposition between mysticism and ethics has no place here either. The religious consciousness here is never without its immediacy, its experience—nor without that which has been commanded and still is to be realized in life. No experience without tasks and no tasks without experience; life dwells only where both are present. In Judaism, all ethics has its mysticism and all mysticism its ethics. This applies to the whole far-flung history of its ideas. For Jewish mysticism the energies welling up out of God are energies of the will. Floods of mystery full of commandments and floods of commandment full of mystery issue from God. And the deed which fulfills God's commandment opens up a gate through which these floods surge into man's day. All absorption in the profundity of God is always also an absorption in the will of God and His commandment. And all Jewish ethics is distinguished by being an ethic of revelation or, one might almost say, an ethic of experience of the divine: it is the tidings of the divine. Every "thou shalt" is confronted with another word which introduces it and simultaneously replies to it—another word which is at the same time the word of mystery: "Thus saith the Lord." And it is followed by this same word both as a conclusion and a new beginning: "I am the Lord thy God." Ethics is here rooted in the profundity of living experience, and it is significant that in the Hebrew language of the Middle Ages the same word is used to designate an ethical disposition and a mystical absorption. The history of Judaism from ancient times to the present could be written as a history of mysticism; and the history of Judaism from its origins until now could also be written as a history of "the Law"—and it would be the same history. And for the most part it would be the history of the very same men. Many of the most influential and decisive teachers of the law have been mystics; for example, the author of the oft-cited *Shulhan Arukh*.

Of course, mystery and commandment were not always emphasized equally in Judaism. Now the one was stressed more, now the other; and this distinguishes different spheres and epochs. Only where one or the other was supposed to constitute the whole of religion, only where the whole of piety was exclusively identified with one or the other, did the religion cease to be Judaism. Judaism ceases where the mood of devotion, that which is at rest and restful, would mean everything; where faith is content with itself, content with mystery; where this mere faith finally extends its darkling glimmer to the point where it drowns the world and dreams become the stuff of life. The religion of mere passivity, devoid of commandments, is no longer Judaism. Nor is Judaism to be found where the commandment is content with itself and is nothing but commandment; where the whole sphere of life is supposed to be embraced by commandments and only that which lies under the rays of their cold light is presumed to be the meaning of life; where man thinks that he has seen everything when he sees the way on which he is to proceed. The religion of mere activity without devotion—this religion which becomes an ethic of the surface, or no more than the custom of the day—is not Judaism. The world of Judaism is to be found only where faith has its commandment, and the commandment its faith.

This is why Paul left Judaism when he preached *sola fide* (by faith alone) and thereby wound up with sacrament and dogma. Mystery became everything for him, not only that which is concealed but also that which is manifest. Hence mystery finally had to become for him something tangible, namely, sacraments, and something that can be molded, namely, dogma. For it is always thus: sacraments are a mystery into which man enters, a mystery of which man can take hold; and dogma, like myth, is a mystery which man can build up and shape. The gospel—that old gospel which had not yet been adapted for the use of the Church and made to oppose Judaism—was still wholly a part of Judaism and conformed to the Old Testament. It is relatively less important that it was written in the language of the Jewish land and thus was a piece of Jewish literature. A full understanding of Jesus and his gospel is possible only in the perspective of Jewish thought and feeling and therefore perhaps only for a Jew. And his words can be heard with their full content and import only when they are led back into the language he spoke. The boundary of Judaism was crossed only by Paul at the point where mystery wanted to prevail without commandment, and faith without the law.

Judaism, however, can be abandoned no less on the other side. The very ground on which it rests is abandoned when these other developments take place: when it is assumed to be merely an ethic or the support for an ethic; when it becomes a mere edifice of ideas, a doctrine; or when that which the mystery intimates is no longer supposed to be the foundation of man's life but merely some postulate of his thought—when Judaism is taken to be a Judaism without paradox. There is no such thing as a Judaism which is nothing but Kantian philosophy or ethical culture, nor a Judaism in which the idea of God is merely a decorative embellishment or a crowning pinnacle. And the distinctive essence of Judaism is lost, too, where the abundance of its laws may still prevail, but merely as something that is performed, severed from its roots in mystery, void of devotion.

Jewish piety and Jewish wisdom are found only where the soul is in possession of the unity of that which is concealed and that which is evident, of the profound and the task—the unity of devotion and deed. What matters is the unity experienced in the soul, a unity which is born of a reality and points toward a truth—not a mere synthesis, and least of all syncretism. A synthesis merely puts two things alongside each other or at best into each other; but however closely it connects them, it merely connects one thing with another. A unity, on the other hand, involves no mere connection but a revelation: one thing is grasped and experienced through the other and each receives its meaning only from the other. Mystery and commandment are not merely connected and interwoven but proclaim each other and give each other their distinctive essences. The commandment is a true commandment only because it is rooted in mystery, and the mystery is a true mystery because the commandment always speaks out of it. Because it is rooted in mystery, the commandment is unconditional and absolute, independent of the ephemeral and useful, urgent and triumphant. It has the force of unconditional unity, of the unity of morality, or—and this is merely another way of putting it—it has the capacity for taking itself absolutely seriously, to think itself through; and this gives it its entire meaning. And because mystery here cannot be without commandment, it has its own blessing and creative power, and remains fertile; it has the power to demand real life and to give real life; it can let the well of profundity rise into the light of day and introduce the eternal into the present hour; it has the gift of being in everything and giving unity to everything or—and this is just another way of putting it—the gift of being real instead of merely existent. And it is this alone that gives mystery its full meaning. This totality and unity—this peculiar way in which each is grasped by way of the other—this is Judaism. . . .

As soon as we understand these traits and trends of Jewish religion, we can also comprehend that which many would consider its only aspect: the profusion of rules and customs with which the community surrounds itself, its so-called Law. In Judaism the attempt has been made to give life its style by causing religion to invade every day and penetrate the whole of everyday. Everything is in a sense divine service and has its mood and its dignity. In the view of the earthly, the spirit is to be safeguarded; and in the view of the desire, the freedom is to be kept. Judaism cannot do without this ascetic trait unless it wants to forego all that is inward and religious. It does not lead man out of his everyday world, but relates him to God within it. Every partition of life into the profane and the sacred is to be avoided, and the sanctuary dare not possess merely one day beside all the other days. The word "remember" is inscribed above this law: "That you may remember and do all my commandments and be holy unto your God." Thoughtlessness is the true Godlessness; it is the homelessness of the soul. And the Law would guard man against this state in which he is without mystery and commandment; it would give every surface its symbolic function and every bit of prose its parable. Every man is to be made the priest of his own life. Therefore are we confronted with such an abundance of customs, arrangements, and orders which surround everything, "when thou sittest in thy house, and when thou walkest by the way, and when thou liest down, and when thou risest up"—all the way to the ample prose of eating and drinking. All this has helped to consecrate the day and especially also the evening; and it is in his evenings perhaps even more than in his days that man really lives, and it is in his evenings that he dies. A form of life has been fashioned here, though it is, of course, not entirely free from the danger which confronts every style of life: it may cease to be something personal and alive and degenerate into something purely external, into mere tradition. The "Law," too, has sometimes been degraded in this way: that which was meant to be consecration has at times become a mere routine, the fulfillment of something handed down. But even then it was preferable to pure lack of style. And it contains the power of always coming to life again and retrieving its soul.

The whole love of the "Law" has been lavished on and has cherished the Sabbath. As the day of rest, it gives life its balance and rhythm; it sustains the week. Rest is something entirely different from a mere recess, from a mere interruption of work, from not working. A recess is something essentially physical, part of the earthly everyday sphere. Rest, on the other hand, is essentially religious, part of the atmosphere of the divine; it leads us to the mystery, to the depth from which all commandments come, too. It is that which re-creates and reconciles, the recreation in which the soul, as it were, creates itself again and catches its breath of life—that in life which is sabbatical. The Sabbath is the image of the messianic; it proclaims the creation and the future; it is the great symbol. In the words of the Bible, it is "a sign between God and Israel"; or, in the words of the Talmud, it is "the parable of eternity." In the Sabbath, life possesses the great contradiction of any end, a perpetual renaissance. A life without Sabbath would lack the spring of renewal, that which opens the well of the depth again and again. An essential and fruitful aspect of Judaism would dry up in such a life; it could still be an ethical life, but it would lack that which defines the Jewish life. Therefore the Jewish community clings to the Sabbath as its possession in spite of all civic difficulties and troubles. The care for the Sabbath is one of the fundamental cares of Judaism.

The Law, and quite especially the sabbatical element in it, has educated that capacity in man which is born only of the depth of life—the capacity to be different. Without this, life cannot be unique. Whoever experiences mystery and command- ment becomes unique among men, different, an individual within the world. Whoever knows only mystery becomes merely unique and knows only the day of silence. Whoever knows only the tasks is only among men and knows only the days of work and times of recess. But whoever experiences both, both in unity, lives in the world and yet is different, is different and yet is in the world, lives for other men and with other men and yet within himself, within himself and yet also for other men and hence also with them. This is the gift and possession of Judaism. And it may well be its historic task to offer this image of the dissenter, who dissents for humanity's sake. . . .

41. Romantic Religion

I f we classify types of piety in accordance with the manner in which they have historically become types of religion, then we encounter two forms above all: classical and romantic religiousness, classical and romantic religion. The distinction and opposition between these two types is exemplified especially by two phenomena of world history. One of these, to be sure, is connected with the other by its origin and hence remains determined by it within certain limits; and yet the significant dividing line separates them clearly. These two religions are Judaism and Christianity. In essential respects they confront each other as the classical religion and the romantic religion.

What is the meaning of romantic? Friedrich Schlegel has characterized the romantic book in these words: "It is one which treats sentimental material in a phantastic form." In almost exactly the same words one might also characterize romantic religion. Tense feelings supply its content, and it seeks its goals in the now mythical, now mystical visions of the imagination. Its world is the realm in which all rules are suspended; it is the world of the irregular, the extraordinary and the miraculous, that world which lies beyond all reality, the remote which transcends all things.

We can observe this disposition of the soul in relative historical proximity when we consider the German romantic of the last century. For him, everything dissolves into feeling; everything becomes mere mood; everything becomes subjective; "thinking is only a dream of feeling." Feeling is considered valid as such; it represents the value of life which the enthusiastic disposition wants to affirm. The romantic becomes enraptured and ecstatic for the sake of ecstasy and rapture; this state becomes for him an end in itself and has its meaning within itself. His whole existence is transformed into longing—not into the longing for God, in which man, raising himself above the earth, overcomes his earthly solitude; nor into the powerful longing of the will which thirsts for deeds; but into that sweet wavelike longing which pours itself out into feelings and becomes intoxicated with itself. Suffering and grief, too, become a good to him, if only the soul is submerged in them. He revels in his agonies as much as in his raptures.

Thus something agitated and excited, something overheated or intoxicated easily enters the feelings—and not only the feelings, but the language, too. Every expression seeks to excel in this direction; voluptuousness becomes a much sought-after word. The feelings talk in terms of superlatives; everything has to be made ecstatic. Fervently, the romantic enjoys the highest delight and the deepest pain almost day after day; he enjoys the most enchanting and the most sublime; he enjoys his wounds and the streaming blood of his heart. Everything becomes for him an occasion of enraptured shuddering, even his faith, even his devotion. Thus Novalis praises his Christianity for being "truly the religion of voluptuousness."

These souls can always be so full of feeling because their abundant suffering is, for the most part, only reverie and dream; almost all of it is merely sentimental suffering. They like so much to dream; the dim distances, twilight and moonlit night, the quiet, flickering hours in which the magic flower lowers its blossoming head, represent the time for which they are wearily waiting. They love the soft, the sweet illusion, the beautiful semblance; and whereas Lessing had said to God, "Give me the wrestling for the truth," the romantics implore, "Accord me lovely illusions." They want to dream, not see; they shun the distinctness of what is clearly beheld in the light, to the very point of antipathy against fact. Disgruntled they confront reality; and in its stead they seek the less clear attraction of fluctuating feelings to the point of outright delight in confusion. What is within and without becomes for them a semblance and a glimmer, resounding and ringing, a mere mythical game; and the world becomes a sadly beautiful novel, an experience to be felt. As Hegel once put it: "The sense for content and substance contracts into a formless weaving of the spirit within itself."

The desire to yield to illusion, justifiable in art, here characterizes the entire relation to the world. In the deliberately sought-out twilight of longing and dream, the border lines of poetry and life are effaced. Reality becomes mere mood; and moods, eventually, the only reality. Everything, thinking and poetry, knowledge and illusion, all here and all above, flows together into a foaming poem, into a sacred music, into a great transfiguration, an apotheosis. In the end, the floods should close over the soul, while all and nothing become one, as the grandson of the romantics celebrates it:

In the sea-like rapture's billowy swell,
In the roaring waves of a drowsy smell,
In the world-breath's flowing all—
To drown—
To sink down—
Unconsciousness—
Highest bliss.

In this ecstatic abandonment, which wants so much to be seized and embraced and would like to pass away in the roaring ocean of the world, the distinctive character of romantic religion stands revealed—the feminine trait that marks it. There is something passive about its piety; it feels so touchingly helpless and weary; it wants to be seized and inspired from above, embraced by a flood of grace which should descend upon it to consecrate it and possess it—a will-less instrument of the wondrous ways of God. When Schleiermacher defined religion as "the feeling of absolute dependence," he condensed this attitude into a formula.

Romanticism therefore lacks any strong ethical impulse, any will to conquer life ethically. It has an antipathy against any practical idea which might dominate life, demanding free, creative obedience for its commandments and showing a clearly determined way to the goals of action. Romanticism would like to "recover from purpose." All law, all that legislates, all morality with its commandments is repugnant to it; it would rather stay outside the sphere of good and evil; the highest ideal may be anything at all, except the distinct demands of ethical action. From all that urges and admonishes, the romantic turns away. He wants to dream, enjoy, immerse himself, instead of clearing his way by striving and wrestling. That which has been and rises out of what is past occupies him far more than what is to become and also more than what wants to become; for the word of the future would always command. Experiences with their many echoes and their billows stand higher in his estimation than life with its tasks; for tasks always establish a bond with harsh reality. And from this he is in flight. He does not want to struggle against fate, but rather to receive it with an ardent and devout soul; he does not want to wrestle for his blessing, but to experience it, abandoning himself, devoid of will, to what spells salvation and bliss. He wants no way of his own choosing. For the romantic the living deed is supplanted by the grace whose vessel he would be; the law of existence, by mere faith; reality, by the miracle of salvation. He wants to exist, without having an existence of his own; he wants less to live than to experience —or, to use the German, he prefers *erleben* to *leben*.

Therefore the romantic "personality" is also something totally different from, say, the Kantian personality who confronts us as the bearer of the moral law and who finds himself, and thus his freedom, in being faithful to the commandment. The romantic, too, loves his own being; but he seeks this individuality in the fluid world of his feelings which, capable of the quasi miraculous, can enter into everything and mean everything. Only out of this emotional experience, which becomes for him the measure of all things, does he derive what is good and evil for him. It is not through ethical action and not through clear knowledge that he expects to find the way to himself. He believes that he can become certain of himself only in self-contained feeling, in emotional self-contemplation which does not give expression to the emotions but dwells on them and all-too-easily becomes sheer virtuosity of feeling, admiring itself in the mirror of introspection and preening its own beautiful soul. There is, therefore, no more unromantic remark than Goethe's when he says that man comes to know himself by doing his duty and living up to the demands of the day. The romantics say instead: experience yourself and revel in yourself.

It is for these reasons that romanticism is usually oriented backwards, that it has its ideal in bygone ages, in the paradise of the past. It does not want to create but to find again and restore. After all, whoever prefers to feel and dream soon sees himself surrounded by ancient images; and only those who direct their will toward fixed tasks know themselves to be standing in a living relationship to the future. Therefore it is also given to romanticism to hearken to the voices from former times. Romanticism is especially qualified for this because, with its abundance of emotion, it is capable of reflecting all the recesses and mysteries of the human soul and to feel its way into different individualities. It has discovered the poetry of transitions, also the poetry of the divisions and clefts of the soul; it has known how to comprehend the radiation that emanates from the individual phenomenon and has cultivated the devotion to what is minute. Man with his contradictions is its subject. Hence romanticism has produced the artists of biography and cultivated the kind of history which demands empathy. But only this kind; it has not shown much vision regarding over-all connections or the ideas of the centuries. Romanticism remains lyrical even when it contemplates the seriousness of great events, and history becomes for it a game in which one becomes absorbed. One will here look in vain for the great message of the past. The strength and weakness of emotion determines the power and the impotence of romanticism.

It is the same everywhere. It is always feeling that is supposed to mean everything. Hence the capacity for feeling defines the dimensions and the limits of romanticism. We see this at close range in its representatives of the last century with their merits and their weaknesses. In opposition to the exclusive rule of the sober understanding, romanticism had legitimately demanded another right and another value. But romanticism itself soon fell victim to the same fundamental mistake which it had arisen to combat; for almost immediately it, too, claimed exclusive validity. It elevated pure feeling above everything else, above all conceptual and all obligatory truth—and eventually not only above everything else but in place of everything else. It strove to drown in beautiful illusion more and more of reality with its commandment, and to let the profound seriousness of the tasks of our life fade into a mere musical mood, to let them evaporate into the floating spheres of existence.

It gave its name to a whole generation in the last century; and yet romanticism is not applicable merely to a particular epoch, to a mere period of history. Romanticism means much more: it designates one of the characteristic forms which have emerged again and again in the development of mankind—a certain type in which, from time immemorial, religious life in particular has manifested itself. To be sure, historical types, just like human types, never appear quite pure. Whatever exists is a mixture; nowhere does life know sharp boundaries and distinctions; it is never an equation without any remainder. There are certain romantic elements in every religion, no less than in every human soul. Every religion has its dream of faith in which appearance and reality seek to mingle; each has its own twilight valley; each knows of world-weariness and contempt for the factual. But in one religion this is merely a quiet path alongside the road, a sound which accompanies, a tone which also vibrates. In another religion it fixes the direction; it is the dominant basic chord which determines the religious melody and gives it its character. Thus, depending on whether this or a wholly different motif is the decisive one, the romantic religion distinguishes itself quite clearly from the classical. And in this sense it may be said: Judaism is the classical religion and Christianity, compared with it, the romantic religion. . . .

FOR FURTHER READING

Books by Leo Baeck

This People Israel: The Meaning of Jewish Experience translated with an introductory essay by Albert H. Friedlander (New York: Holt, Rinehart and Winston, 1965). This is a translation of an important work of Baeck's.

Books about Leo Baeck

BACH, H.I., *The German Jew: A Synthesis of Judaism and Western Civilization* (New York: Oxford University Press, 1984). Includes a biography and analysis of his career and thought.

FRIEDLANDER, Albert H., *Leo Baeck: Teacher of Theresienstadt* (New York: Holt, Rinehart and Winston, 1968). This is the best biography of Baeck to date.

BOROWITZ, Eugene B., *Choices in Modern Jewish Thought: A Partisan Guide* (New York: Behrman House, 1983). Pages 53-74 includes a Baeck essay: "Religious Consciousness."

"Leo Baeck" in *Encyclopedia Judaica*, Volume 4: pp. 77-78 (Jerusalem: 1972). Includes a brief biography and overview of his career.

FRANZ ROSENZWEIG

(1886–1929)

EDITOR'S NOTE

Judaism in the early part of the twentieth century was interpreted from a variety of philosophical standpoints including positivism, mysticism, intuitionism and rationalistic German idealism. In the period after the First World War, a new kind of thinking emerged, a highly personal and individualistic type of philosophizing known as existentialism. Franz Rosenzweig, a leader in the Jewish renaissance in Germany, was one of the outstanding exponents of this point of view. An original philosopher of great profundity, Rosenzweig's call for a renewal of Jewish learning, his emphasis on the classical sources of Judaism, his understanding of the problems of the marginal Jew who wanted to return to Judaism, and the inspiration of his saintly personality have all contributed to the impact of the "new thinking" on American Jewish thought in the 1950's and 1960's.

Franz Rosenzweig was born in Cassel, Germany of a well-to-do and socially prominent Jewish family, with only a nominal affiliation with the Jewish community. He studied history and philosophy at the University of Leipzig, where he began to feel the need for a personal faith. Influenced by the example of Eugen Rosenstock-Huessy, a young philosopher of Jewish origin whom he admired, and of his cousin Hans Ehrenberg, both of whom had converted to Christianity, Rosenzweig decided on a similar step. Wanting to enter Christianity as its founders had done, through Judaism, he arranged to attend synagogue services in preparation for his conversion. However, his visit to the small Orthodox synagogue in Berlin on *Yom Kippur*, 1913, marked a dramatic turning point in his life. By the end of that day he had made up his mind to remain a Jew and to devote his life to the study and teaching of Judaism.

Rosenzweig therefore remained in Berlin where he attended the lectures of Hermann Cohen at the *Hochschule*. When the First World War broke out in 1914, he joined the army as a non-commissioned officer and was sent to the Balkan front. It was during these years that he wrote his most important work *Stern der Erlösung* (*Star of Redemption*) in small sections on postal cards which he mailed to his mother who copied them for later publication.

On his release from the army, Rosenzweig settled in Frankfurt where he founded the Lehrhaus, an institute for adult Jewish studies which became one of the distinguished cultural institutions in Germany. During the seven years of its existence, more than two hundred fifty courses and seminars were given to many hundreds of students. Among the lecturers were Martin Buber, Ernst Simon and Erich Fromm.

Franz Rosenzweig himself headed the school for only two years. Early in 1922 he was afflicted with a paralysis which gradually robbed him of his ability to write and to speak. Nevertheless, by dint of will and faith Rosenzweig continued his scholarly and philosophical interests. For a time he used a special typewriter to facilitate communication, and later, when he was unable to move, he maintained contact by the almost imperceptible signals which he made to his wife and which she in turn tried to sense and write down. In this manner he published a volume on the poetry of Judah Halevi, an essay on Jewish law, and wrote an introduction to the Jewish essays of Hermann Cohen. He also collaborated with Buber in a new translation of the Bible into German. After seven years of suffering, Franz Rosenzweig died on December 10, 1929.

To Franz Rosenzweig, the chief task of the Jewish thinker in the modern world was a redefinition of Judaism. It is this redefinition which he attempted in the first passage *On Being a Jewish Person*. It was addressed as an open letter to a friend, Eduard Strauss, in January, 1920. Rosenzweig preferred this essay to almost all his other occasional writings and he said of it, "It was not written at all, it was almost danced."

In consonance with his approach, Rosenzweig saw the great need of his time not in the writing of books about Judaism, but in the development of "Jewish human beings" to whom nothing Jewish is alien. In his view, such human beings will not come about through formulas or recipes such as Zionism, Orthodoxy or liberalism. In the pre-emancipation period there had been a unity in Jewish life based on Jewish law, the Jewish home and synagogue services. These three elements of Jewish existence had been whole and unseparated. Emancipation, however, led to a breakdown in each of these areas. To restore unity there must take place an individual turning to Jewishness, a "readiness" and "resolve" to be Jewish without the renunciation of the non-Jewish world in which one lives.

One of the fundamental ways for achieving this return to Judaism was through a new kind of learning centered in the student rather than in concepts. Rosenzweig regarded the Jewish adult education movement in Germany as perhaps the "most important movement among contemporary German Jews." His view of adult education, however, was not that of listening to lectures. The new learning was to take the form of discussions or dialogue where "in the same discussion hour the same person may be heard as both master and student."

In our second passage, which was an address given at the opening of the new term of the Lehrhaus, Rosenzweig describes this new learning. Unlike the old method, it would begin, not with the text but with life itself and move from the "periphery to the center." The teachers were not to be rabbis or specialists, but rather Jews of various backgrounds, who themselves wanted to find their way back to the heart of Judaism through a study of the classical sources of Jewish faith.

At the Lehrhaus, great importance was put on Hebrew as the key to the tradition. Translations were used only because they were necessary in a period of transition. But in Rosenzweig's view, Hebrew, which he himself taught, was inextricably related to the Jewish past and the total Jewish heritage (selection 44).

To live as a Jew, to Rosenzweig, also meant a concern for Jewish law. In reply to his friend Martin Buber, who was unable to accept the discipline of law, Rosenzweig addressed an epistle entitled *The Builders* in which he dealt with the importance of the law in Judaism. Rosenzweig did not accept the Orthodox view with its precise distinction between the "forbidden" and the "permissible." To him not everything that is permissible should necessarily be allowed. The original intention of the law as well as Jewish customs may be equally as important as the law itself.

Nor did he accept the liberal view which had repudiated much of the traditional code. To Rosenzweig, observance of the law remained a matter of inner personal decision. Just as in Jewish learning each individual arrives at his own conclusions from the text, so in Jewish law, he believed, each person must be free to make a choice from the body of the law, out of inner affirmation and out of a deep sense of responsibility.

In the next passage which is taken from a book review entitled *Sermonic Judaism*, Rosenzweig touches on some of the "vices" and temptations of preaching in the modern synagogue—the lack of motivation and immediacy, the unprepared listeners and the temptation to play-acting. Though written for German Jewry in the 1920's, his words also have implications for our day.

In the final selection Rosenzweig discusses the significance of the

Bible in world history—its direct effect on the Jewish people and its indirect effects through its fusion with the New Testament and through Christianity on European civilization. In his view, even the continuing secularization of religious communities, which began a century and a half before, would not lessen this significance.

42. On Being a Jewish Person

THE state of the world today may force us to postpone many desirable things, not for a better day but for a better century. It could hardly be asserted that the great urgency of the present moment is to organize the science of Judaism (*Wissenschaft des Judentums*) or to prompt both Jews and non-Jews to the endless writing of books on Jewish subjects. Books are not now the prime need of the day. But what we need more than ever, or at least as much as ever, are human beings—Jewish human beings, to use a catchword that should be cleansed of the partisan associations still clinging to it.

This term should not be taken in its (ostensibly loose) meaning, which is actually a very narrow one—it should not be taken in what I would call the petty-Jewish sense that has been assigned to it by exclusively political or even exclusively cultural Zionism. I mean it in a sense that though certainly including Zionism goes far beyond it. *The Jewish human being*—this does not mean a line drawn to separate us from other kinds of humanity. No dividing walls should rise here. A reality that only sheer stubbornness can deny shows that even within the individual many different spheres can touch or overlap. Yet sheer stubbornness and its counterpart, a cowardly renunciation, seem indeed to be the two main features of our present-day Jewish life.

Just as Jewishness does not know limitations inside the Jewish individual, so does it not limit that individual himself when he faces the outside world. On the contrary, it makes for his humanity. Strange as it may sound to the obtuse ears of the nationalist, being a Jew is no limiting barrier that cuts the Jew off from someone who is limited by being something else. The Jewish human being finds his limitation not in the Frenchman or German but only in another human being as unlimited as himself: the Christian or heathen. . . . Only in them does he find individuals who claim to be and are as all-embracing as himself, above and beyond all divisions of nationality and state, ability and character (for these too divide human beings from one another). . . .

But how? Does not this mean the revival of that old song, already played to death a hundred years ago, about Judaism as a "religion," as a "creed," the old expedient of a century that tried to analyze the unity of the Jewish individual tidily into a "religion" for several hundred rabbis and a "creed" for several tens of thousands of respectable citizens? God keep us from putting that old cracked record on again—and was it ever intact? No, what we mean by Judaism, the Jewishness of the Jewish human being, is nothing that can be grasped in a "religious literature" or even in a "religious life." . . . The point is simply that it is no entity, no subject among other subjects, no one sphere of life among other spheres of life; it is not what the century of emancipation with its cultural mania wanted to reduce it to. It is something inside the individual that makes him a Jew, something infinitesimally small yet immeasurably large, his most impenetrable secret; yet evident in every gesture and every word —especially in the most spontaneous of them. The Jewishness I mean is no "literature." It can be grasped through neither the writing nor reading of books. . . . It is only lived—and perhaps not even that. One *is* it. . . .

Jewish study and teaching, Jewish learning and education— they are dying out among us. This assertion may offend many ears, but in making it, I feel myself one with the best among the young, and among the old too—thank goodness for the last, for otherwise I should not feel sure of myself. Since the time of Mendelssohn and Zunz our Jewish learning no longer has the courage to be itself, but instead runs at a respectful distance behind the learning of the "others." At a respectful distance— what others find an old story is so readily marveled at among ourselves as the very latest thing—at least by the small (and rightly so) circle of those who still pay any attention at all to this dance of shadows. What the sparrows chirp from the rooftops of intellectual Germany still seems terrible heresy to us. Leaving the old ghetto, we have very quickly locked ourselves up in a new one. Only this time we do not want to admit it to ourselves. . . .

—Emancipated Jewry lacks a platform of Jewish life upon which the bookless present can come into its own. Up to the time of emancipation, such a platform was provided by existence within the bounds of old Jewish law and in the Jewish home and synagogal service. Emancipation shattered this platform. True, all three parts exist still, but because they are now only parts, they are no longer what they were when they were joined together—the single platform of a real and contemporaneously lived life, which learning and education had but to serve and from which they drew their greatest strength.

Wherever the Law is still kept among Western Jewry it is no longer a living "Jewishness," one that while largely based on legal paragraphs, was taken naturally and as a matter of course. This sort of Judaism has acquired a polemical point that quite contrary to any original intent—is turned, not against the outsider, but mainly against the large majority of those within Jewry who no longer keep the Law. Today the Law brings out more conspicuously the difference between Jew and Jew than between Jew and Gentile.

Just as the Law, wrenched from its unity with home and worship, is no longer what it once was, so the two other planks of the platform are not what they used to be. And thus the Jewish home, wherever it is still maintained intact, is no longer the heart from which the bloodstream of all Jewish life is pumped, and to which it returns. Slowly but surely the home has lost its dominating position in Jewish existence. Life comes from outside and makes its own demands. The Jewish home can and probably will try to assert itself against the outside world, but the most it can still do is maintain itself. The unity between home and occupation has been destroyed beyond hope; and even the strictest Jewish orthodoxy is forced to initiate its pupils in two different worlds of culture, and to exaggerate the quite new and positive importance of the opposition between Torah and *derekh eretz*, which was of so little significance for the old

Judaism. And thus the home has become at best but "one thing" in life, with "another thing" by the side of it, and *outside* it. That "other thing"—one's occupation, one's public activity— is no longer the natural radiation of the home into the outside world; it obeys requirements and laws of its own. The home no longer binds Jewish life into a unity.

And finally there is the synagogue. Thence at least a stream of Jewish life still seems to flow, and though it is pitifully thin it does trickle through the modern Jew even if it does not wash over and around him. The most assimilated assimilationist does as a rule still take some part in its life, be it but for an hour's memorial service, or for his marriage, or at least for his funeral. Those who know and have experienced personally what forces still slumber in a mere Yom Kippur Jewishness—which many have held on to as the only coin, in an inherited fortune, that still retains its full value—will be careful not to speak disparagingly of the synagogue. But for the same reason that the Jewish home and Law cannot become what they once were, the synagogue cannot become what it once was for our collective existence.

Even if it were possible—and I think it is!—gradually to restore the synagogue's connection with the whole of life out of the small remnant of it which is all that many of us have left, the restored connection would be with a whole that is no longer a whole. For the synagogue no longer acts as a member completing the body of a living life. . . . How many synagogues still have a study room with the heavy folios of the Talmud and its commentaries right next to the room of worship? The synagogue has become, quite in keeping with the spirit of the culture-obsessed, pigeonholing nineteenth century, a "place of religious edification" (or at least it claims to have become this). "Religion," to which life has denied a real place—and rightly, for life rightly rejects such lifeless, partial demands—seeks a safe and quiet little corner. And it is indeed a little corner: life flows past it unconcerned. Nor can the synagogue, either, do what the Law and the home cannot—give Jewry a platform of Jewish life.

What, then, holds or has held us together since the dawn of emancipation? In what does the community of our contemporary life show itself, that community which alone can lead from the past to a living future? The answer is frightening. Since the beginning of emancipation only one thing has unified the German

Jews in a so-called "Jewish life": emancipation itself, the Jewish struggle for equal rights. This alone covers all German Jews, and this alone covers Jews only. From this alone, therefore, those contemporary impulses will have to come which will open up the past to the seeking eyes of the student, and open the future to the capacity for leadership of a determined will. Everyone knows what the true situation is. Here, really, is the final reason why our Jewish scholarship and our Jewish education are in such a bad way. This struggle for equal rights—civil as well as social —has been the only actual "stimulant" our scholarship and our education have got from real life. Which is why neither the one nor the other has been able to free itself from the blinkers of apologetics. Instead of feeling and teaching the enjoyment of that which is ours, and which characterizes us, they have again and again tried but to excuse it. And so we have come to our present pass. . . .

43. On Jewish Learning

*From the Draft of the Address at the
Opening of the Lehrhaus in Frankfurt*

. . . L E A R N I N G—there are by now, I should say, very few
among you unable to catch the curious note the word sounds,
even today, when it is used in a Jewish context. It is to a book,
the Book, that we owe our survival—that Book which we use,
not by accident, in the very form in which it has existed for
millenia: it is the only book of antiquity that is still in living use
as a scroll. The learning of this book became an affair of the
people, filling the bounds of Jewish life, completely. Everything
was really within this learning of the Book. There have been
[Apocrypha] "outside books," but studying them was looked
upon as the first step toward heresy. Occasionally such "outside"
elements—Aristotle, for example—have been successfully natu-
ralized. But in the past few centuries the strength to do this
would seem to have petered out.

Then came the Emancipation. At one blow it vastly enlarged
the intellectual horizons of thought and soon, very soon afterwards, of actual living. Jewish "studying" or "learning" has not
been able to keep pace with this rapid extension. . . .

The old style of learning is helpless before this new development. In vain have both Orthodoxy and religious Liberalism
tried to expand into and fill the new domains. No matter how
much Jewish law was stretched, it lacked the power to encom-
pass and assimilate the life of the intellect and the spirit. The

mezuzah may have still greeted one at the door, but the book-case had, at best, a single Jewish corner. And Liberalism fared no better, even though it availed itself of the nimble air squadron of ideas rather than trying to master life by engaging it in hand-to-hand combat with the Law. There was nothing to be done apparently, except dilute the spirit of Judaism (or what passed for it). High-sounding words were always on tap, words that the Judaism of old had had, but which it was chary of uttering for fear of dulling their edges with too frequent use. High sound-ing words, like "humanity," "idealism," and so forth, which those who mouthed them thought as encompassing the whole world. But the world resists such superficial embraces. It is im-possible to assimilate to Judaism a field of intellectual and spiritual life through constantly reiterating a catchword and then claiming it to have kinship with some Jewish concept or other. The problems of democracy, for instance, cannot be Judaized merely by referring to the sentence in the Torah: "One law and one ordinance shall be both for you and for the stranger that sojourneth with you" (Numbers 15:16), nor those of social-ism by citing certain social institutions or social programs in ancient Israel. If we insist on trying, so much the worse for us! For the great, the creative spirits in our midst, have never allowed themselves to be deceived. They have left us. They went every-where, they found their own spiritual homes, and they created spiritual homes for others. The Book around which we once gathered stands forlorn in this world, and even for those who regard it as a beloved duty to a turning away from life, a turn-ing one's back on life. Their world remains un-Jewish even when they still have a Jewish world to return to. "Learning"—the old form of maintaining the relationship between life and the Book —has failed. . . .

A new "learning" is about to be born—rather, it has been born.

It is a learning in reverse order. A learning that no longer starts from the Torah and leads into life, but the other way round: from life, from a world that knows nothing of the Law, or pretends to know nothing, back to the Torah. That is the sign of the time.

It is the sign of the time because it is the mark of the men of the time. There is no one today who is not alienated, or who does not contain within himself some small fraction of alienation. All of us to whom Judaism, to whom being a Jew, has again become the pivot of our lives—and I know that in saying this here I am not speaking for myself alone—we all know that in being Jews we must not give up anything, not renounce anything, but lead everything back to Judaism. From the periphery back to the center; from the outside, in.

This is a new sort of learning. A learning for which—in these days—he is the most apt who brings with him the maximum of what is alien. That is to say, *not* the man specializing in Jewish matters; or, if he happens to be such a specialist, he will succeed, not in the capacity of a specialist, but only as one who, too, is alienated, as one who is groping his way home.

It is not a matter of pointing out relations between what is Jewish and what is non-Jewish. There has been enough of that. It is not a matter of apologetics, but rather of finding the way back into the heart of our life. And of being confident that this heart is a Jewish heart. For we are Jews.

That sounds very simple. And so it is. It is really enough to gather together people of all sorts as teachers and students. Just glance at our prospectus. You will find, listed among others, a chemist, a physician, a historian, an artist, a politician. Two-thirds of the teachers are persons who, twenty or thirty years ago, in the only century when Jewish learning had become the monopoly of specialists, would have been denied the right of teaching in a Jewish House of Study. They have come together here as Jews. They have come together in order to "learn"—for Jewish "learning" includes Jewish "teaching." Whoever teaches here—and I believe I may say this in the name of all who are teaching here—knows that in teaching here he need sacrifice nothing of what he is. We take life as we find it. Our own life and the life of our students; and gradually (or, at times, suddenly) we carry this life from the periphery where we found it to the center. And we ourselves are carried only by a faith which certainly cannot be proved, the faith that this center can be nothing but a Jewish center.

This faith must remain without proof. It carries further than our word. For we hail from the periphery. The oneness of the center is not something that we possess clearly and unambiguously, not something we can be articulate about. Our fathers were better off in that respect. We are not so well off today. We must search for this oneness and have faith that we shall find it. Seen from the periphery, the center does not appear invariably the same. In fact, the center of the circle looks different from each point of the periphery. There are many ways that lead from the outside in. Nevertheless, the inside is oneness and harmony. Only the outset, only the point of departure, will be different for everyone. . . .

It is in this sense that now, at the opening of the new term in this hall, I bid you welcome. May the hours you spend here become hours of remembrance, but not in the stale sense of a dead piety that is so frequently the attitude toward Jewish matters. I mean hours of another kind of remembrance, an inner remembering, a turning from externals to that which is within, a turning that, believe me, will and must become for you a returning home. Turn into yourself, return home to your innermost self and to your innermost life.

44. Hebrew Language

... THE holiness of the Hebrew language never signified holiness in the original sense of "seclusion," a meaning which has been overcome in classic Judaism. The holy language, the language of God, has always drawn strength for renewal from the spoken language, from the spoken languages of man; and this was so not only in the times of Moses and Isaiah. In other words, holy though it was, Hebrew never stiffened into something rigid and monumental; it always stayed alive. The Hebrew of the Torah and of the Book of Esther, the majesty of the great central prayers, the exquisite proportions of the Mishnah, the baroque of Kalir, the classicism of the great Spanish authors, the pious sobriety of Maimonides, Rashi's serene yet impassioned instruction, the absence of linguistic scruples of the Tibbonides, the crudeness of the Shulhan Arukh, the historicism of the Haskalah in the historical nineteenth century—all this is Hebrew. Numerous tongues contributed to the work on word and phrase, on the fabric of the Hebrew language: the spoken Hebrew of time immemorial, the common Aramaic of the Persian era, the Greek of the times after Alexander the Great, then—stronger and more enduring than all—the Aramaic of the Palestinian and Babylonian academies, and, simultaneously, the language of the armies and law courts of Rome and that of the rulers and subjects of the new Persian empire, the Arabic of the physicians and philosophers of Islam. and the languages of Europe, developing their own structures in the shadow of the widespread tree of the Latin of the universal church.

By the fabric of language so wrought, the Holy of Holies of this priestly people is both veiled from and indicated to the eyes of the peoples of the world. The difference between its vitality and the vitality of a profane language is that nothing once received into it can ever be lost. The holy language grows richer and richer, while the other languages must obey the law of a continual and at times critical self-purification. . . . One may read a novel by Thomas Mann without gaining a better understanding of any of the characteristic locutions of the . . . *Nibelungenlied*, the *Heliand*, or the Gothic Bible, but one cannot read even a Hebrew newspaper, without deriving something that would help to understand Ibn Ezra's commentaries, or talmudic argumentations, or the original text of the Bible. To read Hebrew implies a readiness ¬o assume the total heritage of the language. Reading German, English, or Latin, one merely harvests the crop raised by a single generation on the acre of language.

The holy language in the mouth of the people lacks the true characteristic of a sacred language, that is, separation from the colloquial, and so it never degenerated into anything like the magic sacredness of church Latin or the Arabic of the Koran, which may be, which even *should* be, incomprehensible to the layman—all that is required of him is adherence in spirit and faith. The holy language demands to be understood, word for word. Moreover, the languages spoken by the Jewish people in their everyday life lack the essential characteristic of secular vitality: complete dedication to the present moment. They swarm with quotations. If the new Hebrew, the Hebrew spoken in the land of Israel should set out to evade this law of Jewish destiny, it might indeed achieve its purpose theoretically, but it would have to bear the consequences. . . .

The point is that one cannot simply speak Hebrew as one would like to; one must speak it as it is. And it is tied up with the past. It does have obligations to the rest of the world, even when spoken by the youngest child in the most recently founded settlement. For the center which the new land Palestine might at best become in a pre-messianic period . . . would become a center in the mathematical sense. For, a circle is indeed drawn around its center, but in terms of construction the center does not in the least determine the area the circle will occupy, while the smallest arc of its periphery indicates the location of the center quite unambiguously. Thus a spiritual center such as we have in mind in regard to the land of Israel can be seen at a great distance and so become representative for all Jewry. But if it is to be a real center, it must depend on the periphery and the laws governing it so long as there is a periphery. To express it plainly and drily to the point of blasphemy: the spirit of this spiritual center cannot grow in the direction of pure, uninhibited nationalism avid for its own development, no matter how much it would like to; just because of its focal character it must constantly keep in sight the periphery which can never be governed by pure nationalism but will always be constrained to regard the national as a function of the religious, . . .

45. The Builders: Concerning the Law

. . . [I s] it really Jewish law with which you try to come
to terms? and, not succeeding, on which you turn your back
only to tell yourself and us who look to you for answer that our
sole task must be to take cognizance of the Law with reverence
—a reverence which can effect no practical difference in our
lives or to our persons? Is that really Jewish law, the law of
millennia, studied and lived, analyzed and rhapsodized, the law
of everyday and of the day of death, petty and yet sublime,
sober and yet woven in legend; a law which knows both the fire
of the Sabbath candle and that of the martyr's stake? . . . the
law that always rises beyond itself, that can never be reached—
and yet has always the possibility of becoming Jewish life, of
being expressed in Jewish faces? . . .

The "only" of orthodoxy should no more frighten us away
from the Law than the "only" of liberalism, once you had taught
us to see, could block our way to the *teaching*. . . . We can
reach both the teachings and the Law only by realizing that we
are still on the first lap of the way, and by taking every step
upon it, ourselves. But what is this way to the Law?

What was it in the case of the teachings? It was a way that
led through the entire realm of the knowable, but really *through*
it; a way that was not content to touch upon a few heights which
yielded a fine view, but struggled along where former eras had
not thought it even worth while to blaze a trail and yet would
not give him who had traveled its whole length the right to say

that he had now arrived at the goal. Even such a one could say no more than that he had gone the whole way but that even for him the goal lay a step beyond—in pathlessness. Then why call it a way—a path? Does a path—any path—lead to pathlessness? What advantage has he who has gone the way over him who right at the outset ventured the leap, which must come in the end in any case? A very small advantage, which most people do not consider worth so much trouble, but which, we believe, justifies the utmost trouble; for only this laborious and aimless detour through knowable Judaism gives us the certainty that the ultimate leap, from that which we know to that which we need to know at any price, the leap to the teachings, leads to *Jewish* teachings. . . .

All this holds also for the Law, for doing. Except that what is doable and even what is not doable yet must be done nonetheless, cannot be known like knowledge, but can only be done. But if, for the time being, we set aside this grave difference, the picture is the same. There the way led through all that is knowable; here it leads through all that is doable. And the sphere of "what can be done" extends far beyond the sphere of the duties assumed by orthodoxy. As in the *teaching*, the rigid difference between the essential and the non-essential, as outlined by liberalism, should no longer exist, so in the sphere of what can be done the difference between the forbidden and the permissible, as worked out, not without precedent, yet now for the first time with so much consequence and efficiency by Western European ortho-doxy of the 19th century, must cease to exist. The separation of the forbidden from the permissible had instituted a Jewish sphere within one's life; whatever remained within constituted the Jewish sphere with its commandments and prohibitions. The method of basing "allowances" on the text of the law permitted an extension of the realm of the permissible as long as the norms valid for the inner sphere were observed; this procedure, recog-nized through the ages as legitimate, had only in modern times been made into a system. Only in earlier periods where the security of Jewish life had been at stake, had that boundary been recognized and its temporary extension been accepted as its necessary complement. Only in modern times, when Jewish survival was considered perpetually at stake, was this treatment of the law given a permanent status. The future must no longer recognize that boundary, that method, nor even the general distinction described above. As in the sphere of the Law, there should be nothing *a priori* "permissible." Exactly those things, generally rendered permissible by orthodoxy, must be given a Jewish form. Outside of the Jewish sphere is the domain that should be formed by the "custom," i.e., by a positive principle, instead of merely the negative concept of "permissible." Where Judaism was alive, this had always been true; but whereas previously this fact had been treated with criticism or with slight irony, it will in the future have to be treated with seriousness. Not one sphere of life ought to be surrendered. To give one example for each of the two possibilities I have in mind: for those who eat Jewish dishes all the traditional customs of the menu as handed down from mother to daughter must be as irreplaceable as the separation of meat and milk and he who refrains from opening a business letter on the Sabbath must not read it even if somebody else has opened it for him. Everywhere the custom and the original intention of the law must have the same rank of inviolability as the law itself. . . .

As in the sphere of *teaching* where, after the non-essential has become essential, the essential itself receives some of the characteristics of the non-essential; so in the sphere of the Law, after customs have clothed themselves with the dignity of law, the law will share the positive character of the custom. Not the negative but the positive will be dominant in the Law. Even the prohibitions may now reveal their positive character. One refrains from working on the Sabbath because of the positive commandment concerning rest; when refraining from eating forbidden food one experiences the joy of being able to be Jewish even in the every-day and generally human aspects of one's material existence. Even an act of refraining becomes a positive act. . . .

. . . [We] have to realize that with this unifying and broadening of the Jewishly do-able, nothing has really been done. Whatever can and must be done is not yet deed, whatever can and must be commanded is not yet commandment. Law (*Gesetz*) must again become commandment (*Gevot*) which seeks to be transformed into deed at the very moment it is heard. It must regain that living reality (*Heutigkeit*) in which all great Jewish periods have sensed the guarantee for its eternity. Like *teaching*, it must consciously start where its content stops being content and becomes inner power, our own inner power. Inner power which in turn is added to the substance of the law. . . .

. . . [What] counts here, too, is not our will but our ability to act. Here too the decisive thing is the selection which our ability—without regard to our will—makes out of the wealth of the possible deeds. Since this selection does not depend on the will but on our ability, it is a very personal one; for while a general law can address itself with its demands to the will, ability carries in itself its own law; there is only my, your, his ability and, built on them, ours; not everybody's. Therefore, whether much is done, or little, or maybe nothing at all, is immaterial in the face of the one and unavoidable demand; that whatever is being done, shall come from that inner power. . . .

The growth of the Law is thus entrusted once again to our loving care. Nobody should be allowed to tell us what belongs to its spheres, as nobody was allowed to tell us what belonged to the sphere of teaching. We should not even wish to know that beforehand, even if we could. Neither our wish nor our knowledge should anticipate that choice. . . . There is no other guarantee for our deed being Jewish, whether it will be found to lie within or beyond the precincts of the do-able. In the latter case the boundaries will be extended by them. In either case, however, it will be today's living law, as well as The Law. For this is what we felt was lacking in the law presented to us by its new observers: that the old law was not at the same time the new. This lack of actuality, of living reality, was recognized when the line of demarcation I mentioned made today's life "permissible." Thereby the law had been denied actuality. Moses' bold words, spoken to the generations who had not experienced the event of Mount Sinai (Deuteronomy 5:3), "The Lord made not this covenant with our fathers, but with us, even us, who are all of us here alive this day,"—those words (the paradox of which was keenly felt by ancient commentators) had fallen into oblivion. It is upon us to accept the challenge of this boldness. The inner line of demarcation has become blurred, and there must be an outer one, for not every deed which fails to find its place in the law known to us broadens its boundaries, as not every piece of our knowledge becomes a part of the *teaching*. But we cannot know whether it will not happen after all. We do not know the boundary, and we do not know how far the pegs of the tent of the Torah may be extended, nor which one of our deeds is destined to accomplish such widening. . . .

46. Sermonic Judaism

A GREAT danger faces the modern rabbi, a danger that
threatened his colleagues of yore only rarely and that does not
exist to the same degree for the Christian clergyman of today.
For the Catholic priest, in whose office the strictly circumscribed
liturgical activity occupies by far the most important place,
this danger exists hardly at all. But even the Protestant minister
usually has in his individual pastoral care a counter-balance
against his Sunday sermons, which, at that, are usually short.
The rabbi, on the other hand, who was once, when his activities
were limited to "learning" and judging, almost completely protected from the dangers of his "spiritual vocation," is now ex-
posed to them more than all others. For he has left behind the
sober air of daily learning; with whom, in truth, should he learn?
Those who may turn to him are at best seekers, not men ready
and prepared for learning in the old sense. And his pastoral
activity, unlike that of the Protestant minister, is usually made
exceedingly difficult by a certain social isolation in which he
finds himself in relation to the most educated and respected circles of his congregation. Thus he is more or less dependent upon
preaching, a preaching, incidentally, which he can direct only
rarely to the large mass of his congregation, a preaching therefore without echo. And thus the vices of preaching grow in him
without restraint. What are these vices?

Preaching is not speaking. The partner in conversation is missing. Consequently motivation and immediacy are lacking. As a

result of this, the preacher lacks a criterion for the volume of his sound; in this he resembles the deaf, for he too hears no reply. These dangers now are increased by the lack of subjects. A text does not seem to the preacher to be interesting enough for his public—and in this he may be right. Therefore, he will abandon it as soon as possible and move into the apparently more interesting realms of timeliness. This ardently wooed timeliness, however, has the peculiarity that it seeks to be more truly timely than those who woo it ever imagine. Whoever loves it only for timeliness' sake, it rejects, demanding to be seized in its own timeliness, at its own time, out of the immediacy of an occasion; then and only then will it be conquered. The forced and artificial timeliness of the sermon, therefore, has always a touch of the outlived, of the antiquated. The preacher acts as if he had been asked. But none has asked him. And thus, also from the point of view of the content, all he says seems empty.

This he feels himself. Because of this feeling he yields to the worst temptation. He believes that he must throw himself into the abyss separating him from his audience. But he thereby does not come closer to the audience, he merely hurtles into the depth. His word becomes just then, when it should least be, play-acting. Not that he acts; but he pays the penalty for speaking for others after despairing of reaching them. Thus the word comes to a stop in front of the others, and instead of being heard it is looked upon. Thus, that which was to overcome the danger of false notes and superficial speech, itself presents the most terrible of dangers, the danger of the shameless pretense. Under such unlucky stars stands the profession, and we may therefore rightly blame them largely for the fact that this well-meant book did not turn out to be what the author had desired—and what this reviewer would desire along with him. . . .

47. On the Significance of the Bible

I T will always be futile to attempt to explain the unique position claimed for the Bible in its very name of Bible, the Book, on the grounds of the quality of its content. For to apply a superlative to a book because of content presupposes dogmatic prejudice. Mohammedanism, for instance, dogmatically states that the Koran is the most beautiful of all books. The only way in which the scholar can grasp and prove the significance of the Bible is by its effect and its destiny: namely, by its effect on, and its destiny in, the course of world history.

Their very first encounters, springing from war or from trade relations, establish certain spiritual contacts among peoples, without however creating between them a world-historical bond. For this, more than a haphazard flow of influences is required; the creation of such a bond demands the conscious transfer into one's sphere of something recognized as alien; in other words, it requires *translation*. The historical moment of the birth of world literature, and hence of supernational consciousness, occurred, in the full light of history, with two events, one of which was only symptomatic while the other had constitutive significance as well. It came when two books, each the very foundation of its national literature, were first translated into another language. At just about the same time, a prisoner of war in Rome translated the Odyssey from Greek into Latin, and Jewish settlers in Alexandria translated the Book of their people into Greek. Whatever unity of spirit and purpose exists on the five continents of this earth today derives from the fusion of these two events, and the consequences thereof, events originally related only because in them the Greeks played the double role of giving and taking.

The origin of the Greek Bible falls between the beginning of the movement that tried to bring Judaism to other peoples and the ebb of that movement before one that was stronger, one that, while accepting the Jewish Bible as its ever present foundation, regarded it merely as the "old" Testament. And from this time on we must distinguish between the direct effects of the Jewish Bible, and the indirect effects springing from its fusion—technical as well as chemical—with the New Testament. Viewed from the standpoint of world history, the former effects are sporadic, no matter how strong they may be at certain junctures, while the latter constitute the indispensable mortar that cements world history into a whole.

Let us first discuss the direct effect. Even that is not direct in the true meaning of the word, for every return to the Jewish Bible occurs with reference to the New Testament, though often in a spirit of opposition. Here we have a more or less deliberate, though rarely fundamental, return to the "Law." Wherever the demands of Christian communal life were not satisfied by the all too primitive model community described in the Acts of the Apostles and in the Epistles, or by the critical attitude toward the world pronounced in the Gospels (critical in both the social and moral aspects), it was—and still is—natural to revert to the Old Testament, to law born of prophecy. The Christian church, the Christian state, Christian economics, and Christian society could not and cannot be established upon the New Testament, which sees the world only in crisis, only face to face with Judgment. In contrast to the pointed paradoxes of the New Testament, the Jewish Bible, sprung from the richness of the life of a whole people, of a whole national literature, offered a solid ground for building the world, and for building in the world, in that its faith in creation was both living and profound—even within the sphere of prophetic criticism and polemics. And so, just because of the manifold origins of the Book, the various edifices could be as different, even opposed to one another, as the various sides and aspects of national life: monarchists and monarchomachists, churches and sects, popes and heretics, reactionaries and revolutionists, protectors of property rights and social reformers, war-enthusiasts and pacifists could and can, did and do, cite the Book as their authority.

But its indirect effect by way of the New Testament is far more important than all these influences and references. The New Testament writings originated in protest against the Jewish Bible, in the belief that salvation had come, that "the time was full," a belief whose burning fervor condensed the long-breathed hope for redemption to a brief span. That Christianity could persist after "this generation" has passed away, while "this world" did not come to an end; or, to express it in terms of Bible history, that the New Testament writings became the canonical New Testament—this Christianity and the New Testament owe to their bond with Judaism. For the way back to the still persisting Creation could be found only if the God of Genesis and he "who has spoken through the prophets" was the same as the one invoked in the Lord's Prayer and not, as the Gnostics claimed, an old God dethroned by the God of a new era. Connection with the created world—this and nothing less is at stake for Christianity both in the theological identification expressed in the dogma of the Trinity and in the identifying of the "word" that "was God" with the Messiah from David's stem. It is no mere chance that in the struggle for these identifications, in this struggle against Marcion's "alien God"—and this "alien" means alien to the Old Covenant—the church created her canon of the New Testament as a counterpart to the Old Testament. This counterpart was not, however, intended to supersede the Old Testament, but only to supplement and outrange it. Whatever cultural strength Christianity has displayed in the two millennia since then, and cultural strength here implies strength to become integrated in the world and to integrate the world into itself, is due to the effort to retain *its* Old Testament.

And so it is no longer a problem of conscious references to the Jewish Bible, or of relationships that could be traced or proved in detail, but of the entire sphere of whatever—in any degree—might be called a cultural effect of Christianity. What matters here is that Christianity has been able to synthesize with the world. What matters is the fruitful tension of such syntheses, which has given Christian Europe her spiritual dominance in the world. Nothing is altered by the fact that Christianity itself has always regarded this tension as a torment it wished to evade. If Christianity ever succeeded in its perpetual attempt to escape from the limitations and strangeness of the Old Testament into the wide region of philosophy or the circumscribed pale of nationalism, then Christendom would come to an end, and with it the Bible's, including the Jewish Bible's, participation in world history. For while the course of the one world history that began with this Book may change its protagonists, it cannot lose connection with its origin and each successive step of its development. This connection is precisely what we call world history. No future can undo the past, just as no past can prevent the coming of that which is to come.

It is quite possible that the secularization of religious communities, which began a hundred and fifty years ago, will march on, and that church and synagogue in the old traditional sense will persist only for a small nucleus, while a worldly agent, the "church people," or, in our case, the "Jewish people," will become the general community. If this should take place, the significance of the Holy Scriptures would not lessen but would even grow—as has already been shown both by church and synagogue in the last century and a half. When dogma and Law cease to be the all-embracing frame of the community and serve only as props from within, the Scriptures must not merely fulfil the task of all Scriptures: to establish a connection between generations; they must also assume another which is likewise incumbent on all Scriptures: they must guarantee the connection between the center and the periphery of the community. Thus, even if church and synagogue no longer arched the portal on the road of humanity, the Bible would still continue to be at beck and call, so that humanity could consult it about this very road, "turn its pages again and again," and find "everything in it."

FOR FURTHER READING

Books about Franz Rosenzweig

GLATZER, Nahum N., *Franz Rosenzweig: His Life and Thought* (New York: Schocken, 1953). The best biography to date, with translations of Rosenzweig's most important writings.

ROSENSTOCK-HUESSY, Eugen, editor, *Judaism Despite Christianity: The Letters of Christianity and Judaism* (New York: Schocken, 1971). Fascinating glimpse at this provocative correspondence.

MARTIN, Bernard, editor, *Great Twentieth Century Jewish Philosophers* (New York: Macmillan, 1970). Pages 118–237 devoted to Rosenzweig; an introduction with five translations.

BACH, H.I. *The German Jew: A Synthesis of Judaism and Western Civilization, 1730–1930* (New York: Oxford University Press, 1984). Pages 235–243 include a discussion of the contributions of Rosenzweig.

"Franz Rosenzweig" in *Encyclopedia Judaica*, Volume 14: pp. 299–303 (Jerusalem: 1972). Brief biography with overview of Rosenzweig's thoughts.

MARTIN BUBER

(1878–1965)

EDITOR'S NOTE

Martin Buber is the best known Jewish religious thinker in the world today. His personal approach to religion with its emphasis on the life of dialogue rather than on ritual or dogma, his interpretations of *Hasidism*, the stress he puts on Biblical faith and the spiritual quality and beauty of his writings have made him the outstanding interpreter of Judaism to the non-Jewish world.

In many ways, Buber's thought is similar to that of Franz Rosenzweig. Both approach life from the standpoint of the individual and his situation; both are spokesmen for the life of dialogue and both held that the Bible should be one of the foundations of the Jewish renaissance in post-war Germany. But Buber differs from his friend and co-worker in his inability to accept the discipline of Jewish law, in his advocacy of Jewish nationalism and in his preoccupation with the teachings of *Hasidism*. Before the Second World War, only one book by Buber was available in English—his *I and Thou*. It is an indication of Buber's extraordinary popularity that since the war more than fifteen of his books have been translated into English.

Martin Buber was born in Vienna in 1878. Because of the divorce of his parents, when Buber was three years old, he went to live in Lemberg, Galicia with his grandfather, a Midrashic scholar and a successful merchant. When Buber was fourteen, he returned to his father's home in Vienna and after graduating from the local *gymnasium*, entered the University of Vienna where he received his doctorate in philosophy and the history of art.

While still a student, he joined the Zionist movement and in 1901 became editor of its periodical, *Die Welt*. Though he remained a Jewish nationalist in the spiritual sense, he withdrew from Zionist political activity because of its lack of interest in cultural and religious matters. For a time Buber went through a period of inner confusion without any clear spiritual direction. On a visit to his grandfather's house in Lemberg at the age of twenty-six, he came on a booklet, *The Testament of Rabbi Israel Baal Shem* and began to read it. As Buber describes the experience, "It was then that I, suddenly overwhelmed, experienced the *Hasidic* soul. Something . . . Jewish rose in me . . . I comprehended the idea of the perfect man. And I perceived my responsibility in proclaiming it to the world." Buber devoted the next five years to an intensive study of *Hasidic* sources. The result of these studies was an approach to life which holds that the spirit of God is present in all life, and that, therefore, life is holy. Eventually he wrote a series of important works interpreting the teachings of *Hasidism*.

From 1916 to 1924 Buber edited the periodical, *Der Jude*, which became the leading organ of German-speaking Jewry. But his major interests remained religion and philosophy. In 1923 he was appointed professor of Jewish thought and comparative religion at the University of Frankfurt and held this position until 1933. Buber remained in Germany for another five years where he was responsible for the teacher training program for the new Jewish schools and where he played a major role in building the inner strength and spiritual resources of his persecuted brethren.

In 1938 Buber emigrated to Palestine, where he was appointed professor of social philosophy at The Hebrew University. He also founded and became head of the Institute for Adult Education which trained teachers for the new immigrant settlements. Since his retirement in 1951, Buber has made three visits to the United States, where he lectured at various universities and before other groups.

A prolific writer and literary artist of distinction whose mastery of the German language has delighted educated readers for the past half century, Buber is not a systematic thinker. His books are of three kinds: speculative writings such as *I and Thou* (1922), *Dialogue* (1929), *The Question of the Single One* (1936); his Biblical and Jewish writings such as *Moses* (1946), *The Prophetic Faith* (1950), *The Legend of the Baal Shem* (1955), *Israel and Palestine* (1944), and his *Tales of the Hasidim* (1948); and his popular works which show the relevance of dialogue to the issues of the day. From among this rich storehouse we have chosen several passages to indicate his basic approach and his attitude toward various aspects of Judaism.

Our first selections consist of several passages from Buber's speculative writings in which he sets down his theory of dialogue. *I and Thou*, his great prose poem which was already a classic in its day, is abstract and not easy to read. But it expresses the heart of his philosophy that "real life is meeting" and contains the fundamental attitude toward the world which is the basis of his writings on Zionism, Bible and *Hasidism*. Buber later published an essay entitled *Dialogue* which he describes as a filling out and application of what was said in

I and Thou. Here he describes the types of dialogue and their meaning in human life.

The perfection of the life of dialogue lies in the relation between man and God who is the "eternal Thou." There are many, however, who are ready to give up the use of the word "God" because it has been misused. In a deeply moving passage from *Eclipse of God* (1952) Buber admits "God" is "the most heavy laden of all human words," but he feels he cannot abandon it. When the "hell tormented and heaven storming generations of men," he writes, "stand over against Him in the darkness and sigh Thou and then add God, it is the one living God they mean, the God who can properly be addressed but not expressed."

We turn next to Buber's unique view of the Bible, as he expresses it in his study of *Moses,* one of his finest works. Buber does not accept the traditional view of the Bible as factual history, nor does he agree with those who regard the Scriptures in terms of literary or symbolical significance. To him there is a third way of classifying the Biblical accounts—as sagas, by which he means the rhythmic, poetic accounts in the text which preserve the historical memories of what happened. The critical student who penetrates to the original core of these events arrives at the "indwelling story of faith which inheres" in these accounts.

In the passage which follows, Buber presents his view of Zionism and Israel. Buber had no sympathy with the point of view which urged Jews to be a nation like all other nations. To him Israel is the only nation in the world which from its earliest beginnings has been both a nation and a religious community, the carrier of revelation and a covenant with God. It therefore has a unique role in history and this uniqueness must be recognized. It is against the background of this spiritual approach to Zionism that the essay *Zion and the Other National Concepts* should be read. It is taken from Buber's outstanding work, *Israel and Palestine,* whose purpose was to shed light on the unique relationship between *Eretz Israel* and the Jewish people and on the "beginning of a new kind of society" which is the "hope for a broken world."

This new society in Buber's view must be based on a positive relationship to tradition in which the Jew will absorb the best elements of the past in accordance with his needs. The trend in some *kibbutzim* in *Eretz Yisrael* of "reviving the forms without their content," Buber found "dilettantish and devoid of reverence." For our generation, alienated from religious content, he urged a truly national education which would bring the people to a faith of their own. Thus Buber did not agree with Ahad Ha-am or with Rabbi Kuk that religious rituals may be performed for nationalistic reasons out of reverence for the Jewish people. The last selection, *The Way of Man*, though not as well known as some of Buber's other works on *Hasidism*, is a gem of Jewish literature. In this little volume he has chosen a few traditional stories from the teaching of the *Hasidim* and interpreted them in six short essays, thus portraying a way of life which to him represents the essence of authentic Judaism—to hallow this life and to bring it closer to the Kingdom of God.

48. Philosophy of Dialogue

A) I AND THOU

T o man the world is twofold, in accordance with his twofold attitude.

The attitude of man is twofold, in accordance with the twofold nature of the primary words which he speaks.

The primary words are not isolated words, but combined words.

The one primary word is the combination *I-Thou*.

The other primary word is the combination *I-It*; wherein, without a change in the primary word, one of the words *He* or *She* can replace *It*.

Hence the *I* of man is also twofold.

For the *I* of the primary word *I-Thou* is a different *I* from that of the primary word *I-It*.

Primary words do not signify things, but they intimate relations.

Primary words do not describe something that might exist independently of them, but being spoken they bring about existence.

Primary words are spoken from the being.

If *Thou* is said, the *I* of the combination *I-Thou* is said along with it.

If *It* is said, the *I* of the combination *I-It* is said along with it.

The primary word *I-Thou* can only be spoken with the whole being.

The primary word *I-It* can never be spoken with the whole being.

There is no *I* taken in itself, but only the *I* of the primary word *I-Thou* and the *I* of the primary word *I-It*.

When a man says *I* he refers to one or other of these. The *I* to which he refers is present when he says *I*. Further, when he says *Thou* or *It*, the *I* of one of the two primary words is present.

The existence of *I* and the speaking of *I* are one and the same thing.

When a primary word is spoken the speaker enters the word and takes his stand in it.

The life of human beings is not passed in the sphere of transitive verbs alone. It does not exist in virtue of activities alone which have some *thing* for their object.

I perceive something. I am sensible of something. I imagine something. I will something. I feel something. I think something. The life of human beings does not consist of all this and the like alone.

This and the like together establish the realm of *It*.

But the realm of *Thou* has a different basis.

When *Thou* is spoken, the speaker has no thing for his object. For where there is a thing, there is another thing. Every *It* is bounded by others; *It* exists only through being bounded by others. But when *Thou* is spoken, there is no thing. *Thou* has no bounds.

When *Thou* is spoken, the speaker has no *thing;* he has indeed nothing. But he takes his stand in relation.

It is said that man experiences his world. What does that mean?

Man travels over the surface of things and experiences them. He extracts knowledge about their constitution from them: he wins an experience from them. He experiences what belongs to the things.

But the world is not presented to man by experiences alone. These present him only with a world composed of *It* and *He* and *Shall* and *It* again.

I experience something. If we add "inner" to "outer" experi-

ences, nothing in the situation is changed. We are merely following the uneternal division that springs from the lust of the human
race to whittle away the secret of death. Inner things or outer
things, what are they but things and things!

I experience something. If we add "secret" to "open" experiences, nothing in the situation is changed. How self-confi-
dent is that wisdom which perceives a closed compartment in
things, reserved for the initiate and manipulated only with the
key. O secrecy without a secret! O accumulation of information!
It, always It!

The man who experiences has no part in the world. For it is
"in him," and not between him and the world, that the experience arises.

The world has no part in the experience. It permits itself to
be experienced, but has no concern in the matter. For it does
nothing to the experience, and the experience does nothing to it.

As experience, the world belongs to the primary word *I-It*.
The primary word *I-Thou* establishes the world of relation.

The spheres in which the world of relation arises are three.

First, our life with nature. There the relation sways in gloom,
beneath the level of speech. Creatures live and move over against
us, but cannot come to us, and when we address them as *Thou*,
our words cling to the threshold of speech.

Second, our life with men. There the relation is open and in
the form of speech. We can give and accept the *Thou*.

Third, our life with intelligible forms. There the relation is
clouded, yet it discloses itself; it does not use speech, yet begets
it. We perceive no *Thou*, but nonetheless we feel we are addressed and we answer—forming, thinking, acting. We speak
the primary word with our being, though we cannot utter *Thou*
with our lips.

But with what right do we draw what lies outside speech into
relation with the world of the primary word?

In every sphere in its own way, through each process of becoming that is present to us, we look out toward the fringe of
the eternal *Thou*; in each we are aware of a breath from the
eternal *Thou*; in each *Thou* we address the eternal *Thou*. . . .

The *Thou* meets me through grace—it is not found by seeking. But my speaking of the primary word to it is an act of my being, is indeed *the* act of my being.

The *Thou* meets me. But I step into direct relation with it. Hence the relation means being chosen and choosing, suffering and action in one; just as any action of the whole being, which means the suspension of all partial actions and consequently of all sensations of actions grounded only in their particular limitation, is bound to resemble suffering.

The primary word *I-Thou* can be spoken only with the whole being. Concentration and fusion into the whole being can never take place through my agency, nor can it ever take place without me. I become through my relation to the *Thou;* as I become *I*, I say *Thou*.

All real living is meeting.

The relation to the *Thou* is direct. No system of ideas, no foreknowledge, and no fancy intervene between *I* and *Thou*. The memory itself is transformed, as it plunges out of its isolation into the unity of the whole. No aim, no lust, and no anticipation intervene between *I* and *Thou*. Desire itself is transformed as it plunges out of its dream into the appearance. Every means is an obstacle. Only when every means has collapsed does the meeting come about.

In face of the directness of the relation, everything indirect becomes irrelevant. It is also irrelevant if my *Thou* is already the *It* for other *I's* ("an object of general experience"), or can become so through the very accomplishment of this act of my being. For the real, though certainly swaying and swinging, boundary runs neither between experience and non-experience, nor between what is given and what is not given, nor yet between the world of being and the world of value; but cutting indifferently across all these provinces, it lies between *Thou* and *It*, between the present and the object.

B) *THE LIFE OF DIALOGUE*

I know three kinds [of dialogue]. There is genuine dialogue—no matter whether spoken or silent—where each of the participants really has in mind the other or others in their present and particular being and turns to them with the intention of establishing a living mutual relation between himself and them. There is technical dialogue, which is prompted solely by the need of objective understanding. And there is monologue disguised as dialogue, . . . A *debate* in which the thoughts are not expressed in the way in which they existed in the mind but in the speaking are so pointed that they may strike home in the sharpest way, and moreover without the men that are spoken to being regarded in any way present as persons; a *conversation* characterized by the need neither to communicate something, nor to learn something, nor to influence someone, nor to come into connexion with someone, but solely by the desire to have one's own self-reliance confirmed by marking the impression that is made, or if it has become unsteady to have it strengthened; a *friendly chat* in which each regards himself as absolute and legitimate and the other as relativized and questionable; a *lovers' talk* in which both partners alike enjoy their own glorious soul and their precious experience—what an underworld of faceless spectres of dialogue!

The life of dialogue is not one in which you have much to do with men, but one in which you really have to do with those with whom you have to do. It is not the solitary man who lives the life of monologue, but he who is incapable of making real in the context of being the community which, in the contest of his destiny, he moves. It is, in fact, solitude which is able to show the innermost nature of the contrast. He who is living the life of dialogue receives in the ordinary course of the hours something that is said and feels himself approached for an answer. But also in the vast blankness of, say, a companionless mountain wandering that which confronts him, rich in change, does not leave him. He who is living the life of monologue is never aware of the other as something that is absolutely not himself and at the same time something with which he nevertheless communicates. Solitude for him can mean mounting richness of visions and thoughts but never the deep intercourse, captured in a new depth, with the incomprehensibly real. Nature for him is either an *état d'âme*, hence a "living through" in himself, or it is a passive object of knowledge, either idealistically brought within the soul or realistically alienated. It does not become for him a word apprehended with senses of beholding and feeling.

Being, lived in dialogue, receives even in extreme dereliction a harsh and strengthening sense of reciprocity; being, lived in monologue, will not, even in the tenderest intimacy, grope out over the outlines of the self.

This must not be confused with the contrast between "egoism" and "altruism" conceived by some moralists. I know people who are absorbed in "social activity" and have never spoken from being to being with a fellow-man. I know others who have no personal relation except to their enemies, but stand in such a relation to them that it is the enemies' fault if the relation does not flourish into one of dialogue. . . .

49. The Word "God"

. . . [O n c e] I was the guest of a noble old thinker. . . . There was a good spirit in his house, the spirit that wills to enter life and does not prescribe to life where it shall let it in.

One morning I got up early in order to read proofs. The evening before I had received galley proof of the preface of a book of mine, and since this preface was a statement of faith, I wished to read it once again quite carefully before it was printed. Now I took it into the study below that had been offered to me in case I should need it. But here the old man already sat at his writing-desk. Directly after greeting me he asked me what I had in my hand, and when I told him, he asked whether I would not read it aloud to him. I did so gladly. He listened in a friendly manner but clearly astonished, indeed with growing amazement. When I was through, he spoke hesitatingly, then, carried away by the importance of his subject, ever more passionately. "How can you bring yourself to say 'God' time after time? How can you expect that your readers will take the word in the sense in which you wish it to be taken? What you mean by the name of God is something above all human grasp and comprehension, but in speaking about it you have lowered it to human conceptualization. What word of human speech is so misused, so defiled, so desecrated as this! All the innocent blood that has been shed for it has robbed it of its radiance. All the injustice that it has been used to cover has effaced its features. When I hear the highest called 'God,' it sometimes seems almost blasphemous."

The kindly clear eyes flamed. The voice itself flamed. Then we sat silent for awhile facing each other. The room lay in the flowing brightness of early morning. It seemed to me as if a power from the light entered into me. What I now answered, I cannot to-day reproduce but only indicate.

"Yes," I said, "it is the most heavy-laden of all human words. None has become so soiled, so mutilated. Just for this reason I may not abandon it. Generations of men have laid the burden of their anxious lives upon this word and weighed it to the ground; it lies in the dust and bears their whole burden. The races of man with their religious factions have torn the word to pieces; they have killed for it and died for it, and it bears their finger-marks and their blood. Where might I find a word like it to describe the highest! If I took the purest, most sparkling concept from the inner treasure-chamber of the philosophers, I could only capture thereby an unbinding product of thought. I could not capture the presence of Him whom the generations of men have honoured and degraded with their awesome living and dying. I do indeed mean Him whom the hell-tormented and heaven-storming generations of men mean. Certainly, they draw caricatures and write 'God' underneath; they murder one another and say 'in God's name.' But when all madness and delusion fall to dust, when they stand over against Him in the loneliest darkness and no longer say 'He, He' but rather sigh 'Thou,' shout 'Thou,' all of them the one word, and when they then add 'God,' is it not the real God whom they all implore, the One Living God, the God of the children of man? Is it not he who *hears* them? And just for this reason is not the word 'God,' the word of appeal, the word which has become a *name*, consecrated in all human tongues for all times: We must esteem those who interdict it because they rebel against the injustice and wrong which are so readily referred to 'God' for authorization. But we may not give it up. How understandable it is that some suggest we should remain silent about the 'last things' for a time in order that the misused words may be redeemed! But they are not to be redeemed *thus*. We cannot cleanse the word 'God' and we cannot make it whole; but, defiled and mutilated as it is, we can raise it from the ground and set it over an hour of great care."

It had become very light in the room. It was no longer dawning, it was light. The old man stood up, came over to me, laid his hand on my shoulder and spoke: "Let us be friends." The conversation was completed. For where two or three are truly together, they are together in the name of God.

50. God and the World's Evil

. . . [I N] history . . . times of great utterance, when the mark of divine direction is recognizable in the conjunction of events, alternate with, as it were, mute times, when everything that occurs in the human world and pretends to historical significance appears to us as empty of God, with nowhere a beckoning of His finger, nowhere a sign that He is present and acts upon this our historical hour. In such times it is difficult for the individual, and the more for the people, to understand themselves as addressed by God; the experience of concrete answerability recedes more and more, because, in the seemingly Godforsaken space of history, man unlearns from taking the relationship between God and himself seriously in the dialogic sense. . . . The Bible knows of God's hiding His face, of times when the contact between Heaven and earth seems to be interrupted. God seems to withdraw Himself utterly from the earth and no longer to participate in its existence. The space of history is then full of noise, but as it were, empty of divine breath. For one who believes in the living God, who knows about Him, and is fated to spend his life in a time of His hiddenness, it is very difficult to live. . . .

In this our own time, one asks again and again: how is a Jewish life still possible after Oswiecim? . . . How is a life with God still possible in a time in which there is an Oswiecim? The estrangement has become too cruel, the hiddenness too deep. One can still "believe" in the God who allowed those things to happen, but can one still speak to Him? Can one still hear His word? Can one still, as an individual and as a people, enter at all into a dialogic relationship with Him? Can one still call to Him? Dare we recommend to the survivors of Oswiecim, the Job of the gas chambers: "Call to Him, He is kind, for His mercy endurest forever"?

But how about Job himself? He not only laments, but he charges that the "cruel" God has "removed his right" from him and thus that the judge of all the earth acts against justice. And he receives an answer from God. But what God says to him does not even touch upon it. The true answer that Job receives is God's appearance only, only this that distance turns into nearness, that "his eye sees Him," that he knows Him again. Nothing is explained, nothing adjusted; wrong has not become right, nor cruelty kindness. Nothing has happened but that man again hears God's address. . . .

And we? We—by that is meant all those who have not got over what happened and will not get over it. How is it with us? Do we stand overcome before the hidden face of God as the tragic hero of the Greeks before faceless fate? No, rather even now we contend, we too, with God, even with Him, the Lord of Being, Whom we once, we here, chose for our Lord. We do not put up with earthly being, we struggle for its redemption, and struggling we appeal to the help of our Lord, Who is again and still a hiding one. In such a state we await His voice, whether it come out of the storm or out of a stillness which follows it. Though His coming appearance resembles no earlier one, we shall recognize again our cruel and merciful Lord.

51. Saga and History

I N order to learn at first hand who Moses was and the kind of life that was his, it is obviously necessary to study the biblical narrative. There are no other sources worthy of serious consideration; comparison of reports, normally the chief means of ascertaining historical truth, is not possible here. Whatever has been preserved of Israel's traditions since ancient times is to be found in this one book. Not so much as the vestige of a chronicle dating from that period, or deriving from the nations with whom the Children of Israel established contact on their journey from Egypt to Canaan, has been preserved; and not the vaguest indication of the event in question is to be found in ancient Egyptian literature.

The biblical narrative itself is basically different in character from all that we usually classify as serviceable historical sources. The happenings recorded there can never have come about, in the historical world as we know it, after the fashion in which they are described. The literary category within which our historical mode of thinking must classify this narrative is the saga; and a saga is generally assumed to be incapable of producing within us any conception of a factual sequence.

Further, it is customary to accept as a fundamental tenet of the non-dogmatic biblical scholarship of our day the view that the tales in question belong to a far later epoch than the events related, and that it is the spirit of that later epoch which finds expression in them; or, even more, the spirit of the sundry and various later periods to which are ascribed the "sources," the different constituent parts of which the story is composed or compiled according to the prevalent view. Thus Homer, for example, to take an analogous case, provides us with a picture of the epoch in which he himself lived rather than of the one in which his heroes did their deeds.

Assuming that to be the case, just as little could be ascertained regarding Moses' character and works as is to be ascertained of Odysseus'; and we would perforce have to rest content with the possession of a rare testimony to the art with which court writers commissioned by the kings of Israel, or the more popular (in the original sense of the word) prophets of the nation, wrought the image of its founder out of material entirely inaccessible to us.

The scholarship of our own epoch, however, has prepared the way for another and deeper insight into the relation between saga or legend and history. For example, the philologist Hermann Usener indicated (in 1897) that what finds expression in the saga is not a post-factum transfiguration of an historical recollection, but a process which follows on the events, "in their footsteps, so to say." At a more recent date (in 1933), the Iranologist Ernst Herzfeld observed that "saga and the writing of history start out from the identical point, the event," and that it is the saga which in particular preserves historical memories, "not of what the consequences show to be 'historical event,' but of that which roused the emotions of the men undergoing the experience." It is possible to formulate even more precisely the nature of the issue involved. The man of early times met the unplanned, unexpected events which transformed the historical situation of his community at a single stroke with a fundamental stirring of all the elements in his being; a state of affairs properly described by the great Germanist Jacob Grimm (1813) as "objective enthusiasm." It is a primeval state of amazement which sets all the creative forces of the soul to work. What happens is therefore not a mere recasting of the event perceived by imagination become paramount; the experience itself is creative. "Periods of a more sensuous religious emotion," says Usener, "see vast, bright, superhuman figures passing before the victorious troops and bringing death and defeat to the ranks of the foe." Here the emphasis should be put on the word "see." The historical wonder is no mere interpretation; it is something actually seen. Even the subsequent comprehension of the flashing lightning-like visions within the consecutive report of the saga is not arbitrary in character. An organic and organically creative memory is here at work.

That this early saga, close as it is to the time of the event, tends to assume rhythmical form, can well be understood. It is not due solely to the fact that enthusiasm naturally expresses itself in rhythm. Of greater importance is the basic idea characterizing this stage of human existence that historical wonder can be grasped by no other form of speech save that which is rhythmically articulated, of course in oral expression (a basic concept which is closely associated with the time-old relation between rhythm and magic). This is sustained by the wish to retain unchanged for all time the memory of the awe-inspiring things that had come about; to which end a transmission in rhythmical form is the most favorable condition. Occasionally, the saga assumes specifically lyrical form; as in the Song of Deborah, where the bard mocks and curses as from the very battle.

Hence, alongside the more registrative forms of historical record, conditioned by the court and its requirements, which constitute a stage preliminary to the scientific writing of history, and which develop from the royal lists of the Sumerians to the well-constructed chronicles of the biblical books of Kings, the historical song and the historical saga exist as spontaneous forms of popular preservation by word of mouth of "historical" events, such events, that is, as are vital in the life of the tribe. It is of importance to investigate the sociological character of these types.

The saga is the predominant method of preserving the memory of what happens, as long as tribal life is stronger than state organization. As soon as the latter becomes more powerful, on the other hand, the unofficial popular forms are overshadowed through the development of an annalistic keeping of records by order of the governing authority.

If a saga assumes poetic form in its early stage, it remains virtually unchanged for a long time, even when it is transmitted by word of mouth alone, save that passages may be introduced which describe the course of events subsequent to the initial incident giving rise to the saga. Reminiscences not included in the poem may under certain circumstances condense into a parallel account, so that, as in the case of the story of Deborah, prose is found side by side with poetry; or, more correctly speaking, a loosely cadenced version accompanies the more strictly versified form. If the saga, however, does not assume this strict form at about the time of the event, but remains in its "mobile" state, it will be variously treated by different narrators, without any need to assume a conscious wish to introduce changes. Differing religious, political, and family tendencies, simultaneous and parallel to one another as well as consecutive, find expression in the treatment, with the result that a product already current in the tradition is "rectified," that is, supplemented or actually transformed in one or another detail. This continuous process of crystallization is something entirely different in character from compilation and welding of elements from various sources.

Such a state of affairs invests research with the duty of establishing a critique of tradition. The student must attempt to penetrate to that original nucleus of saga which was almost contemporary with the initial event. The attempt is rendered difficult, *inter alia*, by the fact that the literature of the ages saw fit to round off the saga material by supplementary data; as, for instance, where it was felt that the unknown or only superficially known birth and childhood story of the hero must not be left untold.

Here the procedure of investigation must necessarily be reductive. It must remove layer after layer from the images as set before it, in order to arrive at the earliest of all.

There can be no certainty of arriving by this method at "what really happened." However, even if it is impossible to reconstitute the course of events themselves, it is nevertheless possible to recover much of the manner in which the participating people experienced those events. We become acquainted with the meeting between this people and a vast historical happening that overwhelmed it; we become conscious of the saga-creating ardor with which the people received the tremendous event and transmitted it to a molding memory. This, however, should certainly not be understood to mean that the only results we can expect to obtain lie in the field of group psychology. The meeting of a people with events so enormous that it cannot ascribe them to its own plans and their realization, but must perceive in them deeds performed by heavenly powers, is of the genuine substance of history. In so far as the saga begins near the event, it is the outcome and record of this meeting.

The critique of tradition involved in the interpretation of the saga approximates us to the original meeting. At the sight of it, we have to stand without being able to educe an "objective state of affairs." We shall not regain an historical nucleus of the saga by eliminating the function of enthusiasm from it. This function is an inseparable element of the fragment of history entrusted to our study. Yet, in every case, we can and should test whether and how the narrative can be connected with and incorporated in the historical circumstances. Here history cannot be dissevered from the historical wonder; but the experience which has been transmitted to us, the experience of events as wonder, is itself great history and must be understood out of the element of history; it has to be fitted within the frame of the historical. Whether Sinai was a volcano cannot be determined historically, nor is it historically relevant. But that the tribes gathered at the "burning mountain" comprehended the words of their leader Moses as a message from their God, a message that simultaneously established a covenant between them and a covenant between him and their community, is essentially an historical process, historical in the deepest sense; it is historical because it derives from historical connections and sets off fresh historical connections. When faced by such tales, it is wrong to talk of an "historization of myth"; it might be preferable to describe them as a mythization of history, remembering that here, unlike the concept familiar in the science of religion, myth means nothing other than the report by ardent enthusiasts of that which has befallen them. And it may very well be doubted whether, in the last resort, the report of an unenthusiastic chronicler could have come closer to the truth. There is no other way of understanding history than the rational one, but it must start off with the overcoming of the restricted and restrictive *ratio*, substituting for it a higher, more comprehensive one.

However, two factors should be emphasized as having contributed greatly to the strength of the historical content of the Moses saga.

To begin with, the central figures of the Bible saga are not, as in so many hero-tales, merged in or amalgamated with persons belonging to mere mythology; the data regarding their lives have not been interwoven with stories of the gods. Here all the glorification is dedicated solely to the God who brings about the events. The human being acting under the God's orders is portrayed in all his untransfigured humanity. The wonder-working staff in his hand does not transform him into a possessor of superhuman powers; when once he uses that staff unbidden, he is subject to judgment. And when he descends from Sinai with radiant face, the radiance is not a shining forth from his own being, but only the reflection of some higher light. This withdrawing of the human being from the mythical element steeps the tale in an atmosphere of august sobriety, a dry atmosphere, one might almost say, which frequently permits a glimpse of an historical nucleus.

Besides, precise inspection goes to show that the early narrator of the deeds of Moses aimed not at beautiful or instructive individual sagas, but at a continuity of events. It is true that in the report of the journey through the wilderness, for example, we meet repeatedly with episodes, but they are introduced in a connection which obviously derives not from later harmonizing literary tendencies (like the Book of Joshua, for instance), but from a powerful primitive emotion which is the passionate recollection of a sequence of unheard-of events. Nor yet does the relation found here appear to show anything of the poetic composition of the epos; it is the practically related sequence of the itinerary. The latter may possibly have been worked up from an inexact or mutilated tradition to a state of questionable completeness; maybe the associated temporal sequence has been transformed by didactic aims and number symbolism; but the origin, the memory of a journey in the course of which the nation came into being, and the zealous purpose of preserving on record the stations of that journey, has remained unobliterated. In the literature of the world, the specifically historical can undoubtedly be found only where the principle of original connection is to be met with; here it cannot be denied.

All this leads to a threefold critical task which, difficult as it may be, nevertheless seems in some degree to be capable of accomplishment. It is necessary to draw a distinction between saga produced near the historical occurrences, the character of which is enthusiastic report, and saga which is further away from the historical event, and which derives from the tendency to complete and round off what is already given. Therefore, it is necessary to establish a further distinction, within the former, between the original components and their subsequent treatment. Finally, it is also necessary to penetrate to the historical nucleus of the saga as far as possible. Naturally, it is impossible to produce a coherent historical picture in this way, which is the only one scientifically permissible; yet we are entitled to hope genuine historical outlines may be ascertained. The distinction drawn should not be understood in the sense of elimination; as we have seen, the saga element too, in so far as it is characterized by closeness to history, is historically important, being a document of the reception of what befell in the minds of those whom it befell. Yet we may go further; what was added later is also of importance for us. Even the men who round off and supplement do what they do not arbitrarily but under the sustained urge of the primeval impulse. Tradition is by its nature an uninterrupted change in form; change and preservation function in the identical current. Even while the hand makes its alterations, the ear hearkens to the deeps of the past; not only for the reader but also for the writer himself does the old serve to legitimize the new. The Moses who had his being long ago is properly expanded by the one who has come into being in the course of long ages. It is our aim to come nearer to the former by our testing and selective work on the text; the latter is given to us directly. We must hold both in view without confusing them; we must comprehend the brightness of the foreground and gaze into the dark deeps of history.

At the same time, we must bear in mind that the forces which formed the saga are in essence identical with those which reigned supreme in history; they are the forces of a faith. For this faith, which is in character a history faith, a faith relating largely to historical time as such, did not merely treat a transmitted material after the fact; it cannot be imagined as absent from this material. The transmitted events are steeped in it; the persons who furthered the events believed in it, did in it what had to be done, and experienced in it what had to be experienced. The research of our day has reached the point, in the course of its radical doubts and queries, of providing fresh ground for an old certainty: that the biblical tales of the early Israelitic days report an early Israelitic faith. Whatever the mixture of fact and legend may be in the events related, the indwelling story of faith which inheres in them is authentic in all its main lines. What we learn of the faith determining the active and the receptive life of those persons is not, as scholarship supposed for some time, a "projection" of a later religious development against the surface of the earlier epoch, but is, in essence, the religious content of the latter. And it is this faith which shaped the saga that was near to history and at subsequent stages also shaped the more distant saga.

In its character, this saga is "sacred legend," since the relation to God of the men of whom it tells is a fundamental constituent. But this history, too, is in its character "sacred history," because the people who work and suffer in it work and suffer as they do in virtue of their relationship to their God.

52. Zion and the Other National Concepts

I T is impossible to appreciate the real meaning of "Zion" so long as one regards it as simply one of many other national concepts. We speak of a "national concept" when a people makes its unity, spiritual coherence, historical character, traditions, origins and evolution, destiny and vocation the objects of its conscious life and the motive power behind its actions. In this sense the Zion concept of the Jewish people can be called a national concept. But its essential quality lies precisely in that which differentiates it from all other national concepts.

It is significant that this national concept was named after a place and not, like the others, after a people, which indicates that it is not so much a question of a particular people as such but of its association with a particular land, its native land. Moreover, the idea was not named after one of the usual descriptions of this land—Canaan or Palestine or Eretz Yisrael—but after the old stronghold of the Jebusites which David made his residence and whose name was applied by poets and prophets to the whole city of Jerusalem, not so much as the seat of the royal fort, however, but as the place of the sanctuary, just as the holy mountain itself is often so called: quite early on the name was constructed as that of a holy place. Zion is "the city of the great King" (Psalms 48, 3), that is of God as the King of Israel. The name has retained this sacred character ever since. In their prayers and songs the mourning and yearning of the people in exile were bound up with it, the holiness of the land was concentrated in it and in the Cabbala Zion was equated with an emanation of God Himself. When the Jewish people adopted this name for their national concept, all these associations were contained in it.

This was inevitable, for, in contrast to the national concepts of other peoples, the one described by this name was no new invention, not the product of the social and political changes manifested by the French Revolution, but merely a continuation, the re-statement of an age-old religious and popular reality adapted to the universal form of the national movements of the nineteenth century. This reality was the holy matrimony of a "holy" people with a "holy" land, the local point of which was the name of Zion.

It has been one of the disastrous errors of modern Biblical criticism to attribute this category of the Holy, as applied in the Scriptures to the people and the land, to the sacerdotalism of a later age for which the claims of public worship were all-important. On the contrary, it appertains rather to the *primitive* conception of the Holy as we find it in tribes living close to nature, who think of the two main supports of national life, man and the earth, as endowed with sacred powers. In the tribes which united to form "Israel" this concept developed and became transformed in a special way: holiness is no longer a sign of power, a magic fluid that can dwell in places and regions as well as in people and groups of people, but a quality bestowed on this particular people and this particular land because God "elects" both in order to lead His chosen people into His chosen land and to join them to each other. It is His election that sanctifies the chosen people as His immediate attendance and the land as His royal throne and which makes them dependent on each other. This is more a political, a theopolitical than a strictly religious concept of holiness: the outward form of worship is merely a concentrated expression of the sovereignty of God. Abraham builds altars where God has appeared to him, but he does so not as a priest but as a herald of the Lord by whom he has been sent, and when he calls on the name of his Lord above the altar he thereby proclaims his Lord's royal claim to possession of the surrounding land. This is not the transforming interpretation of a later age but has its roots in primitive language, analogies of which are to be found in other early peoples but nowhere in such historical concreteness as here. Here "holiness" still means to belong to God not merely through religious symbols and in the times and places consecrated to public worship but as a people and a land, in the all-embracing range and reality of public life. It is only later that the category of the Holy becomes restricted to public worship, a process which increases the more the sphere of public life is withdrawn from the sovereign rule of God.

That it is God who joins this people to this land is not a subsequent historical interpretation of events; the wandering tribes themselves were inspired again and again by the promise made to their forefathers and the most enthusiastic among them saw God Himself leading His people into the promised land. It is impossible to imagine a historical Israel as existing at any time without belief in its God or previously to such belief: it is precisely the message of the common Leader that unites the tribes into a people. It is no less impossible to imagine this belief as existing before and outside Israel: it is an absolutely historical belief, the belief in a God leading first the fathers and then the whole people into the promised land at historically determined times for divinely historical purposes. Here is no "nation" as such and no "religion" as such but only a people interpreting its historical experiences as the actions of its God.

This belief in divine leadership is, however, at the same time the belief in a mission. However much of the legislation that has come down to us in the Bible may be attributed to later literary accretions, there is no doubt at all that the exodus from Egypt was bound up with the imposing of a law that was taken to be a divine charter and the positive nucleus of all the later developments was essentially the instruction to establish a "holy" national community in the promised land. For these tribes divine leadership certainly implied an ordinance concerning the future in the land and from this basis a tradition and a doctrine were evolved. The story of Abraham, which connects the gift of Canaan with the command to be a blessing, is a most concise résumé of the fact that the association of this people with this land signifies a mission. The people came to the land to fulfil the mission, even by each new revolt against it they recognized its continuing validity; the prophets were appointed to interpret the past and future destiny of the people on the basis of its failure as yet to establish the righteous city of God for the establishment of which it had been led into the land. This land was at no time in the history of Israel simply the property of the people; it was always at the same time a challenge to make of it what God intended to have made of it.

Thus from the very beginning the unique association between this people and this land was characterized by what was to be, by the intention that was to be realized. It was a consummation that could not be achieved by the people or the land on its own but only by the faithful co-operation of the two together and it was an association in which the land appeared not as a dead, passive object but as a living and active partner. Just as, to achieve fullness of life, the people needed the land, so the land needed the people, and the end which both were called upon to realize could only be reached by a living partnership. Since the living land shared the great work with the living people it was to be both the work of history and the work of nature. Just as nature and history were united in the creation of man, so these two spheres which have become separated in the human mind were to unite in the task in which the chosen land and the chosen people were called upon to co-operate. The holy matrimony of land and people was intended to bring about the matrimony of the two separated spheres of Being.

This is the theme, relating to a small and despised part of the human race and a small and desolate part of the earth, yet worldwide in its significance, that lies hidden in the name of Zion. It is not simply a special case among the national concepts and national movements: the exceptional quality that is here added to the universal makes it a unique category extending far beyond the frontier of national problems and touching the domain of the universally human, the cosmic and even of Being itself. In other respects the people of Israel may be regarded as one of the many peoples on earth and the land of Israel as one land among other lands: but in their mutual relationship and in their common task they are unique and incomparable. And, in spite of all the names and historical events that have come down to us, what has come to pass, what is coming and shall come to pass between them, is and remains a mystery. From generation to generation the Jewish people have never ceased to meditate on this mystery.

When the national movement of this people inherited the

mystery, a powerful desire to dissolve it arose in spite of the protests of the movement's most important spiritual leaders. It seemed to belong to the purely "religious" sphere and religion had become discredited for two reasons: in the West, because of its attempt to denationalize itself in the age of Emancipation, in the East, because of its resistance to the Europeanization of the Jewish people on which the national movement wanted to base itself. The secularizing trend in Zionism was directed against the mystery of Zion too. A people like other peoples, a land like other lands, a national movement like other national movements—this was and still is proclaimed as the postulate of common sense against every kind of "mysticism." And from this standpoint the age-long belief that the successful reunion of this people with this land is inseparably bound up with a command and a condition was attacked. No more is necessary—so the watchword runs—than that the Jewish people should be granted the free development of all its powers in its own country like any other people; that is in fact what is meant by "Regeneration."

The certainty of the generations of Israel testifies that this view is inadequate. The idea of Zion is rooted in deeper regions of the earth and rises into loftier regions of the air, and neither its deep roots nor its lofty heights, neither its memory of the past nor its ideal for the future, both of the selfsame texture, must be repudiated. If Israel renounces the mystery, it renounces the heart of reality itself. National forms without the eternal purpose from which they have arisen signify the end of Israel's specific fruitfulness. The free development of the latent power of the nation without a supreme value to give it purpose and direction does not mean regeneration but the mere sport of a common self-deception behind which spiritual death lurks in ambush. If Israel desires less than it is intended to fulfil then it will even fail to achieve the lesser goal.

With every new encounter of this people with this land the task is set afresh, but every time it is rooted in the historical situation and its problems. If it is not mastered, what has already been achieved will fall into ruin. Once it is really mastered this may be the beginning of a new kind of human society. To be sure, the problem proves to be more difficult every time it is tackled. It is more difficult to set up an order based on justice in the land if one is under the jurisdiction of a foreign power, as after the return from Babylon, than if one is comparatively free to determine one's own way of life, as after the first appropriation of the land; and it is still more difficult if one has to reckon with the coexistence of another people in the same country, of cognate origin and language but mainly foreign in tradition, structure and outlook, and if this vital fact has to be regarded as an essential part of the problem. On the other hand, there seems to be a high purpose behind the increasing difficulty of the task. Even in the life of the individual what has once been neglected can never be made up for in the same sphere and under the same conditions; but one is sometimes allowed to make amends for lost opportunities in a quite different situation, in a quite different form, and it is significant that the new situation is more contradictory and the new form more difficult to realize than the old and that each fresh attempt demands an even greater exertion to fulfil the task; for such is the hard but not ungracious way of life itself. The same process seems to be true of the life of Israel.

53. Education and Tradition

. . . N A T I O N A L movements can have three possible relationships to tradition. The first is positive. The adherents of the movement open their hearts to the tide of the elements, absorb, and transform what they have absorbed, in response to the demands of the hour. They allow the forces inherent in the beginnings to shape present-day life in accordance with present-day needs.

The second form of relationship is negative. The impact of the age-old tidings is warded off as neither credible, nor usable, nor timely.

The third approach I should call the fictitious. Those who follow it exalt the works and values of national tradition, regard them as the subject of pride and piety, and point to them with the air of collectors and owners, as though they were coronation robes in a museum, not, of course, suitable apparel for a living sovereign. While they boast of their tradition, they do not believe in it. They teach it in school, but not with the purpose of seriously integrating it into actual life. All that seems necessary to them is to "have" it. Unfortunately, the relationship of our national movement and national education to tradition is mainly a mixture of the second and third forms.

No mere good intentions can work a thoroughgoing change in the status quo. The power to transform life must spring from life itself. Already the halutz and his communes, the kibbutzim, are beginning to feel that something is lacking in the structure of their existence. Somewhere in the life of the week, there is a dead end; somewhere in the web of the work, there is a hole. No one knows just what it is, and certainly no one will name it. There is silence on that score, silence and suffering. I am under the impression that this suffering will increase in the course of the next decade and penetrate consciousness until it breaks the silence.

I do not believe that it is important for the halutz, or the national type of which he is the best representative, to accept en bloc either a ready-made tradition, or one or another part of it. Any such acceptance would be purely arbitrary and would share the fate of all arbitrary actions; it would be wholly unfruitful. One project, in particular, which is bruited about in the country, seems to me quite hopeless: the project of reviving religious forms without their religious content. Forms in themselves are nothing. What values they have accrues to them only through that which has been expressed in them, what has pervaded them as the soul pervades the body. The secret of their origin is the secret of their effectiveness. Once they have grown empty, one cannot fill them with a new, timely content; they will not hold it. Once they have decayed, they cannot be resuscitated by infusion with a spirit other than their own. They will seem only as life-like as dolls. All such attempts are dilettantish, devoid of reverence and vigor; they are unblessed. A Passover seder which is held to celebrate the national liberation as such will always be lacking in the essential, and that essential can only be gained when we feel that self-liberation enfolds the redemption of man and the world through a redeeming power as the husk enfolds the kernel. The Feast of Weeks is, of course, a nature festival, a festival in honor of a season and its abundance, the festival of the farmer who time and again experiences the miracle that earth gives him so much more than he has given her. But one cannot do justice to this festival by explaining it as a nature symbol. One must also know that nature herself is a symbol, that man can attain to true life only by surrendering himself to the unknown, and that the reward, the manifold harvest, is called revelation. No matter how devotedly the Sabbath is kept, the rite will be threadbare if the Joy in a day of rest for everybody is not filled with the divination of a cosmic mystery of work and rest which is reflected in that day. This mystery is figuratively expressed with a childlike ingenuousness—in the idea that the Creator of heaven and earth "draws breath" after his labors on that day just as well as the "son of thy handmaid." Thus, the breath of relaxation which we draw merges with the breath of the world.

But what shall we do when a generation, like that of today, has become alienated from the religious content of the forms?

We must provide them with a truly national education, and this means that we must convey the primordial utterances of their people to their ears and their hearts. We must surmount the prejudice of this era which claims that those utterances can have interest for us only as literary history, as cultural history, religious history, etc., and that instruction should treat them only as the chief literary creation of the nation, as the source for the study of its ancient culture and the oldest document of its religious beginnings. We must surmount the superstition of the era which seems to hold that the world of faith to which those utterances bear witness is the subject of our knowledge only, and not a reality which makes life worth living. We must keep the younger generation free from the bias that says: "We know all about ourselves and the world, and in any event these utterances can no longer exert an authoritative influence on our lives." This generation must be taught to despise the inflexible self-assurance which says: "I am well prepared. Nothing can happen to change me fundamentally and transform the world before my eyes. I know what I know; I am what I am; tomorrow can be not different than today." This generation must be made receptive to the Unforeseen, which upsets all logical arrangements. Their ears and hearts must be opened to the voice of the mystery which speaks in those utterances. And we should do all this not with the purpose of preparing them to repeat the teachings and perform prescribed rites, but so that they may acquire the power to make the original choice, that—listening to the voice with that power—they may hear the message it has for their hour and their work; that they may learn to trust the voice, and through this trust, come to faith, to a faith of their own.

54. The Way of Man According to the Teaching of Hasidism

I. Heart Searching

R A B B I Shner Zalman, the Rav of Northern White Russia (died 1813), was put in jail in Petersburg, because the *Mitnaggdim* had denounced his principles and his way of living to the government. He was awaiting trial when the chief of the gendarmes entered his cell. The majestic and quiet face of the rav, who was so deep in meditation that he did not at first notice his visitor, suggested to his chief, a thoughtful person, what manner of man he had before him. He began to converse with his prisoner and brought up a number of questions which had occurred to him in reading the Scriptures. Finally he asked: "How are we to understand that God the all-knowing, said to Adam: 'Where art thou?' "

"Do you believe," answered the rav, "that the Scriptures are eternal and that every era, every generation and every man is included in them?"

"I believe this," said the other.

"Well then," said the zaddik, "in every era, God calls to every man: 'Where are you in your world? So many years and days of those allotted to you have passed, and how far have you gotten in your world?' God says something like this: 'You have lived forty-six years. How far along are you?' "

When the chief of the gendarmes heard his age mentioned,

he pulled himself together, laid his hand on the rav's shoulder, and cried: "Bravo!" But his heart trembled.

What happens in this tale? . . . Adam hides himself to avoid rendering accounts, to escape responsibility for his way of living. Every man hides for this purpose, for every man is Adam and finds himself in Adam's situation. To escape responsibility for his life, he turns existence into a system of hideouts. And in thus hiding again and again "from the face of God," he enmeshes himself more and more deeply in perversity. A new situation thus arises, which becomes more and more questionable with every day, with every new hideout. "This situation can be precisely defined as follows: Man cannot escape the eye of God, but in trying to hide from him, he is hiding from himself. True, in him too there is something that seeks him, but he makes it harder and harder for that 'something' to find him." This is the situation into which God's question falls. This question is designed to awaken man and destroy his system of hideouts; it is to show man to what pass he has come and to awake in him the great will to get out of it.

Everything now depends on whether man faces the question. Of course, every man's heart, like that of the chief in the story, will tremble when he hears it. But his system of hideouts will help him to overcome this emotion. For the Voice does not come in a thunderstorm which threatens man's very existence; it is a "still small voice," and easy to drown. So long as this is done, man's life will not become a *way*. Whatever success and enjoyment he may achieve, whatever power he may attain and whatever deeds he may do, his life will remain way-less, so long as he does not face the Voice. Adam faces the Voice, perceives his enmeshment, and avows: "I hid myself"; this is the beginning of man's way. The decisive heart-searching is the beginning of a human way. But heart-searching is decisive only if it leads to the way. For there is a sterile kind of heart-searching, which leads to nothing but self-torture, despair and still deeper enmeshment. . . . There is a demonic question, a spurious question, which apes God's question, the question of Truth. Its characteristic is that it does not stop at: "Where art thou?", but continues: "From where you have got to, there is no way out." This is the wrong kind of heart-searching, which does not prompt man to turn, and put him on the way, but, by representing turning as hopeless, drives him to a point where it appears to have become entirely impossible and man can go on living only by demonic pride, the pride of perversity.

II. The Particular Way

Rabbi Baer of Radoshitz once said to his teacher, the "Seer" of Lublin: "Show me one general way to the service of God."

The zaddik replied: "It is impossible to tell men what way they should take. For one way to serve God is through learning, another through prayer, another through fasting, and still another through eating. Everyone should carefully observe what way his heart draws him to, and then choose this way with all his strength."

In the first place, this story tells us something about our relationship to such genuine service as was performed by others before us. We are to revere it and learn from it, but we are not to imitate it. The great and holy deeds done by others are examples for us, since they show, in a concrete manner, what greatness and holiness is, but they are not models which we should copy. However small our achievements may be in comparison with those of our forefathers, they have their real value in that we bring them about in our own way and by our own efforts. . . . Every person born into this world represents something new, something that never existed before, something original and unique. . . . Every man's foremost task is the actualization of his unique, unprecedented and never-recurring potentialities, and not the repetition of something that another, and be it even the greatest, has already achieved. . . . The same idea was expressed with even greater pregnancy by Rabbi Zusya when he said, a short while before his death: "In the world to come I shall not be asked 'Why were you not Moses?' I shall be asked: 'Why were you not Zusya?' "

We are here confronted with a doctrine which is based on the fact that men are essentially unlike one another, and which therefore does not aim at making them alike. All men have access to God, but each man has a different access. Mankind's great chance lies precisely in the unlikeness of man, in the unlikeness of their qualities and inclinations. God's all-inclusiveness manifests itself in the infinite multiplicity of the ways that lead to him, each of which is open to one man. . . . Thus, the way by which a man can reach God is revealed to him only through the knowledge of his own being, the knowledge of his essential quality and inclination. "Everyone has in him something precious that is in no one else." But this precious something in a man is revealed to him only if he truly perceives his strongest feeling, his central wish, that in him which stirs his inmost being.

Of course, in many cases, a man knows this his strongest feeling only in the shape of a particular passion, of the "Evil Urge" which seeks to lead him astray. Naturally, a man's most powerful desire, in seeking satisfaction, rushes in the first instance at objects which lie across his path. It is necessary, therefore, that the power of even this feeling, of even this impulse, be diverted from the casual to the essential, and from the relative to the absolute. Thus a man finds his way. . . .

By no means, however, can it be our true task in the world into which we have been set, to turn away from the things and beings that we meet on our way and that attract our hearts; our task is precisely to get in touch, by hallowing our relationship with them, with what manifests itself in them as beauty, pleasure, enjoyment. Hasidism teaches that rejoicing in the world, if we hallow it with our whole being, leads to rejoicing in God. . . .

Though detachment from nature, abstinence from natural life, may, in the cases of some men, mean the necessary starting-point of their "way" or, perhaps, a necessary act of self-isolation at certain crucial moments of existence, it may never mean the whole way. Some men must begin by fasting, and begin by it again and again, because it is peculiar to them that only by asceticism can they achieve liberation from their enslavement to the world, deepest heart-searching and ultimate communion with the Absolute. But never should asceticism gain mastery over a man's life. A man may only detach himself from nature in order to revert to it again and, in hallowed contact with it, find his way to God. . . .

III. Resolution

A Hasid of the rabbi of Lublin once fasted from one Sabbath to the next. On Friday afternoon he began to suffer such cruel thirst that he thought he would die. He saw a well, went up to it, and prepared to drink. But instantly he realized that because of the one brief hour he had still to endure, he was about to destroy the work of the entire week. He did not drink and went away from the well. Then he was touched by a feeling of pride for having passed this difficult test. When he became aware of it, he said to himself, "Better I go and drink than let my heart fall prey to pride." He went back to the well, but just as he was going to bend down to draw water, he noticed that his thirst had disappeared. When the Sabbath had begun, he entered his teacher's house. "Patchwork!" the rabbi called to him, as he crossed the threshold.

When in my youth I heard this tale for the first time, I was struck by the harsh manner in which the master treats his zealous disciple. The latter makes his utmost efforts to perform a difficult feat of asceticism. He feels tempted to break off and overcomes the temptation, but his only reward, after all his trouble, is an expression of disapproval from his teacher. . . .

What the master—apparently after watching the progress of the venture with true understanding—says to the disciple, means undoubtedly: "This is not the proper manner to attain a higher rung." He warns the disciple of something that perforce hinders him from achieving his purpose. What this is becomes clear enough. The object of the reproof is the advance and subsequent retreat; it is the wavering, shilly-shallying character of the man's doing that makes it questionable. The opposite of "patchwork" is work "all of a piece." Now how does one achieve work "all of a piece"? Only with a united soul.

Again we are troubled by the question whether this man is not being treated too harshly. As things are in this world, one man—"by nature" or "by grace," however one chooses to put it —has a unitary soul, a soul all of a piece, and accordingly performs unitary works, works all of a piece, because his soul, by being as it is, prompts and enables him to do so; another man has a divided, complicated, contradictory soul, and this, naturally, affects his doings: their inhibitions and disturbances originate in the inhibitions and disturbances of his soul; its restlessness is expressed in their restlessness. What else can a man so constituted do than try to overcome the temptations which approach him on the way to what is, at a given time, his goal? What else can he do than each time, in the middle of his doing, "pull himself together," as we say, that is, rally his vacillating soul, and again and again, having rallied it, re-concentrate it upon the goal —and moreover be ready, like the hasid in the story when pride touches him, to sacrifice the goal in order to save the soul?

Only when, in the light of these questions, we subject our story to renewed scrutiny, do we apprehend the teaching implied in the Seer's criticism. It is the teaching that a man can unify his soul. The man with the divided, complicated, contradictory soul is not helpless: the core of his soul, the divine force in its depths, is capable of acting upon it, changing it, binding the conflicting forces together, amalgamating the diverging elements—is capable of unifying it. This unification must be accomplished *before* a man undertakes some unusual work. Only with a united soul will he be able so to do it that it becomes not patchwork but work all of a piece. The Seer thus reproaches the hasid with having embarked on his venture without first unifying his soul; unity of soul can never be achieved in the middle of the work. . . .

One thing must of course not be lost sight of: unification of the soul is never final. Just as a soul most unitary from birth is sometimes beset by inner difficulties, thus even a soul most powerfully struggling for unity can never completely achieve it. But any work that I do with a united soul reacts upon my soul, acts in the direction of new and greater unification, leads me, though by all sorts of detours, to a *steadier* unity than was the preceding one. Thus man ultimately reaches a point where he can rely upon his soul, because its unity is now so great that it overcomes contradiction with effortless ease. Vigilance, of course, is necessary even then, but it is a relaxed vigilance. . . .

IV. Beginning with Oneself

Once when Rabbi Yitzhak of Vorki was playing host to certain prominent men of Israel, they discussed the value to a household of an honest and efficient servant. They said that a good servant made for good management and cited Joseph at whose hands everything prospered. Rabbi Yitzhak objected. "I once thought that too," he said. "But then my teacher showed me that everything depends on the master of the house. You see, in my youth my wife gave me a great deal of trouble, and though I myself put up with her as best I could, I was sorry for the servants. So I went to my teacher, Rabbi David of Lelov, and asked him whether I should oppose my wife. All he said was: 'Why do you speak to me? Speak to yourself!' I thought over these words for quite a while before I understood them. But I did understand them when I recalled a certain saying of the Baal-Shem: 'There is thought, speech and action. Thought corresponds to one's wife, speech to one's children, and action to one's servants. Whoever straightens himself out in regard to all three will find that everything prospers at his hands.' Then I understood what my teacher had meant: everything depended on myself."

This story touches upon one of the deepest and most difficult problems of our life: the true origin of conflict between man and man. . . .

. . . [In] *Hasidism* man is not treated as an object of examination but is called upon to "straighten himself out." At first, a man should himself realize that conflict-situations between himself and others are nothing but the effects of conflict-situations in his own soul; then he should try to overcome this inner conflict, so that afterwards he may go out to his fellow-men and enter into new, transformed relationships with them.

Man naturally tries to avoid this decisive reversal—extremely repugnant to him in his accustomed relationship to the world—by referring him who thus appeals to him, or his own soul, if it is his soul that makes the appeal, to the fact that every conflict involves two parties and that, if he is expected to turn his attention from the external to his own internal conflict, his opponent should be expected to do the same. But just this perspective, in which a man sees himself only as an individual contrasted with other individuals, and not as a genuine person, whose transformation helps towards the transformation of the world, contains the fundamental error which hasidic teaching denounces. The essential thing is to begin with oneself, and at this moment a man has nothing in the world to care about than this beginning. Any other attitude would distract him from what he is about to begin, weaken his initiative, and thus frustrate the entire bold undertaking. . . .

The origin of all conflict between me and my fellow-men

is that I do not say what I mean, and that I do not do what I say. For this confuses and poisons, again and again and in increasing measure, the situation between myself and the other man, and I, in my internal disintegration, am no longer able to master it but, contrary to all my illusions, have become its slave. By our contradiction, our lie, we foster conflict-situations and give them power over us until they enslave us. From here, there is no way out but by the crucial realization: everything depends on myself, and the crucial decision: I will straighten myself out.

But in order that a man may be capable of this great feat, he must first find his way from the casual, accessory elements of his existence to his own self; he must find his own self, not the trivial ego of the egotistic individual, but the deeper self of the person living in a relationship to the world. And that is also contrary to everything we are accustomed to. . . .

V. Not to Be Preoccupied with Oneself

Rabbi Hayyim of Zans had married his son to the daughter of Rabbi Eliezer. The day after the wedding he visited the father of the bride and said: "Now that we are related I feel close to you and can tell you what is eating at my heart. Look! My hair and beard have grown white, and I have not yet atoned!"

"O my friend," replied Rabbi Eliezer, "you are thinking only of yourself. How about forgetting yourself and thinking of the world?"

What is said here seems to contradict everything I have hitherto reported of the teachings of *Hasidism*. We have heard that everyone should search his own heart, choose his particular way, bring about the unity of his being, begin with himself; and now we are told that man should forget himself. But if we examine this injunction more closely, we find that it is not only consistent with the others, but fits into the whole as a necessary link, as a necessary stage, in its particular place. One need only ask one question: "What for?" What am I to choose my particular way for? What am I to unify my being for? The reply is: Not for my own sake. This is why the previous injunction was: to *begin* with oneself. To begin with oneself, but not to end with oneself; to start from oneself, but not to aim at oneself; to

comprehend oneself, to start from oneself, but not to be pre-
occupied with oneself.

We see a *tzaddik*, a wise, pious, kindly man, reproach himself
in his old age for not yet having performed the true turning. The
reply given him is apparently prompted by the opinion that he
greatly overrates his sins and greatly underrates the penance he
has already done. But what Rabbi Eliezer says, goes beyond this.
He says, in quite a general sense: "Do not keep worrying about
what you have done wrong, but apply the soul-power you are
now wasting on self-reproach to such active relationship to the
world as you are destined for. You should not be occupied with
yourself but with the world."

First of all, we should properly understand what is said here
about turning. It is known that turning stands in the center of
the Jewish conception of the way of man. Turning is capable
of renewing a man from within and changing his position in
God's world, so that he who turns is seen standing above the
perfect *tzaddik*, who does not know the abyss of sin. But turning
means here something much greater than repentance and acts
of penance; it means that by a reversal of his whole being, a
man who had been lost in the maze of selfishness, where he had
always set himself as his goal, finds a way to God, that is, a way
to the fulfilment of the particular task for which he, this particular man, has been destined by God. Repentance can only be
an incentive to such active reversal; he who goes on fretting
himself with repentance, he who tortures himself with the idea
that his acts of penance are not sufficient, withholds his best
energies from the work of reversal. In a sermon on the Day of
Atonement, the Rabbi of Ger warned against self-torture:

"He who has done ill and talks about it and thinks about it
all the time does not cast the base thing he did out of his
thoughts, and whatever one thinks, therein one is, one's soul is
wholly and utterly in what one thinks, and so he dwells in baseness. He will certainly not be able to turn, for his spirit will grow
coarse and his heart stubborn, and in addition to this he may be
overcome by gloom. What would you? Rake the muck this way,
rake the muck that way—it will always be muck. Have I sinned,
or have I not sinned—what does Heaven get out of it? In the
time I am brooding over it I could be stringing pearls for the

delight of Heaven. That is why it is written: 'Depart from evil and do good'—turn wholly away from evil, do not dwell upon it, and do good. You have done wrong? Then counteract it by doing right."

But the significance of our story goes beyond this. He who tortures himself incessantly with the idea that he has not yet sufficiently atoned, is essentially concerned with the salvation of his soul, with his personal fate in eternity. By rejecting this aim, Hasidism merely draws a conclusion from the teachings of Judaism generally. One of the main points in which Christianity differs from Judaism is that it makes each man's salvation his highest aim. Judaism regards each man's soul as a serving member of God's creation which, by man's work, is to become the Kingdom of God; thus no soul has its object in itself, in its own salvation. True, each is to know itself, purify itself, perfect itself, but not for its own sake—neither for the sake of its temporal happiness nor for that of its eternal bliss—but for the sake of the work which it is destined to perform upon the world.

The pursuit of one's own salvation is here regarded merely as the sublimest form of self-intending. Self-intending is what Hasidism rejects most emphatically, and quite especially in the case of the man who has found and developed his own self. . . .

The greatest of Rabbi Bunam's disciples, a truly tragic figure among the *tzaddikim*, Rabbi Mendel of Kotzk, once said to his congregation: "What, after all, do I demand of you? Only three things: not to look furtively outside yourselves, not to look furtively into others, and not to aim at yourselves." That is to say: firstly, everyone should preserve and hallow his own soul in its particularity and in its own place, and not envy the particularity and place of others; secondly, everyone should respect the secret in the soul of his fellow-man, and not, with brazen curiosity, intrude upon it and take advantage of it; and thirdly, everyone, in his relationship to the world, should be careful not to set himself as his aim.

VI. Here Where One Stands

Rabbi Bunam used to tell young men who came to him for the first time the story of Rabbi Eizik, son of Rabbi Yekel of Cracow. After many years of great poverty which had never shaken his faith in God, he dreamed someone bade him look for a treasure in Prague, under the bridge which leads to the king's palace. When the dream recurred a third time, Rabbi Eizik prepared for the journey and set out for Prague. But the bridge was guarded day and night and he did not dare to start digging. Nevertheless he went to the bridge every morning and kept walking around it until evening. Finally the captain of the guards, who had been watching him, asked in a kindly way whether he was looking for something or waiting for somebody. Rabbi Eizik told him of the dream which had brought him here from a faraway country. The captain laughed: "And so to please the dream, you poor fellow wore out your shoes to come here! As for having faith in dreams, if I had had it, I should have had to get going when a dream once told me to go to Cracow and dig for treasure under the stove in the room of a Jew—Eizik, son of Yekel, that was the name! Eizik, son of Yekel! I can just imagine what it would be like, how I should have to try every house over there, where one half of the Jews are named Eizik and the other Yekel!" And he laughed again. Rabbi Eizik bowed, traveled home, dug up the treasure from under the stove, and built the House of Prayer which is called "Reb Eizik Reb Yekel's Shul." . . .

There is something that can only be found in one place. It is a great treasure, which may be called the fulfilment of existence. The place where this treasure can be found is the place on which one stands.

Most of us achieve only at rare moments a clear realization of the fact that they have never tasted the fulfilment of existence, that their life does not participate in true, fulfilled existence, that, as it were, it passes true existence by. We nevertheless feel the deficiency at every moment, and in some measure strive to find—somewhere—what we are seeking. Somewhere, in some province of the world or of the mind, except where we stand, where we have been set—but it is there and nowhere else that the treasure can be found. The environment which I feel to be the natural one, the situation which has been assigned to me as my fate, the things that happen to me day after day, the things that claim me day after day—these contain my essential task and such fulfilment of existence as is open to me. . . .

If we had power over the ends of the earth, it would not give us that fulfilment of existence which a quiet devoted relationship to nearby life can give us. If we knew the secrets of the upper worlds, they would not allow us so much actual participation in true existence as we can achieve by performing, with holy intent, a task belonging to our daily duties. Our treasure is hidden beneath the hearth of our own home.

The Baal Shem teaches that no encounter with a being or a thing in the course of our life lacks a hidden significance. The people we live with or meet with, the animals that help us with our farmwork, the soil we till, the materials we shape, the tools we use, they all contain a mysterious spiritual substance which depends on us for helping it towards its pure form, its perfection. If we neglect this spiritual substance sent across our path, if we think only in terms of momentary purposes, without developing a genuine relationship to the beings and things in whose life we ought to take part, as they in ours, then we shall ourselves be debarred from true, fulfilled existence. It is my conviction that this doctrine is essentially true. The highest culture of the soul remains basically arid and barren unless, day by day, waters of life pour forth into the soul from those little encounters to which we give their due; the most formidable power is intrinsically powerlessness unless it maintains a secret covenant with these contacts, both humble and helpful, with strange, and yet near, being.

Some religions do not regard our sojourn on earth as true life. They either teach that everything appearing to us here is mere appearance, behind which we should penetrate, or that it is only a forecourt of the true world, a forecourt which we should cross without paying much attention to it. Judaism, on the contrary, teaches that what a man does now and here with holy intent is no less important, no less true—being a terrestrial indeed, but none the less factual, link with divine being—than the life in the world to come. This doctrine has found its fullest expression in Hasidism. . . .

"Where is the dwelling of God?"

This was the question with which the Rabbi of Kotzk surprised a number of learned men who happened to be visiting him.

They laughed at him: "What a thing to ask! Is not the whole world full of his glory?"

Then he answered his own question:
"God dwells wherever man lets him in."
This is the ultimate purpose: to let God in. But we can let
him in only where we really stand, where we live, where we live
a true life. If we maintain holy intercourse with the little world
entrusted to us, if we help the holy spiritual substance to accomplish itself in that section of Creation in which we are living,
then we are establishing, in this our place, a dwelling for the
Divine Presence.

FOR FURTHER READING

Books by Martin Buber

On the Bible: Eighteen Studies edited by Nahum N. Glatzer (New York:
Schocken, 1982). One volume of many translations of Buber's work
that is currently available.

Books about Martin Buber

MARTIN, Bernard, editor, *Great Twentieth Century Jewish Philosophers* (New
York: Macmillan, 1970). Introduction to his work with four translations, pages 238-334.

BOROWITZ, Eugene B., *Choices in Modern Jewish Thought: A Partisan's
Guide* (New York: Behrman House, 1983). "Religious Existentialism:
Martin Buber," pages 141-164.

FRIEDMAN, Maurice, *Martin Buber's Life and Work*—3 volumes (New
York: Dutton, 1985). Without question, the definitive biography.

"Martin Buber" in *Enclycopedia Judaica*, Volume 4: pp. 1429-1433 (Jerusalem: 1972). An excellent introduction to his thought.

AMERICAN
JEWISH
THINKERS

KAUFMANN KOHLER

(1843–1926)

EDITOR'S NOTE

With Kaufmann Kohler we turn back to the world of nineteenth-century rationalism and evolution and to the optimistic and univer-salistic approach which characterized Reform Judaism in America until after the First World War. Scholar, pioneer theologian and radical reformer, Kohler served as head of the Hebrew Union College during the first two decades of the century. He shared with Leo Baeck, spokesman for liberal Judaism in Germany, his emphasis on the ethical affirmations of Judaism and its optimistic spirit. But Kohler was more radical in his attitude toward traditional rituals and the use of Hebrew and more vehement in his opposition to political Zionism. Their differences in outlook are an indication of the distance which separated American Reform from German liberalism.

Kaufmann Kohler was born in 1843 in Fuerth, Bavaria to pious Orthodox parents who gave him a traditional upbringing. He studied for a time with Samson Raphael Hirsch, the leading exponent of Orthodox Judaism in Germany. Though he later rejected his teacher's point of view, Kohler acknowledged the lifelong influence Hirsch had on him. At the University of Munich and later at Berlin, Kohler went through a period of inner doubt and spiritual confusion (as was true of Ahad Ha-am, Buber and Kaplan in their youth) until he finally arrived at a historical evolutionary approach to the Bible. Kohler's progressive views antagonized some of his former teachers and hindered his rabbinic career. On the advice of Abraham Geiger, the noted Reform leader, Kohler, therefore, decided to emigrate to America.

On his arrival in the United States in 1869 he was befriended by Rabbi David Einhorn (a leading spokesman for Reform Judaism) whose daughter he married the following year. After serving as rabbi in Detroit and Chicago for several years, Kohler succeeded his father-in-law at Temple Beth El in New York in 1879 and soon emerged as chief spokesman for Reform Judaism in the United States. He was the guiding spirit in drafting the "Pittsburgh Platform," the declaration of principles for Reform Judaism, in November, 1885.

In 1903, at the age of sixty, Kohler was elected president of the

Hebrew Union College in Cincinnati. During his presidency he introduced a series of new courses and raised the academic standards of
the institution which became the recognized center of Reform
Judaism. He was one of the moving spirits in launching the Jewish
Encyclopedia and wrote a number of its major articles. He also served
on the Board of Editors which prepared the new translation of the
Holy Scriptures for the Jewish Publication Society of America.

In 1910, at the request of the Society for the Promotion of the
Science of Judaism in Germany, Kohler wrote his most important
work, *Jewish Theology Systematically and Historically Considered*,
which a few years later he enlarged and had translated into English.
It is this pioneer work, in which he surveyed the whole field of Jewish
theology from its earliest beginnings to his own time, on which his
fame rests. In 1916 Kohler published *Hebrew Union College and
Other Addresses* as a companion to Solomon Schechter's *Seminary
Addresses*. After his death two collections of his writings, *Studies,
Addresses and Personal Papers* (1931) and *A Living Faith* (1948)
were issued. From among these writings the late Dr. Samuel Cohon,
professor of theology at the Hebrew Union College and author of
the chapter on Kohler in the companion volume, chose a group of
representative selections shortly before his death.

We begin with a lecture Kohler gave on *Evolution and Religion* at
Temple Beth El in New York in 1887. At the time a lively debate
was under way on the relation of science to religion as a result of
Darwin's epoch-making works which had appeared a few years
before. Kohler accepted the idea that religion, like all human phenomena, was constantly evolving. He sought to show, however, that
the new scientific theories of Darwin were not incompatible with a
moral and religious outlook. The doctrine of evolution, to him, did
not eliminate the need for eternal moral truths.

In the next passage, taken from his volume on theology, Kohler
presents his concept of God, stressing His "unique self-consciousness," rationality and moral qualities, and the many stages the Jewish
God idea went through before it reached the concept of a spiritual
God—transcendent and yet "an ever-present helper in trouble." This
selection is followed by one giving his interpretation of creation.
Here again, Kohler sees no conflict between the "facts established by
natural science" and the religious view of the world as the "free act
of a creator." In Kohler's view, the Bible accentuates truths with
which science is not concerned such as the unity, goodness and harmony of the universe.

The passage on ethics is taken from an address given in 1911, in
reply to a number of publications which had appeared advocating the

introduction of "pure non-sectarian ethical lessons in our public and high schools." Kohler pointed out that in actuality the writers stressed "the Christian character of the ethics to be taught." He further noted that "even among the most liberal and most learned men there prevail very confused notions about the relation of the New Testament ethics to prior teachings of Judaism." In this excerpt he indicates the error of those who claim Christian ethics to be "the highest standard of morality for human society," and points to some of its fundamental weaknesses.

The selection on the *Mission of Israel* brings to our attention a fundamental idea which is still very much a part of Reform ideology and has been discussed in recent conventions of the Central Conference of American Rabbis. In our final passage, Kohler reveals a greater traditionalism than in his early period. While he still minimized the use of Hebrew in daily services, he now stressed the importance of the Sabbath as opposed to Sunday services, the values of such festivals as *Shavuot* and *Simhat Torah* and the role that the home should play, together with the synagogue, in the revitalization of Jewish life.

55. Evolution and Religion

W H A T is Evolution? To put it in fewest and plainest words: The things around about us and the ideas within us have not, as was the belief hitherto, been created and fixed by single creative acts of God, but have all along been and are still growing and developing from lower to ever higher and more complicated forms. Not only suns and stars, plant and animal life of all shape and size, but the speech, the conscience and reason we possess, and the religion we own, have been and are in constant process of growth, ever changing, moving, shifting. Of course, it is asked: What becomes of the divine sanctity of religion, of the authority and influence of morality, if the conscience is, as our evolutionists say, the product of society rather than the voice of the heavenly judge?

Let me, in answer to this, state that in these evolution doctrines there is a great deal of philosophical error mixed with the scientific truth. When Darwin first struck upon that grand idea of evolution, he staunchly held and asserted the belief in a divine creator. Only when, in search of the mechanical forces operating in response to the creative fiat, he after long scientific observation arrived at the conception of the "survival of the fittest in the great struggle for existence," the spectacle of that great fierce warfare carried on throughout the universe so bewildered him that he lost sight of the sublime Leader of Hosts marshalling all these forces from behind the scene. Yet does not each victory tell of a triumphant idea? Does the interacting of all these wheels within wheels in the great fabric of life not sufficiently betray the all-surveying Master-Mind? Chance will never drive your vessel into the safe harbor when left to the sway of wave and wind. There must be a captain at the helm somewhere to move and to guide it. And whether you trace the oak tree to the acorn, and the hen to the egg, or not, time alone produces nothing unless there is a sperm that promises the future growth. Evolution accounts only for the *How*, not for the *What*. Far from excluding, it includes and necessitates a designing intellect at the start, and a great and holy moral purpose at the end. Instead of alienating us from God, it brings us right face to face with God; for we see steadily at work fashioning worlds and lives without number here and carving out new destinies for all beings there. In fact, evolution, as I conceive it, is the unfolding of divine life, the un- broken revelation of God first in endless varieties of *matter*, then in marvellous productions of the conscious *mind*.

And since matter and mind emanate from the same God, why should the lines not merge? If man forms the pinnacle of evolution, the blossom and fruit of earth-life, the sanctuary of the mind, why should there be no root, no threshold, no court-yard leading to the holy? . . . There is one little word in the human vo- cabulary which eludes the scientist's crucible. . . . He cannot reduce it to mere chemical affinity or to animal sensation of pleasure or pain. . . . It is the word *Ought*. Whether high up among the most civilized, or far down among the lowest types of life, you find man always measuring his steps by duty's rule, by a voice dimly or clearly heard calling: Thou oughtst and thou oughtst not! The voice of conscience may err, the judgment may mislead; but the judging and dictating power is there, not as the power of human society, but as its original and everlasting shaping-power. Morality made man, not man morality. I am sure, no evolutionist dares say: Truth is the invention of man. It is there from eternity, waiting for the human mind to grasp it, just as the light waits for the flower to give it life and beauty. Not all the people of the world can change the simple arithmetical fact and make twice two five instead of four. Neither can they declare theft and murder to be right, and honesty wrong. They may, as savage tribes do, misapply the rules, and for instance, allow theft or murder under certain conditions to be committed where we from a higher standpoint cannot: but they cannot change them. Morality, as a principle, is eternal like truth. . . .

Need I then ask you which of the two is the higher conception of God: the one which has man fashioned by God of a piece of clay as by a potter and equipped with all the faculties of heart and mind befitting the Divine Mould, and then allowing him from his high station in Paradise to fall so low in intellect and manners as to become next-door neighbor to the orang-outang? Or the one which makes star and flower, worm and ape sigh for the moment when, as the highest and the most fitted in the scale of beings, man at last emerges with the conscious longing after a better state of things, which enables him to grope and work his way up into an ever nobler and finer stature until the Divine Life, unfolded all along, is mirrored in his world-encompassing mind and heart? Yes, man *is* made in the image of God; only that is dimly felt or seen at the base, and grows ever brighter and grander the nearer it reaches the top.

I think evolution offers a religion of hope, of life grander than any other system. It accounts better for all our errors and failings, for the shortcomings of our moral and religious life, for the very evils that surround us within or from without. As it took all the notes on the key-board to discover the law of harmony and arrive at the true secret of music, so man had first to learn the letters of the alphabet of morals before the true name of God could be spelled out. Neither the Decalogue nor the Bible presents a complete code of ethics. They only drew the outline, they laid the foundation to the world's morality. Justice begins with: Thou shalt not! Love whispers: Thou shalt! The warning against sin and vice in one age leads to the practice of virtue in the next. Conditional toleration of polygamy, slavery and retaliation by the Mosaic law points to the recognition of the higher dignity of man and woman, of the sanctity of human life arrived at by later Judaism and Christianity. And what are all the conceptions of reward and punishment, what the notions of heaven and hell but symbols and suggestions of a celestial justice, leading to the realization of a higher righteousness? Judaism, the Bible, all the given religions are but evolutions of morality.

56. The Essence of God

. . . A L L efforts of philosophy to define the essence of God are futile. "Canst thou by searching find out God?" Zophar asks of his friend Job. Both Philo and Maimonides maintain that we can know of God only that He *is*; we can never fathom His innermost being or know what He is. Both find this unknowability of God expressed in the words spoken to Moses: "If I withdraw My hand, thou shalt see My back—that is, the effects of God's power and wisdom—but My face—the real essense of God—thou shalt not see."

Still, a divinity void of all essential qualities fails to satisfy the religious soul. Man demands to know what God is—at least, what God is to him. In the first word of the Decalogue God speaks through His people Israel to the religious consciousness of all men at all times, beginning, "I am the Lord, *thy* God." This word *I* lifts God at once above all beings and powers of the cosmos, in fact, above all other existence, for it expresses His unique self-consciousness. This attribute above all is possessed by no being in the world of nature, and only by man, who is the image of his Maker. . . .

Judaism, accordingly, teaches us to recognize God, above all, as revealing Himself in self-conscious activity, as determining all that happens by His absolutely free will, and thus as showing man how to walk as a free moral agent. In relation to the world, His work or workshop, He is the self-conscious Master, saying "I am that which I am"; in relation to man, who is akin to Him as a self-conscious rational and moral being, He is the living Fountain of all that knowledge and spirituality for which men long, and in which alone they may find contentment and bliss. Thus the God of Judaism, the world's great *I Am*, forms a complete contrast, not only to the lifeless powers of nature and destiny, which were worshiped by the ancient pagans, but also to the God of modern paganism, a God divested of all personality and self-consciousness, such as He is conceived of by the new school of Christian theology, with its pantheistic tendency. . . .

The Jewish God-idea, of course, had to go through many stages of development before it reached the concept of a transcendental and spiritual god. It was necessary first that the Decalogue and the Book of the Covenant prohibit most stringently polytheism and every form of idolatry, and second that a strictly imageless worship impress the people with the idea that Israel's God was both invisible and incorporeal. Yet a wide step still intervened from that stage to the complete recognition of God as a purely spiritual Being, lacking all qualities perceptible to the senses, and not resembling man in either his inner or his outer nature. Centuries of gradual ripening of thought were still necessary for the growth of this conception. This was rendered still more difficulty by the Scriptural references to God in His actions and His revelations, and even in His motives, after a human pattern. Israel's sages required centuries of effort to remove all anthropomorphic and anthropopathic notions of God, and thus to elevate Him to the highest realm of spirituality. . . .

The rabbis are . . . emphatic in their assertions that the Torah merely intends to assist the simple-minded, and that unseemly expressions concerning Deity are due to the inadequacy of language, and must not be taken literally. "It is an act of boldness allowed only to the prophets to measure the Creator by the standard of the creature," says the Haggadist, and again, "God appeared to Israel, now as a heroic warrior, now as a venerable sage imparting knowledge, and again as a kind dispenser of bounties, but always in a manner befitting the time and circumstance, so as to satisfy the need of the human heart." This is strikingly illustrated in the following dialogue: "A heretic came to Rabbi Meir asking, 'How can you reconcile the passage which reads, "Do I not fill heaven and earth, says the Lord," with the one which relates that the Lord appeared to Moses between the cherubim of the ark of the covenant?' Whereupon Rabbi Meir took two mirrors, one large and the other small, and placed them before the interrogator. 'Look into this glass,' he said, 'and into that. Does not your figure seem different in one than in the other? How much more will the majesty of God, who has neither figure nor form, be reflected differently in the minds of men! To one it will appear according to his narrow view of life, and to the other in accordance with his larger mental horizon.' "

In like manner Rabbi Joshua ben Hanania, when asked sarcastically by the Emperor Hadrian to show him his God, replied: "Come and look at the sun which now shines in the full splendor of noonday! Behold, thou art dazzled. How, then, canst thou see without bewilderment the majesty of Him from whom emanates both sun and stars?" This rejoinder, which was familiar to the Greeks also, is excelled by the one of Rabban Gamaliel II to a heathen who asked him, "Where does the God dwell to whom you daily pray?" "Tell me first," he answered, "where does your soul dwell, which is so close to thee? Thou canst not tell. How, then, can I inform thee concerning Him who dwells in heaven, and whose throne is separated from the earth by a journey of 3500 years?" "Then do we not do better to pray to gods who are near at hand, and whom we can see with our eyes?" continued the heathen, whereupon the sage struck home, "Well, you may see your gods, but they neither see nor help you, while our God, Himself unseen, yet sees and protects us constantly." . . .

Probably the rabbis were at their most profound mood in their saying, "God's greatness lies in His condescension, as may be learned from the Torah, the Prophets, and the Writings. To quote only Isaiah also: 'Thus saith the High and Lofty One, I dwell in high and holy places, with him that is of a contrite and humble spirit.' For this reason God selected as the place of His revelation the humble Sinai and the lowly thornbush." In fact, the absence of any mediator in Judaism necessitates the doctrine that God—with all His transcendent majesty—is at the same time "an ever present helper in trouble," and that His omnipotence includes care for the greatest and the smallest beings of creation.

The doctrine that God is above and beyond the universe, transcending all created things, as well as time and space, might lead logically to the view of the deist that He stands outside of the world, and does not work from within. But this inference has never been made even by the boldest of Jewish thinkers. The Psalmist said, "Who is like the Lord our God, that hath His seat on high, that humbleth Himself to behold what is in heaven and on earth?"—words which express the deepest and the loftiest thought of Judaism. Beside the all-encompassing Deity no other divine power or personality can find a place. God is in all; He is over all; He is both immanent and transcendent. . . .

57. God in Relation to the World

The World and Its Master

I N using the term world or *universe* we include the totality of all beings at once, and this suggests a stage of knowledge where polytheism is practically overcome. Among the Greeks, Pythagoras is said to have been the first to perceive "a beautiful order of things" in the world, and therefore to call it *cosmos*. Primitive man saw in the world innumerable forces continually struggling with each other for supremacy. Without an ordering mind no order, as we conceive it, can exist. The old Babylonian conception prevalent throughout antiquity divided the world into three realms, the celestial, terrestrial, and the nether world, each of which had its own type of inhabitants and its own ruling divinities. Yet these various divine powers were at war with each other, and ultimately they, too, must submit to a blind fate which men and gods alike could read in the stars or other natural phenomena.

With the first words of the Bible, "In the beginning God created the heavens and the earth," Judaism declared the world to be a unity and God its Creator and Master. Heathenism had always beheld in the world certain blind forces of nature, working without plan or purpose and devoid of any moral aims. But Judaism sees in the world the work of a supreme Intellect who fashioned it according to His will, and who rules in freedom, wisdom, and goodness. "He spoke, and it was; He commanded, and it stood." Nature exists only by the will of God; His creative *fiat* called it into existence, and it ceases to be as soon as it has fulfilled His plan.

That which the scientist terms nature—the cosmic life in its eternal process of growth and reproduction—is declared by Judaism to be God's creation. Ancient heathen conceptions deified nature, indeed, but they knew only a cosmogony, that is, a process of birth and growth of the world. In this the gods participate with all other beings, to sink back again at the close of the drama into fiery chaos—the so-called "twilight of the gods." Here the deity constitutes a part of the world, or the world a part of the deity, and philosophic speculation can at best blend the two into a pantheistic system which has no place for a self-conscious, creative mind and will. In fact, the universe appears as an ever growing and unfolding deity, and the deity as an ever growing and unfolding universe. Modern science more properly assumes a self-imposed limitation; it searches for the laws underlying the action and interaction of natural forces and elements, thus to explain in a mechanistic way the origin and development of all things, but it leaves entirely outside of its domain the whole question of a first cause and a supreme creative mind. It certainly can pass no opinion as to whether or not the entire work of creation was accomplished by the free act of a Creator. Revelation alone can speak with unfaltering accents: "In the beginning God created heaven and earth." However we may understand, or imagine, the beginning of the natural process, the formation of matter and the inception of motion, we see above the confines of space and time the everlasting God, the absolutely free Creator of all things.

No definite theological dogma can define the order and process of the genesis of the world; this is rather a scientific than a religious question. The Biblical documents themselves differ widely on this point, whether one compares the stories in the first two chapters of Genesis, or contrasts both of them with the poetical descriptions in Job and the Psalms. And these divergent accounts are still less to be reconciled with the results of natural science. In the old Babylonian cosmography, on which the Biblical view is based, the earth, shaped like a disk, was suspended over the waters of the ocean, while above it was the solid vault of heaven like a ceiling. In this the stars were fixed like lamps to light the earth, and hidden chambers to store up the rain. The sciences of astronomy, physics, and geology have abolished these child-like conceptions as well as the story of a six-day creation, where vegetation sprang from the earth even before the sun, moon, and stars appeared in the firmament.

The fact is that the Biblical account is not intended to depreciate or supersede the facts established by natural science, but solely to accentuate those religious truths which the latter disregards. These may be summed up in the following three doctrines:

First. Nature, with all its immeasurable power and grandeur, its wondrous beauty and harmony, is not independent, but is the work, the workshop, and the working force of the great Master. His spirit alone is the active power; His will must be carried out. It is true that we cannot conceive the universe otherwise than as infinite in time and space, because both time and space are but human modes of apperception. In fact, we cannot think of a Creator without a creation, because any potentiality or capacity without execution would imply imperfection in God. Nevertheless we must conceive of God as the designing and creating intellect of the universe, infinitely transcending its complex mechanism, whose will is expressed involuntarily by each of the created beings. He alone is the living God; He has lent existence and infinite capacity to the beings of the world; and they, in achieving their appointed purpose, according to the poet's metaphor, "weave His living garment." . . .

Second. The numberless beings and forces of the universe comprise a unity, working according to one plan, subserving a common purpose, and pursuing in their development and interaction the aim which God's wisdom assigned them from the beginning. However hostile the various elements may be toward each other, however fierce the universal conflict, "the struggle for existence," still over all the discord prevails a higher concord, and the struggle of nature's forces ends in harmony and peace. "He maketh peace in His high places." Even the highest type of heathenism, the Persian, divided the world into mutually hostile principles, light and darkness, good and evil. But Judaism proclaims God as the Creator of both. No force is left out of the universal plan; each contributes its part to the whole. Consequently the very progress of natural science confirms more and more the principle of the divine Unity. The researches of science are ever tending toward the knowledge of universal laws of growth; culminating in a scheme of universal evolution. Hence this supports and confirms Jewish monotheism, which knows no power of evil antagonistic to God.

Third. The world is good, since goodness is its creator and its final aim. True enough, nature, bent with "tooth and claw" upon annihilating one or another form of existence, is quite indifferent to man's sense of compassion and justice. Yet in the wise, though inscrutable plan of God she does but serve the good. We see how the lower forms of life ever serve the higher, how the mineral provides food for the vegetable, while the animal derives its food from the vegetable world and from lower types of animals. Thus each becomes a means of vitality for a higher species. So by the continuous upward striving of man the lower passions, with their evil tendencies, work more and more toward the triumph of the good. Man unfolds his God-likeness; he strives to

"Move upward, working out the beast,
And let the ape and tiger die."

The Biblical story of Creation expresses the perfect harmony between God's purpose and His work in the words, "And behold, it was good" spoken at the end of each day's Creation, and "behold, it was very good" at the completion of the whole. A world created by God must serve the highest good, while, on the contrary, a world without God would prove to be "the worst of all possible worlds," as Schopenhauer, the philosopher of pessimism, quite correctly concludes from his premises. The worldview of Judaism, which regards the entire economy of life as the realization of the all-encompassing plan of an all-wise Creator, is accordingly an energizing optimism, or, more precisely, meliorism. This view is voiced by the rabbis in many significant utterances, such as the maxim of R. Akiba, "Whatsoever the Merciful One does, is for the good," or that of his teacher, Nahum of Gimzo, "This, too, is for the good."

58. The Nature and Purpose of Prayer

. . . A C C O R D I N G to our modern thinking there can be no question of any influence upon a Deity exalted above time and space, omniscient, unchangeable in will and action, by the prayer of mortals. Prayer can exert power only over the relation of man to God, not over God Himself. This indicates the nature and purpose of prayer. Man often feels lonely and forlorn in a world which overpowers him, to which he feels superior, and yet which he cannot master. Therefore he longs for that unseen Spirit of the universe, with whom alone he feels himself akin, and in whom alone he finds peace and bliss amid life's struggle and unrest. This longing is both expressed and satisfied in prayer. Following the natural impulse of his soul, man must pour out before his God all his desires and sighs, all the emotions of grief and delight which sway his heart, in order that he may find rest, like a child at its mother's bosom. Therefore the childlike mind believes that God can be induced to come down from His heavenly heights to offer help, and that He can be moved and influenced in human fashion. The truth is that every genuine prayer lifts man up toward God, satisfies the desire for His hallowing presence, unlocks the heavenly gate of mercy and bliss, and bestows upon man the beatific and liberating sense of being a child of God. The intellect may question the effect of prayer upon the physical, mental, or social constitution of man, or may declare prayer to be pious self-deception. The religious spirit experiences in prayer the soaring up of the soul toward union with God in consecrated moments of our mortal pilgrimage. This is no deception. The man who prays receives from the God-head, toward whom he fervently lifts himself, the power to defy fate, to conquer sin, misery, and death. "The Lord is nigh to all them that call upon Him, to all that call upon Him in truth." . . .

Self-expression before God in prayer has thus a double effect; it strengthens faith in God's love and kindness, as well as in His all-wise and all-bountiful prescience. But it also chastens the desires and feelings of man, teaching him to banish from his heart all thoughts of self-seeking and sin, and to raise himself toward the purity and the freedom of the divine will and demand. The essence of every prayer of supplication is that one should be in unison with the divine will, to sum up all the wishes of the heart in the one phrase, "Do that which is good in Thine own eyes, O Lord." On the other hand, only the prayer which avoids impure thoughts and motives can venture to approach a holy God, as the sages infer from the words of Job, "There is no violence in my hands, and my prayer is pure."

Every prayer, teach the sages, should begin with the praise of God's greatness, wisdom, and goodness, in order that man should learn submission and implicit confidence before he proffers his requests. While looking up to the divine Ideal of holiness and perfection, he will strive to emulate Him, and seek to grow ever nearer to the holy and the perfect. But only when he prays with and for others, that is, in public worship, will he realize that he is a member of a greater whole, for then he prays only for that which advances the welfare of all. "He who prays with the community," say the rabbis, "will have his prayer granted."

Another saying of theirs is that he who prays should have his face directed to the sanctuary, and when he stands on its sacred precincts, he should turn his face toward the Holy of Holies. By this they meant that the attitude of the suppliant should ever be toward the highest, making the soul soar up to the Highest and Holiest in reverent awe and adoration, transforming the worshiper into a new character, pure from all dross.

Therefore prayer offered with the community upon the sanctified ground of the house of God exerts a specially powerful influence upon the individual. In the silent chamber the oppressed spirit may find calm and composure in prayer; but the pure atmosphere of heavenly freedom and bliss is attained with overwhelming might only by the united worship of hundreds of devout adorers, which rings out like the roaring of majestic billows: "The Lord is in His holy temple; let all the earth keep silence before Him." . . . In the ardor of communal worship the traditional words of the prayer-book obtain invigorating power; the heart is newly strengthened; the covenant with heaven sealed anew. To such communal prayer, which springs from the heart, the rabbis refer the Biblical words, "to serve Him with the whole heart." . . .

59. Ethics and Religion

. . . [W E] may distinguish three types of ethics that have determined the moral growth of humanity, to wit: the Greeks, the Hindoo and the Jewish; Greek ethics . . . is aristocratic throughout. Cradled under a serene blue sky, it aims—not to include, of course, the harsh Spartan type—at a beautiful type of humanity. . . . Perfect harmony of the inner and outer man, a symmetrical development of his powers for the benefit of the commonwealth, is the highest aim and ideal. It is at once utilitarian and hedonistic, though in Plato it endeavors to rise above the mists of the earth. It provides at best only for the privileged upper classes, taking no regard of the toiling slave, the suffering poor, the subjected woman and the unprotected stranger. . . .

Quite different in character is the system set forth by the Hindoo prince, Gautama Buddha, who exchanged his royal robe for the garb of a mendicant friar in order to go forth preaching the gospel of charity and benevolence for all fellow creatures. Sympathy with the ailing and suffering is the cry and self-sacrifice, self-effacement, the principle and motive power. It was the first to build hospitals for the sick, even the sick animals. It endeavored to remove all distinction of class and caste. But while touching true chords of humanity, it declared life to be a burden, joy and illusion, the world a large cemetery and existence a misery from which the hermit's cell is the only means of escape. However noble its efforts to overcome pain, to extinguish passion, to create a permanence of virtue in the ever-reborn *Kharma*, its highest ideal is resignation, the annihilation of all thought and feeling. . . . Only the morbid pessimism of a Schopenhauer could give a responsive ear to this deep sigh for non-existence.

Between the two ethical systems, of which the one views life as a banquet within to feast man on earthly joy, and the other as a graveyard to bathe him in tears, stands *Jewish ethics* which through synagogue and church alike declares true life to be a great and noble strife after *holiness*. "Be *holy*, for I the Lord your God am *Holy*," or as the Greek New Testament renders the words: "Ye shall be *perfect*, as your Father in Heaven is *perfect*." This is the ethical principle and the moral idea of the Jew, and through him also of the *Christian*. It at once points to the source of all human excellence. It denotes that state of purity and perfection which the soul in its highest aspiration longs for as the very acme of happiness, the highest harmony of life . . .

Little do they understand Judaism or even the Old Testament, who find its ethics circumscribed by the letter of the law or confined to the boundaries of tribe, land or sect. The law could only by way of compromise and step by step educate the people that was prone to idolatry, for higher views and purposes and like the rest of the nations addicted to the barbarous customs of slavery, polygamy, sextatonis and cruel warfare. In order to know Jewish ethics you must search after the spirit which dictated the law, created the Decalogue, produced the nineteenth chapter of Leviticus with the commandment of holiness as the *initatio Dei* at the beginning and the commandment, "Love thy neighbor as thyself" in the center; the laws that insist on the recognition of the human rights of the laborer, the slave, the stranger, yea, even of the criminal. . . . To be sure, there is gold and dross, wheat and chaff, lofty and low utterances, strangely mixed in the Old Testament, as this, in fact, can be seen also in the New Testament, but let those who charge the Hebrew with clannishness and tribalism read the twenty-ninth and thirty-first chapters of Job, wherein the obligation is voiced to be a help to the orphan and widow, eyes to the blind, feet to the lame and father to the needy, kind protector to the slave as being our equal before our Maker, or the fifteenth and twenty-fourth Psalms, wherein cleanness of hand, purity of heart and sincerity of speech are declared to be the sole conditions of a citizen in the kingdom of God, . . .

It is the Jewish genius working in an Amos, Hosea, Isaiah and Micah, and again in a Hillel and Philo, Jesus and Paul, that gave to ethics its vital essence, its compelling force, by revealing the God within, by pointing, as Matthew Arnold so beautifully expresses it, to "the Power not ourselves that maketh for righteousness." Neither Moses and Isaiah nor Jesus, to mention only these three, have a word for either virtue or duty, and yet they and their compeers in the realm of prophetic vision have laid bare the very core of all ethics in showing us that the glory of the Divinity is mirrored in the virtues of justice, mercy, purity and holiness, which man is to strive for. In other words, Ethical Theism, or the insistence on the purely ethical qualities of God as the Ruler of life, gave humanity its vigorous idealism. The fundamental error of those who belittle Jewish ethics as defective and narrow is that, guided or misguided by the gospel of Matthew, they contrast the Mosaic Law as the old Dispensation, with the Sermon on the Mount as the New Dispensation, being entirely unaware of the fact that the Pharisean doctors of the law interpreted the words of the scripture exactly in the same spirit of greater mildness and benevolence of a larger freedom and broader humanity, as did the Nazarene preacher. Centuries before the New Testament was written the law demanding "an eye for an eye and a tooth for a tooth" had been changed by the Pharisees, and the Golden Rule taught all those that desired to espouse the Jewish faith, "Do not do unto others what you do not want others to do unto you." . . .

I could quote dozens of similar sayings believed by Christian readers of the New Testament to have originated with the Nazarene preacher, but are not only found in the Talmud as ancient teachings of the wise, and especially of the pious Essenes, but it can easily be shown that the New Testament writers, even Paul the Apostle, had made use of older ethical writings . . .

Before a tribunal of impartial judges, therefore, Christian ethics can by no means claim a higher standard than Jewish . . .

There are, in my opinion, mainly two false notes sounded in the New Testament ethics that prevent it being held up as the highest standard of morality for human society. First of all, it cares only for the individual soul and overlooks the greater task of social justice. . . . Secondly, it has, as George Eliot so well expressed it, the character of other-worldliness and consequently its ethics are eudemonistic. . . .

What system of ethics, then, shall it be that we should teach in our schools and colleges and choose for our own guidance of life? Humanitarian ethics patterned after the Greek, or after the modern positivist or non-religious system? Never are the foundations of society sound and safe, so long as the commandments: "Thou shalt not murder! Thou shalt not commit adultery! Thou shalt not steal!" are not followed by the command: "Thou shalt not covet!" and given by a holy and stern lawgiver and judge who watches the scale, and holds the pillars of life, looking to the heart with its motives, and springs of action. Here is the difficulty. Morality must be autonomous and yet of God, the essence and ideal of morality. Morality must be the law and fruitage of religion and yet religion dares not divide humanity into sects, into Jews and Christians, believers and unbelievers. So Christian ethics will not do. Only when the teachers and leaders of the various sects and classes of humanity, the workers for a Church Universal will as believers in the God and Father of all dare to meet on a common ground and gather all that is good and true, beautiful and elevating in their holy writings and sayings into one storehouse of ethical teachings which reflects the glory of the Unseen, yet All-seeing God in the strivings and workings of God-like man, then the question of ethical teachings can be satisfactorily solved. . . .

60. The Mission of Israel

. . . T H E Church in her efforts to conquer the heathen world was to a large extent conquered herself by the heathen view. Having started in the name of Israel's God, she had, in order to win the nations for her faith, to enter into all kinds of compromise, whether in regard to the unity and spirituality of God or in regard to the unity of mankind and of the cosmos. So under the influence of the Egyptian and other trinitarian systems God was divided into three personalities and, in consequence thereof, also mankind into believers and unbelievers, and the Cosmos between the good and evil power represented by Christ and Satan. Thus faith and reason, religion and science, the sacred and the secular were opposed to one another, and instead of having religion made "the all-uniting mother leading mankind to God as the Father of All," as Maimonides calls it at the close of his Commentary to *Eduyot,* it became a disuniting force for the human race. And the same holds, of course, still more true to the other religious systems.

Against all this the Jewish people had, amidst oppression and persecution, the peculiar mission assigned to them of being 'witnesses' to God in His absolute Unity and sublime Holiness. And to be witnesses meant, as the Greek translation 'martyrs' suggests, to testify to the truth held forth by them by offering up their very lives in martyrdom for it. Noble as the heroic task accomplished by many a Christian missionary indisputably was, the task of the Jew during the dark medieval centuries of withstanding all the trials, the threats, the taunts, the auto da fes and the alluring baits of the Church was by all means far nobler and more heroic, and it was performed not by individuals, but by the entire people. It was a passive, not an active mission. Had they then gone forth among the nations to win the world for their teachings, they might have long ago been swallowed up by the surrounding multitude. Instead of this, the Jew proved to be the "Servant of the Lord" who "gave his back to the smiters," "the man of sorrows, despised and forsaken of men," . . . A two thousand years' history of martyrdom, a tragedy without parallel in the world and yet sustained by a faith which never faltered and with words of praise and sanctification of the Most High which resounded throughout the centuries—this was the wondrous realization of the Deutero-Isaianic prophecy, for the grandeur of which our Nationalists have as little appreciation as have our anti-Semitic enemies. Well may the words of the English poet be applied here: "They also serve who only stand and wait." And for what did the Jew wait all these centuries? Not for his mere national resurrection or for the rebuilding of a state like any other, but for the new and grander revelation of God's glory, for the establishment of God's Kingdom on earth.

Nor was the mission of the medieval Jew altogether a passive one. He stood out indeed as "a light to the nations and a covenant of the people." In the midst of the dense darkness that covered the nations all around, his lamp of learning shone brightly in the humblest hut and diffused its rays into the cells of the monastery and into the abode of the solitary thinker of Christendom. Jews, intermediating between Arabic culture and Christian Europe, held the torch of philosophy and science aloft to enlighten and nurture the minds of the scholastics and the pioneers of the universities, and usher in the era of the Renaissance and of the Reformation. So also did the Jewish men of commerce, while carrying material goods from land to land, transport the popular wisdom and folklore of the East to the West to interlink distant civilizations. Like Lessing's Nathan the Wise, the Jew, standing between Moslem and Christian, typified a broader cosmopolitan humanity. True, this was rather the achievement of individuals and cannot be characterized as the mission of the people in general. Nevertheless the fact remains that the Jew excelled everywhere by his zeal for truth, his love of knowledge and wisdom and, owing to his religious fervor, his study of the Torah, to which he was trained from childhood up, he became actually the instructor of an illiterate environment.

But above all, he remained ever-conscious of the mission assigned to Israel as a "kingdom of priests and a holy nation." He led a consecrated life. In the midst of a world full of profanity and vulgarity, of coarse sensuality and drunkenness he displayed the virtues of chastity and modesty in his domestic and social sphere. . . . Each Jew was a living protest against the dogma of the Church which placed a man born of woman on God's throne, and defied human reason in order to save the soul. He was God's priest and prophet pointing to a better day, to God's kingdom on earth. . . .

61. The Scholar and the Preacher

I n quoting the familiar saying of Hillel to the heathen: "Do not do unto thy fellowman what thou hatest to have done unto thee; this is the principal law; the rest is mere commentary," people as a rule omit the closing words of the Master: "Go, then, and study!" The study of the law must form the basis of the ethical teaching. Behind the preacher must stand the scholar to give weight to his utterances. But it is no easy matter, either, for the rabbi, or for him who prepares for the rabbinical career, to find the right relation between these two functions, and many a failure in, or surrender of, the pulpit is due to this embarrassing difficulty. As long as the main object of the rabbi was to expound the law and to decide ritual questions in accordance with the codified tradition, there could be no conflict between private study and public utterance, even though medieval exegesis and philosophy, and even the older *Haggadah* differed widely from the *Halakhic* interpretation of Scripture, because the life of the people was regulated by the *Halakhic* code. The preaching was of secondary importance. . . .

Nor did the situation materially change when in the post-Mendelsohnian era modern preaching was introduced. Zunz, Salomon, Kley, and Mannheimer officiated as preachers whereas the rabbinical office with all its power and authority was in the hands of the orthodox rabbi. Zunz, as may be learned from his letters, looked with a certain disdain and sneer upon the title of rabbi—*Hatarat Horah*—and his sermons, like those of the rest of the Jewish preachers of his time, were patterned after Protestant models, lacking substantial Jewish thought and learning. Hence the ridicule cast by Heinrich Heine upon the inane preaching he heard from the Hamburg pulpit. A higher and far more genuinely Jewish type of sermons was produced afterwards by preachers who knew how to utilize the various *Midrashic* passages for the illustration or elucidation of their subjects. Among these the successor of Mannheimer in Vienna, Adolf Jellinek, stands out as the foremost pulpit orator who made the ancient Hagadists voice striking truths in modern form as no other preacher could. But he, too, was satisfied with the title of preacher. It was Abraham Geiger who as the pioneer of the Reform theologians insisted in his controversy with Tiktin and the Prussian government upon his title of *rabbi*. He justly claimed that only because he was conversant with the entire Rabbinical as well as Biblical literature and the whole history of Judaism from its beginning to modern times, was he entitled to voice the demands of the modern phase of Judaism and, in the name of the divine forces governing Jewish history, to introduce the needed reform. He stated clearly and emphatically the necessity of having the scholar and preacher combined in the rabbi. And yet he could not fail to see that the rabbi in his new position of teacher and leader of the people was confronted with new difficulties arising from his studies and investigations as scholar and historian. And so he wrote in 1839 in his *Wissenschaftliche Zeitschrift fuer juedische Theologie*, p. 321f, the interesting article on the two different points of view: that of the author and the rabbi (*Die zwei verschiedenen Betrachtungsweisen: Der Schriftsteller und der Rabbiner.*) Here he claims for the scholarly writer, who views religion from the standpoint of the historian and beholds in it a continual process of growth, and the right and the duty to assign to the present state of religious life its place and scope, and accordingly to lay down the general principles of reform and apply them to all such cases as show retrogression or aberration from the high aim and purpose of Judaism. On the other hand he holds that the rabbi must consult first of all the spiritual needs of his congregation and should, therefore, proceed with caution in introducing reforms, lest he give offense to the people by assailing views and practices held dear by them. . . .

Certainly our American Congregations have been trained to look upon the rabbi as their real leader. They honor him for his courage of opinion and want the pulpit to echo forth a living truth and a living faith. The pulpit in America is a power, because it voices the best and the highest in the people that sit in the pew. Our great reformers were also great preachers. Einhorn and Isaac M. Wise became the prophets of American Judaism. In fact, the preacher of today must have the prophets of old as models; he must have a message for his hearers. He must furthermore be able to translate the truths of the past into the language of the age, and, therefore, be also what has been called a backward looking prophet; that is, one endowed with profound insight into the history of the past in order to obtain a real understanding of the task assigned to our time and point out its leading ideas and ideals. This, however, means that he must have the ammunition of the scholar; that he must be sufficiently acquainted with various epochs of Jewish history and their currents of thought under the influence of the various civilizations in order to recognize the historic forces at work in the shaping of the religious and cultural life in the Biblical, the Hellenistic, the Rabbinical and the Arabic-Spanish period, and thus learn to understand the trend of events in our own era and the mission assigned therein to Judaism. Only thus equipped with knowledge in the light and after the method of modern critical and historical research can he be a true defender and expounder of the faith.

Right here again arises the difficulty caused by the wide diversity between the standpoint to be taken by the preacher and that of the scholar. The scholar in his search for truth cannot, and should not, be satisfied with half truths. The mere tabooing of Higher Bible Criticism resorted to by the Conservative Schools seldom prevents the truth-seeking student from eating from the forbidden fruit of the tree of knowledge which will, sooner or later, open his eyes to the naked facts of the late origin of the Mosaic books and the Mosaic laws and so forth. But these very facts as well as Bible Criticism in general do not belong to the pulpit. The function of the pulpit is to strengthen the faith, not to unsettle it; to build up, not to destroy. To speak in a sermon of the Priest Code and Deuteronomic Code, of an Elohistic and Jahvistic author, or of the late origin of the Atonement Day and of the Immortality belief is to cast stumbling blocks in the way of the devout worshipper instead of leading him up the hill of God. You can not inspire the people with reverence for the scroll of the law which you hold up as Israel's banner of truth through the ages and at the same time dissect this very book, as the botanist does the beautiful flower when endeavoring to show its component parts. There is a fine psychological lesson conveyed by the law concerning the vessels of the sanctuary: "They should not come in to look at the uncovered sanctuary lest they die." (Numbers IV, 20) Holy things must be treated with reverential awe; when reduced to the level of the common life by obtrusive glance, they are robbed of the character of sanctity.

The rabbis of old already made the wise distinction between the language of the religion, the Torah, and the language of scientific wisdom-Hokhmah. In a lecture to be given to more or less enlightened audiences, or for the purpose of enlightening them, you are perfectly justified in presenting to them the results of modern investigations, be they of the nature of critical-historical or of comparative religious research. Here you are also at liberty to speak of *Jahveh* as the God of Scripture in accordance with modern Biblical exegesis. It is, however, an offense against the entire spirit of Judaism to use this, merely scientific or historic, name for Israel's Only One God whose name has ever since the second temple period become ineffable and is, according to a tradition sanctioned by the centuries, to be pronounced *Adonai*, a term rendered by the Greek translators *the Lord*. Superfluous to say that name *Jehovah*—which owes its origin to an erroneous application of the vowel signs referring to Adonai to the Tetragram made by Galatinus, a Catholic writer, in 1518—should have no place in the Synagogue, whether in sermons or in songs.

Of course, it often requires tact and discretion to draw the line between what is fit for the pulpit and what should be confined to the sphere of the scholar, between what may be called esoteric and what is exoteric. But just as the pedagogue knows how to apply the rule of giving bread and milk to the babe in his teaching, so must the preacher who has to appeal to the people at large guard against offering to souls that hunger for righteousness a stone instead of bread.

This does not by any means imply that we should have in

matters of religion a double standard of truths, one for the people and one for personal conviction. It only means that the religious truth has two different aspects. The one is that of historical analysis which traces the evolutionary stages of the past in an exclusive scientific spirit, which is that of the learned; the other is that of reverential devotion which is eager to preserve the continuity with the time-honored past to which we, with all our progressive views, owe the best we have and are— and this is that of the religious community at large. The problem how to reconcile the two may cause many an hour of heart-burning and misgiving to the young theologian. Still, if he but hears the knocking of the spirit within and listens to his calling as the true man of God, he will find the solution in himself by personal equation. As the Psalmist says (62:12): "The thing God has spoken, but two-fold have I heard it." The truth for mind and the truth for heart is one.

Research and reverence must, therefore, ever go hand in hand. "Turn it and again turn it, for all is therein, and thine all is therein; swerve not therefore, for thou canst have no greater nobility than the one offered by it."

62. A Revaluation of Reform Judaism

I T ought today no longer be denied that Reform Judaism, which rallied the progressive elements in Germany, came as a saving force at a time when religion was at a decline, and apostasy had become almost epidemic among the higher classes. The assertion made by its detractors that Reform is nothing but the outcome of convenience and levity in disregard of the traditional laws and customs, or that it arose from a mere desire for social assimilation may be dismissed as a wilful slander. As a matter of fact, the Reform movement roused Orthodoxy itself from its medieval slumber, warning it that in adhering to its Ghetto form and spirit it will lapse into utter stagnation and decay. The changed conditions of the new era demanded reform everywhere, though the people were not yet ripe for a systematic reform. The first attempts at innovation were made to improve the mode of worship by a better decorum in the Synagogue and better methods of education in the school, and these led to a wise consideration of the needs of the girl together with those of the boy. This gave the impulse to the elevating rite of confirmation, soon also adopted by numerous Conservative congregations. And so followed, step by step, the introduction of the sermon and of prayers in the vernacular, of the organ and choral song. In other words, aesthetic and linguistic reforms lent the Synagogue an unforeseen and attractive and impressive character. They gave Judaism a modern aspect, calling forth the jealousy and opposition of the reactionaries from without and from within. Still these exterior measures did not touch the spirit, nor deserve the name of Reform Judaism. Only the earnest endeavor to so interpret the heritage of the past for an enlightened generation as to make the people realize that, although they can no longer accept or observe the views and practices of their fathers who for centuries lived in seclusion from the world, they still hold fast to the same ancestral faith in a rejuvenated form. Only an inner reconciliation of the ancient truth with modern thought could bring about what has since been called Reform Judaism. . . . It is, accordingly, utterly erroneous to speak, as so many do, of a *Reformed* Judaism, as if the Reform leaders had ever intended to create a schism, a new system of religion or creed fixed and final, such as is the Reformation of Luther, Calvin and Wesley. . . .

Neither can the name Liberal Judaism, which is now in vogue, be accepted as a substitute. It is altogether too vague and arbitrary. With some it denotes a certain reduction of the old ceremonies and traditional prayers or a dropping of the non-Mosaic festivals and the like; with others, as with Claude G. Montfiore in his recent work "The Old Testament and After," p. 565, it is nothing less than the *"harmony of the law and the Gospels."* In the one case it makes allowance for the old synagogal prayers for the restoration of the Temple with its sacrificial cult and for the resurrection of the Jew, though they belie the conviction of the enlightened modern Jew; in the other case, concessions are made to a creed which totally differs from our monotheistic faith, and which for more than eighteen hundred years stood out as a hostile force to Jew and Judaism, sowing hatred instead of fostering the spirit of justice, of love and humanity in the name of God, the Father of mankind. Reform Judaism stands firmly and positively for principles, the principle of liberalism, and loyalty, for progress and steadfast continuity with the past, for the one Revelation of God as recorded in our Scriptures and the one undivided humanity which is finally to share in our truth, for the God of righteousness and the God of love, but above all, for the covenant of Sinai which never grows *old!* Liberal Judaism, however, often wavers and halts between the two sides.

Let us now see whether the name American Judaism should be used, with omission of the characteristic epithet Reform. It is true, American Judaism has features of its own which distinguish it from German or English or Russian Judaism, just as Hellenic and Babylonian Judaism differed from each other. But this applies to Orthodoxy as well as to Reform Judaism. America with its broadness of view, its practical common sense and large-hearted tolerance, its freedom and independence, which places democracy and progress above authority of the past, has been influencing all religious denominations and systems of thought, and it naturally created a more congenial atmosphere for our Reform, whereas the reactionary powers in Europe did their best to restrain or suppress it. But after all, the majority of Jews in America do not subscribe to our principle of progress. . . .

Whether multiform and much divided American Israel will ever consolidate and coalesce into a uniform American Judaism, is a matter of great doubt and beyond our control. The great problem which we have to solve in our days is to find new and more efficacious ways of implanting our sublime faith and our glorious hope and confidence in the future into the generation brought up under the present American conditions, . . . Indeed, the main issue today is no longer between Orthodoxy and Reform, but between a world *with* or a world *without* God, and the question is how to counteract the intellectualism and outward culturalism which pervades our entire educational and social system by a strong appeal to our emotional nature, to the spiritual needs of man. We need a constructive force of a more conservative, rather than liberalizing, tendency in our religious life, one that draws the youth again to the Synagogue as the center of Judaism. Yet this can only be brought about by certain Reform methods, by a regeneration of our divine service which makes it attractive, instructive and impressive for the young generation. Minimize the reading of lengthy Hebrew passages which are unintelligible to the great majority of worshippers and have more lessons of a real devotional character such as stir the soul that hungers and thirsts after the living God and bring our hearts into closer communion with the spirit of the Most High.

However much good has been accomplished by our Sunday services, which aroused a new interest in, and a warmer love for our religion in many that had been estranged from us all these years, the historical Sabbath remains for us the day of the Lord, and since most of our business and professional men are of necessity kept away from the divine service on this day, all the more must we make every possible effort to have our women and children made active participants in the same. To this end our Religious School should be brought into closer connection with the Synagogue, and our children should be trained first of all to choral song instead of having all the singing left to a non-Jewish choir, and likewise to responses. As the *Shabvoth* festival was saved from falling into abeyance by the Confirmation—which, by the way, ought to be annual renewal of the Sinai Covenant by the entire Congregation and not a mere parade of the children—so might the last *Sukkot* day be rendered an actual feast of Joy with the Torah by having it made the solemn Opening Day of the school year, just as the first Sukkoth day has in many Synagogues been rejuvenated by the children's procession with the various plants of the land. . . .

But after all, our Reform must not be confined to the Synagogue. Our home must again be made what it was, the sanctuary of piety. Of course, this great duty devolves first of all on the mother. She must again teach her child to recite its morning and evening prayer and say the grace at every meal. But what lent the Jewish home at all time its beauty of holiness was the ceremonial systems so rich in elevating power, and since these old traditional forms have lost their appealing force, Reform has to step in and replace them by more attractive ones. . . . Well did Professor Lazarus in his *Treu and Frei* recommend the reintroduction of the parental blessing at each family reunion on Sabbath and Holy Day Eve to bring the hearts of the children near to their parents and the hearts of the parents to the children. And have we done all we could to kindle the spirit of Hanukah and the pride in our heroic past in our children at their homes in the face of the alluring Christmas tree with its radiating splendor? All our festivals ought to offer their peculiar charm to susceptible youth to awaken the sentiment of loyalty and love in them anew. And what about the almost forgotten lesson of reverence which is the beginning of all religion? True reform begins at home. . . .

FOR FURTHER READING
Books about Kaufmann Kohler

"Kaufmann Kohler" in *Enclycopedia Judaica*, Volume 10: 1142–1143 (Jerusalem: 1972). Including a brief biography and introduction to his thought.

RUDAVSKY, David, *Modern Jewish Religious Movements: A History of Emancipation and Adjustment* (New York: Behrman House, 1979). Includes a short discussion of Kohler's contributions to Reform Judaism.

DIMONT, Max, *The Jews in America: The Roots and Destiny of American Jews* (New York: Simon and Schuster, 1978). With a brief discussion of Kohler's part in the development of Reform Judaism in America.

GRINSTEIN, Hyman B., *A Short History of the Jew in the United States* (London: Soncino, 1980). Includes several references to Kohler.

MORDECAI M. KAPLAN
(1881–1983)

EDITOR'S NOTE

Mordecai Menahem Kaplan is one of the most controversial and at the same time one of the most influential thinkers in American Jewry today. Rabbi, teacher, philosopher of Judaism and religious reformer, Kaplan represents a total synthesis of the cultural nationalism of the Russian Jewish thinkers in this book and the religious concern of the German theologians. Though his original naturalistic approach to religion has met with opposition in some quarters, his concept of Judaism as an evolving religious civilization, his insistence that the Jewish religion cannot be separated from Jewish peoplehood, his vision of an organic Jewish community, his constructive educational proposals and his deep interest in American democracy have had a great impact on Jewish educators, social workers and on the Jewish center movement. Many rabbis and laymen both in the Conservative and Reform wings of Judaism during the past four decades have acknowledged their debt to him as a guide to the perplexed of our time.

Mordecai M. Kaplan was born in 1881 in a small town in the Pale of Settlement in Russia and came to the United States at the age of eight. He entered the Jewish Theological Seminary at twelve and was graduated from that institution in 1902. For a time he served as rabbi of a large Orthodox congregation on New York's upper East Side. In 1909 he accepted the invitation of Solomon Schechter to serve as dean of the newly organized Teachers Institute of the Seminary. The following year he was appointed professor of homiletics in the Rabbinical School where he has continued to teach for half a century.

During the First World War, Kaplan organized the first synagogue center in American Jewry. But when controversy arose over some of his religious and social views, he and a small group of followers seceded and founded the Society for the Advancement of Judaism in New York City. In 1934 *Judaism as a Civilization*, his first major work, appeared. It presented, in comprehensive form, his bold new concept of Judaism. His ideas were also disseminated through the *Reconstructionist* magazine which he launched in 1935 with the help of Ira Eisenstein, Milton Steinberg and others and through a series of books he has published. These include *Judaism in Transition* (1935), a collection of essays on various phases of Jewish life, *The Meaning of God in Modern Jewish Religion* (1936), described by one of his disciples as "the most fundamental, illuminating and courageous of his writings," and in later years *The Future of the American Jew* (1948), *Questions Jews Ask* (1956) and *The Greater Judaism in the Making* (1960). The Jewish Reconstructionist Foundation established in 1940 has been the main instrument for the dissemination of Kaplan's views.

Ira Eisenstein, president of the Jewish Reconstructionist Foundation and author of the chapter on Mordecai M. Kaplan in the companion volume, has chosen a number of passages from the writings of Dr. Kaplan to introduce the reader to his thought.

In our first selection Kaplan presents his viewpoint that religion, like all human life, is subject to change and if it is to retain its vitality and relevance, it must undergo a transformation. In the past the technique for revitalizing spiritual values was an unconscious one. Men read their own beliefs and ideals into the religious traditions they had inherited. This method of the ancients Kaplan calls "transvaluation." We, however, need a new method which is in keeping with our historical sense—that of "revaluation." By this term Kaplan means singling out from the traditional content the really significant elements and the implications which can help us meet our moral and spiritual needs.

Kaplan's new naturalistic understanding of God is discussed in the second selection. In place of the traditional view of God as a supernatural being or entity, Kaplan advances the concept of God as a process. By this he means that God is the power in the universe, not ourselves, which makes for order, justice and goodness and helps man to achieve self-fulfillment. The analogy he uses of the magnetic needle is particularly revealing of Kaplan's point of view. Just as the needle assumes a north-south position of its own accord, so man normally veers in the direction of that which makes for the fulfillment of his destiny as a human being. Kaplan, however, understands that the average person will have to undergo a long period of training in scientific thought in order to learn to associate the divine with life's creative forces and to think of the divine as a quality or process instead of a being.

In contrast to Rosenzweig and Buber, who see the chosen people idea as basic to the covenant between God and Israel, Kaplan rejects the concept of chosenness both in its traditional supernatural form as well as the modern attempts to reinterpret it. To him this idea is neither necessary for Jewish survival nor compatible with the ethical basis of American democracy. In its place he suggests the idea of vocation or calling by which every individual as well as nation strives to use and develop its best powers so that they may make their contribution to the welfare of mankind.

Kaplan has been accused of indifference to traditional forms of ritual. Though he does not see religious ritual as part of a supernaturally revealed code of Jewish law or as divine commandment and would therefore allow variations in observance, he feels that these rituals play an important preservative role in group survival and are a means of personal enrichment. In the next selection they are described as "sancta" because they represent the sacred values of the group. Nevertheless, in a growing and changing civilization old forms become obsolete and new forms of religious expression take their place.

Jewish education must also undergo reconstruction if Judaism is to be saved from disintegration. Kaplan sees education as having a revolutionary function—to reinterpret traditional values and to create a new social structure. This means a curriculum which will find a place for Jewish history "with a clear distinction between the legendary and the historical in Jewish traditional material," the development of special areas of study in ethics and religion and the organization of projects in what he calls "Jewish civics" which will lead to a cohesive community.

Kaplan's ideas on Zionism and Israel are to be found in *A New Zionism* (1955), from which the next excerpt has been taken. To Kaplan as to Ahad Ha-am, whose influence he has always acknowledged, fulfillment of the ultimate goals of Zionism involves the regeneration of the Jewish people from its present state of disintegration. Now that the State of Israel has been established, world Jewry, in Kaplan's opinion, should reconstitute itself as an international fellowship with the Jewish community in the State of Israel as its nucleus. In the present passage Kaplan urges that Zionism in our time be seen in religious terms as part of the Messianic movement which will reawaken the Jewish people to its sense of destiny.

The emancipation of the Jew during the past century and a half has led to a breakdown in Jewish communal solidarity. To retrieve this solidarity and to build a strong Jewish community without the existing divisiveness, there is needed an organic, comprehensive social structure organized on a regional basis to which every Jew can feel he belongs. Our final selection discusses the principles which should govern such an organic community and some of the problems it will have to overcome. Only through such an organized social structure, Kaplan feels, can his concept of Judaism as an evolving religious civilization become a living reality.

63. An Approach to Jewish Religion

. . . THERE are many who assume that religious truth differs from the truth about the material world in being absolute
and immutable. Religious teaching, they maintain, must belong
to the eternal verities, otherwise it is delusion. According to
them, no change in circumstances or in our pattern of thinking
should affect a religious tradition. It is futile to argue with those
who subscribe to these assumptions; the very trend of all modern
thinking is to repudiate them as false. With our tendency to
oppose the division of truth into separate compartments and to
insist that all our ideas be mutually consistent and integrated,
we cannot help demanding of religion that it be organic with the
rest of our life and inherently relevant to it. Since the rest of
human life changes, religion must change with it. The religion of one age cannot be transferred whole into a subsequent
age without being frozen into inertness. If we find that a religion
manages to retain its vitality in a new age, we may be sure that
it has undergone transformation. If its teachings and practices
continue to have meaning long after the conditions of life and
thought under which they arose have changed, it is because
that meaning is not the same they had originally.

Even the technique for revitalizing the spiritual values of the
past is not the same in one age as it is in another. We need a
new technique for our day; neither the one employed by the
Tannaim and *Amoraim*, nor the one employed by the Hellenist
allegorists or the medieval theologians, will answer our purpose.

In the past, the process by which the continuity of Jewish life and thought was maintained was an unconscious one. Before historic research or before any of the social sciences was born, men lacked the historic perspective which might have made them aware of the discrepancy between the original meaning of a sacred text or a ritual practice and their understanding of it, however unwarranted such understanding actually was. They were not troubled in the least by scruples about anachronism, and were therefore not inhibited from reading their own needs, beliefs and ideals into the religious traditions which had come down to them. We, on the other hand, must seek to maintain the continuity of the Jewish religion by a method which is in keeping with the modern historical sense, and which takes into account our repugnance to anachronisms. The method which the ancients employed may be termed *transvaluation;* the method we must employ may be termed *revaluation.*

Transvaluation consists in ascribing meanings to the traditional content of a religion or social heritage, which could neither have been contemplated nor implied by the authors of that content. The Jewish religious tradition often underwent this kind of transvaluation. The teachers and sages of a later period did not hesitate to read their own beliefs and aspirations into the writings of the teachers and sages of an earlier period. Both the sense of national continuity and the faith in the divine origin of the religious tradition made transvaluation seem perfectly plausible. Practically any rabbinic rendering of a scriptural text reveals considerable disparity from the literal meaning of that text. To the *Tannaim* and *Amoraim* there was scarcely a verse in the Bible that retained merely its original significance. Whole mountains of teachings, to use a rabbinic figure, hang by a hair to the text of the Bible. In ancient times the continuity of the Jewish religion was attained by means of this process of transvaluation. This is how the Jewish religion developed from the henotheism, which it was during the First Commonwealth, into a religion based on a monotheistic and universal conception of God; this is also how later it transformed itself from the theocratic religion which it was during the Second Commonwealth into a religion based on otherworldliness. . . .

But the method of transvaluation cannot do that for the modern Jew. The very use of it implies that those who resort to it are themselves unaware that they are adjusting or reconstructing tradition to meet the needs of their own day. This resource, however, is no longer possible. The transition from traditional Judaism to the Judaism of the future can be effected only in the glaring light of complete awareness of the change involved. The problem of maintaining the continuity of the Jewish religion can be solved only in one way, and that is by being convinced that the continuity is genuine. Such conviction is compatible only with the certainty that whatever ancient meanings or values we choose to conserve and develop are read out of, and not into, the traditional teachings or practices. For that reason we have to avoid transvaluation and resort to revaluation.

Revaluation consists in disengaging from the traditional content those elements in it which answer permanent postulates of human nature, and in integrating them into our own ideology. When we revaluate, we analyze or break up the traditional values into their implications, and single out for acceptance those implications which can help us meet our own moral and spiritual needs; the rest may be relegated to archeology. It is highly essential that we acquire the ability of getting at the really significant implications. They need not necessarily be such as the ancients themselves would have been able to articulate, but they should have psychological kinship with what the ancients did articulate. One advantage we surely have over those who lived in the remote past, when most of our religious teachings and practices took form; we are the heirs of all the experiences of the generations between them and ourselves. With the aid of these experiences, we should be able to unfold what is implied in the traditional teachings and practices. . . .

The Jewish religious content which is in need of being subjected to the process of revaluation may be divided into three distinct layers. The first layer consists of the greater part of the material recorded in the Bible. It reflects the formative period, or the first stage, of the Jewish religion. To be recognized, it has to be retrieved through the scientific study of the Bible. The second layer which reflects the religious development of the Jews during the Second Commonwealth to about the beginning of the common era is, in part, also found in the Bible, but, on the whole, is contained in the Jewish literature later described as "extraneous books." The third layer consists of the rabbinic and theological writings which cover the period of about two thousand years preceding the modern era. The last two layers would never have been produced out of the first, were it not for the process of transvaluation. Yet they are representative of the Jewish spirit in their own right. Though they are not, as the ancients believed, part of the pristine revelation to Israel, they are, nonetheless, the creation of the Jewish spirit, and must therefore function in any Jewish life in which that spirit is to be continued. The only way, however, in which the second and third layers of the Jewish religious tradition can be made to function in our day is by our *revaluating*, not by our transvaluating, their content.

64. A Conception of God

W HATEVER general idea we hold in our minds and regard as pointing to, or representative, of Reality, or of any phase of it, derives from something seen, heard, felt, believed or assumed. It proceeds, in other words, from the known to the unknown. That fact is true also of the belief in God. In most religions of the past, that belief was derived from *traditions* concerning self-revelations of God through visions and oracles. Those traditions are now discounted by all who have become habituated to scientific and philosophic thought. Though such people are in the minority, their influence is bound to increase with time, and their rejection of the traditional basis of the belief in God is certain to be followed by a like attitude on the part of the multitude. This may take a long time, but it is bound to come sooner or later.

Those who are not content with the superficiality of merely rejecting a belief that has been so universal, spontaneous and persistent as the belief in God, have turned their attention to the study of human nature and its needs. They have rightly concluded that there must be something in the very nature of man which has led him to create that vast and complex edifice of religion with its creeds, rituals, institutions and polities. What is that something? Some maintain that religion is the product of fear of whatever is beyond man's control, and that it is nothing but a disguised form of primitive magic to which man resorted, expecting the supposed gods, demons, spirits and angels to fulfill his wishes. As man learns to bring under control more and more of the forces in his own body and in his environment, he feels he can dispense with religion, or belief in God; what he cannot control, he has to accept with resignation. Others, however, and I among them, assume that man, once his physiological needs are satisfied, begins to experience the need to overcome such traits as self-indulgence, arrogance, envy, exploitation and hatred, or to bring under control the aggressive forces of his nature. That constitutes man's true destiny. Therein lies his salvation.

From that point, it is natural to arrive at the next step, which requires no blind leap into the dark. The next step is to conclude that the cosmos is so constituted as to enable man to fulfill this highest human need of his nature.

A magnetic needle, hung on a thread or placed on a pivot, assumes of its own accord a position in which one end of the needle points north and the other south. So long as it is free to move about, all attempts to deflect it will not get it to remain away from its normal direction. Likewise, man normally veers in the direction of that which makes for the fulfillment of his destiny as a human being. That fact indicates the functioning of a cosmic Power which influences his behavior. What magnetism is to the magnetic needle, Godhood or God is to man.

To carry the analogy one step further, just as the magnetic needle is the source of our knowledge of the earth's magnetism, so is man's salvational behavior the source of our knowledge of God. And just as we learn from the action of the magnetic needle the laws of magnetism so do we learn from man's salvational behavior, which we come progressively really to understand, the law or will of God.

There is, to be sure, a large element of faith in the foregoing type of analogical reasoning. But it is the kind of faith without which we could not live. When we count upon the sun's rising tomorrow morning, we act upon that kind of indispensable faith. You cannot compare that kind of faith to faith in the Biblical story that the sun stood still for Joshua. Likewise, you cannot say that faith in God as the process that makes man's salvation possible, is as "unprovable" as faith in an anthropomorphic God. For that matter, the human person, too, is not a ghost double of each of us, that walks out on us when we go to bed. The human person, too, is part of the salvation-making process, and is as much an object of *faith* as is God.

The universality and persistence of religion, in whatever form it has manifested itself, can thus be easily accounted for. Even the intellectuals who claim that religion has been motivated by fear and by the attempt to bring under control the inexplorable elements in the world, experience this highest need of human nature, the need for salvation, however they conceive it. Though they do not articulate it through worship, they seek some outlet like poetry, art or a social cause. All this implies that human life, and the cosmos which is its source, demand more of man than that he be able to split the atom or traverse the interplanetary spaces.

The fact that the cosmos possesses the resources and man the abilities—which are themselves part of those resources—to enable him to fulfill his destiny as a human being, or to achieve salvation—is the Godhood of the cosmos. That is the fact which we should have in mind when we worship God and glorify Him in inexhaustible variations on the motif of "Halleluyah." Even when we conceive God as Process, we do not pray to a *what* or to a *fact*. When we pray, we *affirm the* what or *the* fact that spells salvation. Likewise, when we address ourselves to God in prayer of petition, we raise to the level of consciousness those desires, the fulfillment of which we regard as a prerequisite to the fulfillment of our human destiny.

All the theologians who deprecate the naive conception of God as an anthropomorphic being, virtually do not themselves believe in God as an identifiable being or entity. When they denounce the notion of God as Process, they apparently try to convey the impression that their own idea of God is at least comprehensible. Actually, they keep on stressing at the same time that God is absolutely unknowable, inscrutable, and ineffable. They use the very terms in which the agnostic Herbert Spencer long ago described God. They keep on repeating that we can know God only through his manifestations, or that He reveals Himself not in objects, but in events. What are manifestations and events, if not process? These theologians are merely hurling at the notion of God as Process the same anathemas that have been hurled at the God idea of medieval theologians by the naive pietists who conceived of God in human form.

65. The Chosen People

. . . THE idea of Israel as the Chosen People, must be understood as belonging to a thought-world which we no longer inhabit. It fits in with a set of ideas that were congruous and rational enough in their day. But it can no longer help us to understand relations, or to orient ourselves to conditions, as they exist today. The very notion that a people can for all time be the elect of God implies an epic or dramatic conception of history, a history predetermined in form and aim. Nowadays for any people to call itself "chosen" is to be guilty of self-infatuation. . . .

The Effort to Reinterpret the Election of Israel

. . . The traditional basis for the belief that Israel was God's Chosen People was the assumption that the miraculous events recorded in the Torah concerning the Patriarchs and their descendants in Egypt represented factual truth. By far the most significant of these miraculous events was God's self-revelation to Israel on Mount Sinai. It was as unthinkable to question the truth of those events as to question the reality of one's own body. Under those circumstances, Jews could not possibly regard themselves as other than the most privileged of all peoples. Those circumstances, however, no longer obtain with the majority of modern-minded men and women. The modern-minded Jew cannot consider the miraculous events recorded in the Torah and in the rest of the Bible as other than legendary. He, therefore, cannot accept them as evidence of the traditional Jewish doctrine that Israel is God's Chosen People. The attempt to supply other evidence is itself a departure from tradition. Such an attempt might be justified, if at least the new evidence were convincing. But is it convincing?

Unable to accept literally the traditional version of the doctrine of the chosen people, the religious wing of the early *Maskilim*, the first *Reformers* and the middle group who designated themselves as the *Historical School* reinterpreted that doctrine to mean one or all of the following propositions as justifying the claim of the Jews to being a chosen people:

1. Jews possess hereditary traits which qualify them to be superior to the rest of the world in the realm of the religious and the ethical.

2. Their ancestors were the first to achieve those religious and ethical conceptions and ideals which will, in the end, become the common possession of mankind and help them to achieve salvation.

3. Jews possess the truest form of the religious and ethical ideals of mankind.

4. Jews are entrusted with the task of communicating those ideals to the rest of the world.

What Is Wrong with the Reinterpretations?

First, the proposition that Jews possess unusual hereditary traits which entitle them to be God's elect is based on a series of unproved generalizations concerning certain qualities as being characteristic only of Jews, and on biological assumptions concerning heredity, which are entirely unwarranted. It is one thing for an ancient sage to express his love for his people by describing them as unique in the possession of the traits of chastity, benevolence, and compassion. But it is quite another thing for a modern person seriously to assert that, because Jewish life has manifested these traits, Jews alone are inherently qualified to grasp and promulgate the truth of religion. We expect a greater regard for objective fact than is evidenced by such sweeping statements about hereditary Jewish traits.

If Jews were to adopt the foregoing reinterpretation of the

doctrine of election, they would, by implication, assent to the most pernicious theory of racial heredity yet advanced to justify racial inequality and the right of a master race to dominate all the rest of mankind. The truth is that historical circumstances, as well as geographic environment and social institutions, are greater determinants of national traits than heredity. Moreover, to represent divine election merely as confirming naturally inherited traits is to identify it virtually with natural selection. It is but one step from such identification to the identification of God with the process by which the physically weak are weeded out. We know all too well from current experience how such a concept of God is only another name for the apotheosis of the will to power.

Secondly, for Jews to claim sole credit for having given mankind those religious and ethical concepts which hold out the promise of a better world smacks of arrogance. The Greek philosophers, the Stoics in the Roman period, the humanists of the Renaissance, and the rationalists of the 18th century have made highly significant contributions to spiritual and moral truth. The religious philosophies of the Hindus antedate all others, and are experiencing a remarkable revival in our day. Even if Jews were the first to enunciate the great moral and spiritual teachings, it would be immodest of them to boast about it. That would not make them better or superior to the rest of the world, in any sense whatever. The first-born has no right to claim that he is better or more beloved than the other children. Special privileges no longer attach to primogeniture. . . .

Thirdly, for Jews to maintain that they possess the truest form of truth would be understandable, if they still believed that the teachings of their religion are immutable and infallible. However, with the modern dynamic conception of Jewish belief and practice being accepted by those of light and leading among them, the only meaning such claim can have is that Jews generally have managed to advance a bit ahead of every new development of spiritual truth. No one, however, who knows how far behind the best thinkers of their day some of our greatest Jewish spiritual leaders have been at times can subscribe to this reinterpretation. Spinoza, who truly did forge ahead of his contemporaries, was excommunicated. . . .

Finally, the fourth proposition confuses the doctrine of Israel's *election*, as expressed in the overwhelming majority of Biblical allusions which deal with Israel's relation to God, with the doctrine of Israel's *mission* which is the subject of less than a dozen passages in the second part of Isaiah. There is not the slightest implication in the multitude of references to Israel as a Chosen People that it is expected to fulfill the mission of making God known to the nations. . . .

There are many apologists for the doctrine who cling to the assertion of divine election, but compromise on its implied claims. They even confess to an awareness of the distaste which the assertion of divine election provokes in many modern-minded people. They seem to understand and even to admit that "extolling God for 'not having made us like other peoples' is grating." Nevertheless, they maintain that properly interpreted, the doctrine still remains valid and should not be discarded.

Though the belief expresses a certain national pride, or a sense of national privilege, "it carries with it also a sense of consecration and responsibility." No one can question the fact that the belief of being divinely elect has long been associated in the Jewish mind with consecration and responsibility. However, we cannot ignore the other implications of that belief, especially those which are often sharply stressed, as in the *Alenu* and the *Havdalah* prayers. In the latter, the invidiousness of the distinction between Israel and the nations is emphasized by being compared with the distinction between light and darkness. It is that invidiousness which is highly objectionable, and should be eliminated from our religion. . . .

The Doctrine of Election Not Necessary for Jewish Survival

. . . Since the proponents of the various reinterpretations of the doctrine of the Chosen People no longer believe in the factual truth of the Patriarchal stories, or of the miracles and the Sinaitic theophany, why are they at such pains to reinterpret that doctrine? . . .

The only reasonable motive to which such zeal can be ascribed is not one which derives from the momentum of tradition, but from considerations of Jewish survival. They seem to think that Jews would give up their struggle to live as an indivisible people, unless they were to believe that they are endowed, either individually or as a group, either biologically or culturally, with some moral or spiritual preeminence over the rest of the world.

In reply, be it said that the very attempt to bolster up the Jewish will to live by reasons or assumptions of questionable validity not only defeats its own purpose, but is injurious, from the standpoint of Jewish self-respect. The Jewish will to live cannot be fortified by spurious means. Any claim to moral or spiritual superiority, that is not based on incontrovertible proof, either supernatural or natural, is spurious and unworthy even of ordinary morals, to say nothing of a high spiritual standard.

Judaism can certainly not afford to harbor any doctrine which is in conflict with the ethical basis of democracy. That basis is the intrinsic worth of the individual human soul, a worth which is independent of the people, race or church to which one belongs. This implies that no people, race or church can confer upon its members a higher human status than does any other. Democracy as such calls for the treatment of individuals, despite their marked differences, as equals, from the standpoint of law and of their right to happiness and salvation. Ethical democracy goes one step further and calls for the treatment of all peoples, races and churches as equals in all respects. Indeed, *societies are far more like one another in their characteristics and behavior than are individuals. Hence, discrimination between one people and another is even more irrational and unethical than between one individual and another.*

Continuity of the Jewish consciousness demands that as large a number as possible of traditional Jewish values be retained. This does not mean, however, that all traditional values must necessarily be retained. Some are inherently of such a character as not to be capable of reinterpretation, or of being fitted into the pattern of the present-day outlook on life. Not even the fact that they suffuse the entire tradition, and that their elimination must produce a radically altered tradition, should be sufficient to save them. . . .

Vocation a Valid Substitute for the Doctrine of Election

. . . The place previously occupied in the Jewish consciousness by the doctrine of election will have to be filled by the doctrine of vocation. The whole course of Jewish history has been so dominated by religious motivation that Jews cannot be true to themselves, as a people, without stressing the religious character of Judaism. Jewish religion would have Jewish civilization make for the enhancement not only of Jewish life but of the life of mankind, and thus help to render manifest the cosmic purpose of human life. Jewish religion expects the Jew to live the civilization of his people in a spirit of commitment and dedication. To live thus is to live with a sense of vocation or calling, without involving ourselves in any of the invidious distinctions implied in the doctrine of the election, and yet to fulfill the legitimate spiritual wants which that doctrine sought to satisfy.

It is generally assumed that the idea of "vocation" is a Christian, particularly a Protestant, idea. As a matter of fact, that idea is no less Jewish than it is Christian. Thus we read in the Talmud: "A familiar saying in the mouth of the Sages of Yabneh was this: 'I (who study Torah) am a creature (of God); my work is in the city, his in the field; I rise early to my work, he rises early to his. Just as he cannot excel in my work, so I cannot excel in his.' Perhaps thou wilt say: I do much and he does little (for the Torah). But we have learned, 'He who offers much and he who offers little are equal, provided that each direct his heart to Heaven.' " Judaism should extend the significance of vocation to include nations as well as individuals. *No nation is chosen, or elected, or superior to any other, but every nation should discover its vocation or calling, as a source of religious experience, and as a medium of salvation to those who share its life.* . . .

All these considerations make it clear that, whether we apply rational or pragmatic criteria, the traditional formula concerning Israel's divine election is objectionable. Rationally, it has no place in the realm of discourse from which belief in the supernatural revelation of religious truth has been excluded. Pragmatically, it is objectionable, as barring the way to peace and harmony among religions, and as making for self-righteousness and cant. All the genuine values that once attached themselves to this belief can be maintained by substituting for it the doctrine of "vocation." What more important calling could a people have than to promulgate, by its way of life, the truth of the universal presence of God in all religions, and the universal obligation of every man to use his traditional *sancta* for glorifying not merely his own people or church, but mankind as a whole?

66. Rituals

. . . B o t h Orthodoxy and Conservatism, insofar as they are logically consistent, make Judaism the exclusive possession of that constantly diminishing minority who are prepared to sacrifice their personal interests for the preservation of Jewish life. The vast multitudes, as they lose the momentum of a Jewish past vividly recollected, cannot be persuaded, in the name of Jewish survival alone, to live under "the yoke of a law," which has become burdensome. An organism fights to live only as long as life yields satisfactions. Our ancestors lived joyously under the law of the Torah, because that life offered them social standing in this world and salvation in the world to come. In our day, too, we can expect Jewish religious practices to be maintained only in the degree that Jews feel their personal lives thereby enriched.

In spite of elements of strength, each of the contemporary formulations of Jewish religion suffers the weakness of its one-sidedness. The Conservative emphasis on the importance of Jewish usage as an expression of the collective will of the Jewish people to survive is correct. *But it is wrong to make the existence and continuation of the group the sole end of Jewish observance.* In doing so, Conservatism impairs the religious significance of Jewish group life, and evades the problem of making the law function as an instrument of salvation. Orthodoxy is correct when it asserts that piety involves more than intellectual assent to a body of dogma, that it involves a constant awareness of

God's presence in the world of nature and man, an awareness which expresses itself in a religious way of life. But Orthodoxy fails to reckon with the need for an adequate theology that can meet the challenge of modern thought, and with the political, social and economic realities that condition Jewish group survival. Reform leaders were right in their emphasis on the supreme importance of ethical ideals and of reenforcing them by faith in God articulated in religious symbols and acts of worship, but they erred in renouncing Jewish nationhood, neglecting the group aspect of Jewish living, and failing to recognize the importance of ritual norms and standards to identify the individual Jew with his people by a specific and distinctive way of life.

The only tenable position is that, in the matter of ritual observance as in so many other phases of life, it is necessary to strike a balance between the interests of the group and the interests of the individual. This is implied in the fundamental principle that Judaism is a religious civilization. For a religious civilization is one which not only identifies the individual with his group, but makes the group responsible for the salvation of the individual, for helping him to experience life as supremely worthwhile or holy, and thus to commune with God. *A satisfactory rationale for Jewish usage is one that would recognize in it both a method of group survival and a means to the personal self-fulfillment, or salvation of the individual Jew.* Through it, the individual Jew will know the exhilaration of fully identifying himself with his people and, thereby, saving his own life from dullness, drabness and triviality. Jewish tradition brings to the daily living of the Jew, to his holiday celebration, to the celebration of turning points in his life, a wealth of beautiful and meaningful symbols embodying the *sancta* of his people, expressive of its ideals and native to its culture. These should be retained and developed; for, no creed, no value, no self-identification of the individual with his people is effective, unless it is translated into action of a systematic and habitual nature.

If we accept this rationale of Jewish usage and recognize its dual function of contributing both to Jewish group survival and to the personal self-fulfillment of the individual, we must accept as a corollary the sanctioning by the group of variations in ritual usage. The circumstances of life are so different for different Jews, their economic needs and opportunities, their cultural background, their acquired skills and inherited capacities are so varied that it is unreasonable to expect all of them to find self-fulfillment in the traditional rituals. That was possible only where the Jewish community lived a self-contained life and could make possible for all its members, without undue sacrifice on their part, the observance of all usages which were the norm in Jewish life. It is not possible when, as in democratic countries, the Jew has to live in two civilizations, and find his place in the economic and cultural life of the civic community as well as of the Jewish.

From this point of view, no stigma attaches to those who permit themselves a wide latitude in their departure from traditional norms. It is not appropriate, in dealing with matters of ritual, sanctimoniously to invoke God's pardon for transgressions which are unavoidable, or to refrain from teaching the law, on the basis of the principle that it is better for Jews to err unwittingly than to sin presumptuously. Adherence to tradition is henceforth to be evaluated not solely in terms of group needs, but also in terms of individual satisfactions. It certainly cannot be considered in terms of a supernaturally revealed code. *The vocabulary of "law," "sin," "pardon," is ideologically and pragmatically unjustified as applied to ritual.* Parental and synagogical insistence on observance of the totality of Jewish ritual has resulted in the complete breakdown of traditional usage. We have asked too much and have received nothing.

For those of us who have been trained to think of ceremonial observance as divine commandments, or as part of a self-sufficient mystic "law" which is the essence of historic Judaism, the elasticity of this new approach will, at first, seem unsatisfactory. There is, however, literally no alternative. Modern thought acknowledges the propriety of the concept of "law" only in nature and in human relationships; in the sphere of ritual, of the relationship between man and God, there can be no law. A modern state is separated from any established church, and refuses to legislate on matters of religious practice. In a Jewish commonwealth, religious usages could be embodied into the law of the land, only insofar as they had social repercussions, as, for instance, in matters of Sabbath observance, where it would be necessary to insure the opportunity for such observance to all who desire it, and in marital law, where the social efficacy of the home has to be protected.

But to deny that ritual usage can appropriately be treated as law does not mean that it can be left solely to the whim of the individual. The benefit which the individual hopes to derive from ritual usages is dependent on their power to effect his self-identification with the Jewish group. Consequently, it is important for those who feel the need of such self-identification through ritual to evaluate the heritage of traditional Jewish usages, and to adopt those that are capable of functioning beneficently in their lives. Moreover, since the obsolescence of much traditional usage is inevitable, they would do well to consider the possibility of also introducing new usages that can similarly contribute to self-identification with the Jewish people and to personal self-fulfillment as Jews.

These are the considerations which make desirable the effort to define what, under various circumstances of life, shall be the norm of Jewish practice for those Jews who cannot accept the traditional attitude toward the Jewish codes, who may even find that some observances are obstacles rather than helps to self-fulfillment, but who wish to remain Jews and to make the most of their Judaism. For Jews who are satisfied with the traditional codes and can find complete self-realization in their observance, such a guide would have no message. Nor would it have a message for those Jews who see no good to be gained by identifying themselves with the Jewish people and its religious tradition. All other thinking Jews, however, should either encourage, or engage in, the effort to arrive at a Jewish way of living which will insure both the survival of the Jewish group and the enrichment of their own lives as Jews.

The time when any one authoritative voice might be sufficient sanction for any law, or code of laws, pertaining to ritual practice is long passed. To wait for an authoritative body that would be recognized by the whole or even a considerable part of Jewry, and that would undertake to draw up a guide of ritual practice, is to postpone the solution *sine die*. The only way to extricate Jewish life from its impasse in the matter of ritual observance is for a group of rabbis to whom people look for religious guidance, together with scholars expert not only in the knowledge of ancient texts but also in the understanding of contemporary human needs, to collaborate in the issues here discussed and to draw up the long awaited guide. In time such a guide would become authoritative. . . .

67. Jewish Education

Modern Jewish teachers and educators, who no longer subscribe to the traditional or Orthodox version of Judaism—and they are unquestionably in the majority—should dedicate themselves to the task of utilizing the very process of education for the purpose of developing an acceptable version of the Jewish tradition, and of preparing the ground for Jewish communal life. This may seem incompatible with conventional education procedure. All cultural and social changes are supposed to be effected directly through, and in, adult society. They are supposed to precede and not to follow the educational process. The usual assumption is that the society of today conditions the education of tomorrow, and not the reverse. But we Jews, in our struggle for existence, have had to resort to extraordinary measures. We have a precedent in our past for the use of the educational process to create a new social structure and a relatively new universe of thought. Such was the achievement of the first few generations of teachers known as *Tannaim*, during the first two centuries of the common era.

When the Second Temple was destroyed, our ancestors were virtually without the kind of tradition and without the kind of corporate frame which the new circumstances of exile and dispersion demanded. They were on the verge of national and religious collapse. It was then that the *Tannaim* made use of the educative process to evolve both the necessary tradition and the requisite corporate frame. This they did first with adults who were to function as the spiritual guides; then they brought their teachings down to the level of the child.

Similarly creative effort in Jewish education must be undertaken in our day, if Judaism is not to die out in this country. Such effort calls for abundant energy, far-seeing initiative and willing sacrifice. In modern times the Jewish teacher, particularly in east-European countries, has shown himself equal to the task of moulding the Jewish consciousness in the spirit of the Hebrew renascence. In Eretz Yisrael, the Jewish teacher succeeded in transforming Hebrew into a living vernacular. There is no reason why the Jewish teacher should not be able to cope with the particular task which devolves upon him now to save Diaspora Jewry from disintegration.

In utilizing the educational process as a means of reinterpreting our traditional values, an important role will have to be played by the way we organize the content of instruction into different kinds of subject matter. In contrast with the tendency of Western education to break up the content of a social heritage into different kinds of subject matter, the traditional type of Jewish education retained the Jewish social heritage in the undifferentiated form in which it was lived. When the youngster studied Torah, he studied simultaneously everything that had to do with making him a worthy member of the Jewish community. The Western habits of thought, however, which our children acquire with their non-Jewish education, necessitate similar differentiation of the Jewish educational content into different subjects. This very differentiation necessarily results in new meanings and emphases. That itself is perhaps the most important step in the process of reinterpretation. There are, however, certain lines of differentiation which must be followed, specifically with a view to their effect on that process.

It is essential, for example, to create in the mind of the child an awareness of the several facets of our tradition, and of the fact that each facet represents a distinct pattern of values. Thus, while, in actual life, Jewish religion and Jewish peoplehood are always found together, it is essential to learn to differentiate one from the other in thought. The first effect of such differentiation, in modern times, has been to create at least one new subject in the Jewish curriculum—Jewish history. Jost, Graetz, Weiss and others, in developing new Jewish historical content, have done what the *Tannaim* and *Amoraim* did for their day. These new content values have been translated by the text-book makers and pedagogues into subject matter for the elementary school.

It is also necessary to draw a distinction between the legendary and the historical. The child should be made to realize that our traditional narrative material has two facets to it, legend and history, with legend predominant in the earlier narratives of the Bible, and history in the later narratives. The practice of ignoring that distinction results in the distorted notions which most Jews have of their people's past. By permitting our children to carry away the impression that the stories in the Pentateuch are meant to be taken as history, we plant in their minds seeds of inner conflict for the rest of their lives. "The folklore and myth of a people," says Henry N. Wieman, "convey in aesthetic form the quality of events critically determinant of their history." Not until Jewish education assimilates the truth expressed in that statement, will the early narratives of the Bible exercise their proper influence on the thinking and conduct of the coming generations of Jews.

Another important area to be delineated in the content of Jewish education is that of ethics and religion. While that area constitutes part of the content of tradition, it must be enlarged, organized and developed into distinct subject-matter. What we mean by such central ideas as God, holiness, personality, responsibility, goodness, truth, human destiny and salvation, must henceforth be clearly articulated and recognized as in need of being studied and translated into action.

In utilizing the educational process for evolving the social structure of Jewish life, which normally should have preceded that process, it is advisable to organize projects in what might be called "Jewish civics." That should not be difficult. Many Jewish schools have succeeded in making Eretz Yisrael the theme of instruction and project activity. By the same token, Jewish civics should come to occupy a place in the curriculum, for the purpose of creating in the mind of the child an appreciation for the need of Jewish communal life in America. Projects should be developed entailing the study of all educational and social service institutions, public relations organizations, community councils, as well as the organization and functioning of congregations, and the huge fund-gathering campaigns like those for welfare funds, the Joint Distribution Committee and the United Jewish Appeal. The purpose of these projects should be to discover the forces at work in all those activities, their accomplishments, their ideologies, their inherent defects, and what would be necessary to integrate them into an organic Jewish community. All this would have to be accompanied by combining the various schools into a kind of youth *Kehillah*, out of which would evolve, in the course of ten to fifteen years, the beginning of real community life.

No doubt, the most difficult problem, which will have to be met in developing the educational content both for the reinterpretation of traditional Jewish values and the establishment of Jewish social structure, is that presented by the vast variety of conflicting ideas and interests. The only possibility of achieving collaboration at least among the majority of those who profess the desire to see Judaism flourish is to have them accept the principle of diversity in unity not grudgingly, but wholeheartedly. With all that, however, there must be a definite pattern of Jewish living, which should constitute the criterion by which to judge all educational effort. The basic principle of that pattern must be that *Judaism is a religio-ethical civilization, to be fostered by the American Jew to the maximum degree compatible with the legitimate claims which American citizenship has upon him.* . . .

This is the only tenable conception of the Jewish way of life to be imparted to the American-Jewish child, from the standpoint of those who are modernist in their general world-outlook and religio-culturist in their attitude to Judaism. The principal aim to be kept in mind in the Jewish education of the American-Jewish child, from the standpoint of his maximum self-fulfillment as an American and as a Jew, is, accordingly, to render the Jewish heritage relevant to his moral and spiritual needs, and to qualify him, when he matures, to establish the kind of Jewish communal environment that will provide opportunities for the satisfaction of those needs.

68. Israel

. . . I N resuming a national life in Eretz Yisrael, the land that embodies its highest aspirations, Judaism demonstrates the principle that it is normal for religion to convert into means of salvation the experiences arising from the social interaction which a common land makes necessary for a People. The organic collective life resulting from the common interests which people, living in close proximity, must of necessity share is, despite the philosophy of existentialism, more existentially real and certainly of far longer duration than any individual member of the group, however great. Even the most distinguished individual is far more in debt to his society than it is to him. Thus a territorial society provides what every man needs for his salvation, and is the initial source of his experiencing the meaning of Godhood.

How readily Jewish national life in Israel can give rise to new cultural and spiritual values is evidenced by the practice, instituted there recently, of using the celebration of Independence Day as an occasion for Israel Awards to scholars, scientists and men of letters in recognition of distinguished work in their various fields. That work embraces poetry, fiction, music, natural and exact science, philosophy, law, education and Bible studies (*Israel Digest*, May 17, 1954).

Jews who live in the Diaspora, by maintaining their oneness with the Jews in Eretz Yisrael, may serve to restrain the chauvinistic tendencies which the Israeli struggle for survival is apt to produce. On the other hand, they will also participate in the experiences of the Jews in Eretz Yisrael, together with the moral and spiritual values which those experiences may yield. We need only recall how closely the average American Jew at present follows the daily events in Israel and how sensitive he is to what goes on there. How long that interest will continue—that is the problem. "The bond with the Jewish People wherever they may live is the solid foundation of our life," declared Prime Minister Moshe Sharett, "just as the spiritual attachment to the State of Israel is the central fact in the life of the Jewish People" (*Ibid.,* May 17, 1954). Sharett speaks advisedly of the attachment to the State of Israel as "spiritual."

If world Jewry will reconstitute itself as a People and achieve a modern national civilization in Eretz Yisrael and a religious cultural life everywhere, it will place itself in the vanguard of an urgently needed new trend in world civilization, already becoming manifest in the more advanced nations of the Western world. On the one hand, they utilize their own historic experiences and their own *sancta* (such as their great personalities, their memorable events and places) as sources of morale and guidance, and on the other hand, they seek to integrate their own collective interest, both material and spiritual, within the common life of mankind. Without such integration, which only the acceptance of some kind of universal religion can make possible, mankind will revert to nationalist idolatry, with all its excesses.

Thus in treating the reclamation of Eretz Yisrael as part of a modern messianic or religious movement, Jews have a unique opportunity to serve mankind by fostering a method of group life directed towards this-worldly salvation. This achievement will justify the age-old refusal of the Jewish People to renounce Eretz Yisrael. When, in an historic demonstration of unexampled loyalty, the East European Zionists rejected the offer of Uganda as a national territory, *they proved that the Zionist movement was basically motivated by Jewish cultural nationalism, with its roots in the Jewish tradition, rather than by modern political nationalism.*

The mistake of the Reform Movement, in its initial stage, was not in maintaining that the Jews have a universal mission. Whenever we try to live a useful and meaningful life, we exert a beneficent influence. If, as a group, we make this our deliberate purpose, we may be said to have a mission. The mistake of the

Reform Movement consisted in having expected the Jews to do what the Talmud describes as "breaking the cask without spilling the wine." Although the leaders of the Movement consented to the fragmentation of the Jewish People and the renunciation of its homeland, they nevertheless expected the Jews as a group to influence all mankind to accept the fatherhood of God and the brotherhood of man. Those leaders made little, if any effort, to indicate what Jews were expected to do, or live up to, in order that they might fulfill so high a mission. They seem to have believed that, if the Jews kept on affirming as emphatically as possible that they had been chosen for that mission, it would somehow get itself fulfilled.

On the other hand, the particularity of a group does not prevent it from developing ways of living and spiritual values capable of being universalized and of stimulating other groups to creativity. The idea of such universal life values is implicit in the form of the Jewish People's attachment to Eretz Yisrael; it must now be made explicit. The process of realizing such values consists in utilizing for self-fulfillment as human beings that wide range of interactivity which is possible only among those who are rooted in a common land. *Earthly interests must constitute the stuff out of which human beings may mold their destiny. That is the Jewish contribution to the method of salvation whose source and guarantor is God.*

To demonstrate the validity of that method of salvation, Judaism needs a home: that is, a land where Jews, as the majority population, can demonstrate how a People may make its civilization an instrument for the maximum human self-fulfillment of its individual members. There is a spiritual advantage in "being true to a particular piece of earth—true to its landscape, its climate, its history, its morality, its tongue."

Only in such a land can enough members of a People live in that propinquity which necessitates interaction in pursuit of common economic, social and political interests. Only such interaction provides that inexhaustible flow of new experience without which cultural, moral and spiritual values are void of content. Only in such a context can develop the freedom which has been defined as "that faculty of man by which he is able to determine his being through history" (Tillich). *Eretz Yisrael is indispensable to Jews as the realm of freedom to be creative as Jews.*

Only thus can the Jewish People make history, instead of being its passive product.

After all is said and done, if it were not for the unparalleled attachment of the Jewish People to Eretz Yisrael, and the inexhaustible meanings for human life that have derived for all mankind from that attachment, the resentment of the Arab world at the Zionist movement would be at least understandable, even if not justified. There can be no question that, without our historic claim to the land, the nations, including Britain, would never have made it possible for Jews to rebuild it as their homeland and ultimately to establish there a political state.

The Arab nations destroyed any possible justification for their anti-Zionism when they flouted the final decision of the United Nations to restore to the Jews at least part of their ancient land. Reasonable in itself, that solution was the only way the civilized nations had to make amends for having looked on while Hitler and his myrmidons were massacring millions of Jews. That brutal genocide could be perpetrated on so vast a scale only because of the heartless failure of the democratic nations, which were brought together before World War II at the conference in Evian, to offer refuge to the Jews who were hit by Hitler's Nuremberg laws.

It therefore devolves upon the Zionist movement, in its effort to reconstitute the Jewish People and arouse in Diaspora Jewry a sense of personal involvement in the consolidation of the State of Israel, to develop fully the far-reaching religious, or salvational, implications of our historical claim to the land of Israel. From the very beginning Zionism presented itself as not merely a movement to salvage human lives, desperately urgent as that was, but as seeking to resurrect a People that had made history and evolved moral and spiritual values which half of mankind have incorporated into their consciousness and made part of their conscience.

*   *   *

Jewish history and values are the product of the interaction between the Jewish People and Eretz Yisrael. *World Jewry without Eretz Yisrael is like a soul without a body; Eretz Yisrael without World Jewry is like a body without a soul.*

The interplay of people and land is more responsible for the individuality of the Jewish People and its contribution to civilization than any other factor in its life, be it even its tradition, or its outstanding spiritual leaders. Those leaders themselves were the product of that interrelationship between land and people, in terms of which they were guided, warned and comforted their contemporaries. That interplay of land and people is without parallel in human history; a fact that has been accepted as fundamental to religion, and which has made Eretz Yisrael a Holy Land for half of mankind. The effort to resume the interaction of the Jewish People with its land cannot succeed if it ignores this.

Zionist leaders should possess the moral courage to present the Zionist movement as a messianic movement to world Jewry. In Jewish tradition, the Messiah represents the reawakening of the Jewish People to a sense of destiny and the resumption of Jewish nationhood in the land of its origin and development. Even in its traditional setting, Messianism belongs to a different dimension from that of other-worldliness. It was conceived as breaking through the bonds of the natural order, but not as destroying it, as inaugurating a new era in the life of mankind and culminating in the rise of a free People, re-wedded to its soil and giving birth to the new man. The twice-told Messianic prophecy that "in the end of days" peace will reign throughout the world and men "will not learn war anymore," is certainly a promise for this, our world.

Such Messianism is of the very essence of Jewish religion. Zionism must make Jews everywhere take Messianism seriously and translate it into religion. In no other way can Zionism make American Jews treat as a moral and religious responsibility the recruitment of *halutzim* to help build the land, and develop all forms of personal involvement in its security and in the achievement of its high purposes. Referring to the sudden change of habits which modern conditions often demand, Karl Mannheim writes: "It can only take place, if enthusiasm or an emotionalization of the new issues accompanies it, and the latter occurs only when the crucial issues of life can be re-defined and gain new significance . . . this general revaluation can only happen if each new objective is part of a new world view and a new way of life" (*Diagnosis of Our Time,* p. 115).

Zionism at long last must do what Judah Halevi, many centuries ago, urged Jews to do. It should put an end to the habit of treating the role which Eretz Yisrael played in the past, and which it is destined to play in the future, as no more than a thema for liturgy. More than ever has it become necessary for Zionism to enlarge its perspective. One of its main purposes should be to deepen our awareness of the extent to which the Jewish being was fashioned by Eretz Yisrael. Zionism should stress that during the centuries of their dispersion Eretz Yisrael played a greater role in the spiritual life of the Jews than the countries which they actually inhabited.

Zionism should urge Jews to read their tradition with fresh eyes. If Jews were to do so, they would discover that they have in the Pentateuch—the basic source of the sanctions, laws, and folkways of the Jewish People—a perfectly recorded deed to the eternal possession of Eretz Yisrael. Moreover, it is stated there in bold and unmistakable terms that even if the children of Israel will be exiled from the land, they will not entirely forfeit it, but that ultimately their descendants will return to it, and rebuild their national life. . . .

69. The Social Structure of American-Jewish Life

Why Jews Need Community

THROUGHOUT the past, wherever a number of Jews lived within reach of one another, they formed a self-governing community. Each Jew was answerable to his community to a greater degree than is the citizen of a modern state to his government. . . .

The self-government which Jews exercised was not granted them as a privilege. It was not even a matter of voluntary choice. It was forced on them by the exclusionist attitude of those among whom they lived, and who refused to incorporate them into their own body politic. To this autonomy, perhaps more than to aught else, Jews owe their survival as a people. It rendered the Jew dependent upon his people for everything he deemed important to his life. . . .

All this has changed. With the granting of civic rights to the Jews, their feeling of mutual dependence has waned. The main reason is that they are not only permitted, but expected, to derive their basic literacy and culture from the social heritage of the majority population. This has removed the principal cohesive factor of Jewish togetherness. From the standpoint of Jewish survival, that is a cataclysm. Yet most Jewish leaders, whether lay or religious, act as though the structure of Jewish life may have been somewhat shaken, but not as though it were in danger of collapsing. Either they are unconcerned about the future of the Jewish people, or they fail to realize that *the inevitable consequence of the generally accepted version of democratic nationalism is to render Judaism superfluous to the Jew.* . . .

In the modern world, the Jew receives few of these benefits from the Jewish community. He does not have the experience of being taken care of by that community, as his fathers had before the Emancipation. . . .

It is obvious that Jews can do little, if anything, to induce the general community to care for them as fully as it does for non-Jews. But Jews can, if they take thought, so reorganize their communal life that the individual Jew may realize that "in this unanimously non-caring world," at least his own *Jewish* community cares for him. . . .

The Jewish community can be so organized that it can help the Jew overcome those political, social and economic disadvantages from which he suffers, by reason of his being identified with a minority group. It should make the individual Jew feel that he is an object of solicitous care to his fellow-Jews, no matter how indifferent the rest of the world may be to his basic interests. . . .

Strange as it may seem, ever since the ghetto walls were officially razed, and the solidarity of the Jewish community life has been undermined, little, if any, thought has been given to the problem of retrieving Jewish communal solidarity. This may be due to various fears and misapprehensions. In the first place, Jews are afraid that, if they became too active in caring for their own, they would segregate themselves from the general community. That might lead to the reestablishment of the ghetto. There is, however, no basis whatever for such fear. Jews can be segregated, or the ghetto reinstated only as a result of a fascist revolution that would destroy the American form of government. . . .

Secondly, it is claimed that, if Jews were to build a strong community of their own they would play into the hands of the anti-Semites who maintain that the Jews are united in a conspiracy to dominate the rest of the world. By this time, it should have become evident that the policy of appeasing the anti-

Semites makes as little sense as the late Neville Chamberlain's policy of appeasing the Nazis. As far as the anti-Semites are concerned, we are damned if we do, and we are damned if we don't. Nothing short of our extinction will suit them. It is folly, therefore, even to take note of their ravings against us.

Finally, few Jews, even among those who are loyal to their people and their tradition, realize the vital connection between Judaism and the social structure of Jewish life. To most Jews anything that has to do with organization smacks of the secular or profane. It is at best an instrument which is serviceable as long as it raises no questions. But as soon as it exposes us to the charge of trying to segregate ourselves from the civic community, it ought to be dispensed with. This dualism between the spirit and the body of Jewish life has to be unlearned. *Without an enduring social structure, such as only a well-organized community can provide, being a Jew is like trying to live as a disembodied soul.*

The main reason, however, for the failure to come to grips with the problem of Jewish communal solidarity is, no doubt, the fact that it is not possible, as it was in the past, to build the community around the synagogue. It is, therefore, necessary to evolve a new conception of communal cohesion. . . .

The synagogue can no longer be the all inclusive community that it was in the past. Both the necessarily limiting character of its specific version of Judaism, and the urge to satisfy needs of a non-religious character, have given rise to a whole network of Jewish organizations. The fraternal order B'nai B'rith, for instance, was formed more than one-hundred years ago because Jews, who were beginning to divide themselves along religious lines, felt the need of some means of fraternal association. Then came the many *Landsmanschaften*. Later, the various philanthropic societies were established to maintain hospitals, orphan asylums and homes for the aged, and to provide relief for the needy. Still later, these were combined into federations and welfare funds. When the Zionist movement came on the scene, it gave rise to different groupings: the Zionist Organization of America, Mizrachi, Hadassah and Labor Zionists. The menace of anti-Semitism led to the formation of the American Jewish Committee and the American Jewish Congress. These organizations and their activities, which are concerned with the secular needs of Jews, consume almost all of the available time and energies of the public-spirited and socially-minded among us.

It is futile to bewail this multiplicity of societies, agencies and organizations outside the synagogue, and to plead that all of them become an integral part of it. . . .

[We] should, therefore, look beyond the synagogue for ways and means of maintaining unbroken the organic character of Jewish life in the face of the overwhelming assimilative power of the environment. *It is the duty of the synagogue—be it Orthodox, Conservative or Reform—to arrive at a formula for Jewish life, which shall satisfy the just demands of the modern state, and which shall make differentiation along religious and functional lines safe for Jewish survival and growth.*

What Should Be the Social Structure of American Jewry?

The basic unit of Jewish life cannot be any one agency. The entire aggregate of congregations, social service agencies, Zionist organizations, defense and fraternal bodies, and educational institutions, should be integrated into an organic or indivisible community. That is the only structure or agency qualified to translate the conception of the Jews as an indivisible people, and of Judaism as a religious civilization, into a living reality. It would be organic, in that *all* matters of Jewish interest would in some way deeply affect the lives of all who desire to remain Jews. The social intelligence of the Jew would be as all-inclusive and as far-reaching as the limits not only of the particular institution or cause he is identified with, but of the entire Jewish people the world over.

In an organic community, all purposes for which Jews unite would converge upon the one purpose of Jewish survival and growth. *In such a community, the structural pattern would be determined by regional propinquity rather than by interest in particular objectives.* This means that all Jewish bodies—all congregations, public-relations organizations, social service agencies, educational institutions within any region or district—would have to collaborate for the express purpose of eliciting fresh energies and tapping new resources for living as Jews and finding Jewish life rewarding.

The spirit in which most of the public-relations and social service activities are presently conducted is far from calculated to render them as a means to the survival and growth of the Jewish people. If they can be said to have any objective in common, it is to forestall the spread of anti-Semitism by preventing Jews from falling a burden on the general community. Ironically, however, helping the individual Jew may be entirely compatible with gradual disappearance of the Jewish people.

It is unfortunate that most of those who are closely associated with Jewish social activities think that it is not only possible but necessary to carry them on, without bothering about Jewish mass survival. This assumption is both theoretically fallacious and, in the long run, also bound to prove a source of inefficiency. . . .

The Principles and Aims of Jewish Community in America

It is neither necessary nor possible to do more than indicate certain principles which have to be followed in the formation of an organic community. The first principle is that *all who definitely desire to see Jewish life fostered, regardless of how they conceive the form or content of that life, should be eligible for membership.* The first step in the self-discipline which the pronounced survivalists among us must take is to cooperate with all who prefer to remain Jews, on any terms whatsoever. No one but a fanatical believer in his own particular brand of Jewish survivalism would withhold membership in the Jewish community from those who conceive of Jewish survival differently from the way he does. One has to be blind to the complexity of our inner problem to claim to have found the only true solution, and to refuse to cooperate with any one who disagrees.

We must have faith in the capacity of the Jewish people to determine for themselves the character of Jewish life. Indeed, not only must no Jew be excluded from the Jewish community for his opinions and beliefs, but the community must provide in its administration for a proper and proportionate representation of every Jewish trend. Each such trend should be given a chance to organize its own adherents and to pursue its own program, so long as it recognizes the right of Jews of other schools of thought to do likewise.

Secondly, if the Jewish community is to be a means of having the individual Jew experience the reality and vitality of the Jewish people, it follows that those institutions and agencies whose main function is to foster Jewish consciousness should occupy a position of primacy. Accordingly, *the synagogues, the communal centers and the institutions of elementary education and higher learning should constitute the nucleus in the organizational pattern.* How to get the various Jewish denominations to operate harmoniously within the communal frame is by no means as insuperable a problem as we have been wont to think. In many large cities, Jewish educational bureaus manage to serve diverse types of Jewish educational institutions, from the most secular to the most Orthodox. This proves that it is possible for widely differing groups to find a common ground. By the same token, it should be possible to establish in each community a synagogue and center bureau that would perform a similar function for the spiritual and cultural needs of the adults.

Thirdly, the multiplicity of organizations and their tendency to perpetuate themselves and to retain their independence might seem to preclude their integration into a united community. The experience, however, with the existing federations and welfare funds throughout this country, which have succeeded in bringing together for common action the most diverse institutions and agencies, shows that the difficulties in the way of their committing themselves to a positive program for Jewish life are not insuperable. Moreover, if we follow the principle that it is always best to avail ourselves of existing forces and agencies instead of liquidating them and beginning *de novo*, there would be no occasion for any of them to feel aggrieved. Being the spontaneous expression of the will to organized effort, they are the medium through which the conservation and growth of Jewish life could best be furthered. *All organizations and agencies at present engaged in specific tasks should, therefore, continue what they are doing, but they should be required, in addition, to be represented in local community councils.* All organizations and agencies that are national in scope should have representation in, and give an accounting to, all the local community councils of those localities where they have branches. The community councils should in each case be a reviewing, coordinating and initiating body, from the standpoint of the all-dominant purpose of giving the Jew the courage, and providing him with the resources, to live as a Jew.

In a number of cities, Jewish community councils have already been formed; in others they are in the process of formation. At present, they virtually have no definite purpose, except that of exploring, or perhaps even generating, the sentiment for Jewish unity. Given the affirmative purpose of strengthening the morale of the Jew, we would have in the community councils the groundwork of an overall national Jewish community. An over-all council, which would constitute the executive committee of that community would be representative of all areas of opinion, and have first-hand acquaintance with local problems. It could, therefore, well be trusted not to treat perfunctorily its task of reviewing and coordinating the activities of the different sections of our people, and initiating needed lines of action.

Many technical problems are bound to arise. How shall we deal, for example, with large Jewish populations in metropolitan centers, or with sparse Jewish populations in rural areas? Such problems are by no means insoluble. In metropolitan centers, a maximum, like twenty or twenty-five thousand, might be entitled to a local community council. In the case of rural areas, on the other hand, a population minimum and a geographic maximum might be combined to form a unit that would be entitled to a community council. These and similar details could be worked out by those who are expert in matters of this kind.

In a word, Jewish communal life should be organized on the following principles:

1. The inclusion of all who desire to continue as Jews.

2. The primacy of the religious and educational institutions in the communal structure.

3. Democratic representation of all legitimate Jewish organizations in the administration of the community.

What can be done by an organic Jewish community to help American Jews achieve self-fulfillment both as Americans and as Jews? The potentialities of such a community cannot be fully envisaged, so long as it is merely a dream. But they would become increasingly apparent, as steps are taken to translate the dream into reality. In the meantime, certain important objectives deserve to be set up as immediate aims. They are the following:

1. To maintain a complete register and vital statistics, and to

establish bureaus for gathering information concerning all matters of importance to contemporary Jewish life.

2. To activate the high ethical standards transmitted in the
Jewish tradition, by the formulation of specific codes and sanctions for various social and economic relationships.

3. To foster Jewish educational, cultural and religious activities.

4. To coordinate all efforts in behalf of the health and social
welfare of Jews and the relief of poverty and suffering among
them.

5. To help Jews to meet economic difficulties due to discrimination, by both Gentiles and Jews, and to defend Jewish rights
against encroachment and Jewish honor against defamation.

6. To organize the collaboration of the Jewish community
with other groups in civic movements for the promotion of the
common welfare.

7. To advance the cause for the rebuilding of Eretz Yisrael
and to collaborate with world Jewry in all matters affecting the
general welfare of Jews. . . .

FOR FURTHER READING

Books by Mordecai M. Kaplan

Judaism as a Civilization: Toward a Reconstruction of American-Jewish Life (New
York: Schocken, 1967). Kaplan's major work. Also available in an
edition published by the Jewish Publication Society in 1981.

Books about Mordecai M. Kaplan

GOLDSMITH, Emanuel S. and Scult, Mel, editors and writers of intro-
ductions, *Dynamic Judaism: The Essential Writings of Mordecai M. Kaplan*
(New York: Schocken, 1985). A Mordecai Kaplan reader.

BOROWITZ, Eugene B., *Choices in Modern Jewish Thought: A Partisan's
Guide* (New York: Behrman House, 1983). "Naturalism: Mordecai
Kaplan," pages 98–120.

JOSPE, Raphael and Wagner, Stanley M., editors, *Great Schisms in Jewish
History* (New York: Ktav, 1981). Includes a discussion of Kaplan's
unique contributions to modern Jewish thought, pages 229–235.

GLATZER, Nahum N., editor, *Modern Jewish Thought: A Source Reader*
(New York: Schocken, 1977). A brief introduction with a translation of
the introductory chapter of Kaplan's "Questions Jews Ask," pages
150–157.

Acknowledgments

Grateful appreciation is expressed to the following publishers for their permission to reprint selections in this book.

Jacob Agus: *Banner of Jerusalem*

Charles Scribner's Sons: *I and Thou*

Doubleday & Company, Inc.: *The Zionist Idea*

East and West Library, London: *Ahad Ha-am: Essays, Letters and Memoirs, Moses and Israel* and *Palestine: The History of an Idea*

Harper & Row, Publisher, Inc.: *Eclipse of God*

Horizon Press, Inc.: *Hasidism and Modern Man*

Jewish Publication Society: *Ahad Ha-am: Selected Essays* and *Judaism and Christianity*

Jewish Reconstructionist Foundation, Inc.: *The Meaning of God in Modern Jewish Religion, Questions Jews Ask, The Future of the American Jew* and *A New Zionism*

League for Labor Palestine: *A. D. Gordon: Selected Essays*

The Macmillan Company: *Between Man and Man*

Schocken Books, Inc.: *Franz Rosenzweig: His Life and Thought, On Jewish Learning, Israel and the World: Essays in a Time of Crisis,* and *The Essence of Judaism*

Sources

AHAD HA-AM

1. *Ahad Ha-Am: Essays, Letters, Memoirs*, translated from the Hebrew and edited by Leon Simon, East and West Library, Oxford, 1946, pp. 130-137.
2. *Ibid.*, pp. 80-82.
3. *Ibid.*, pp. 59-64.
4. *Ahad Ha-am: Selected Essays*, edited by Leon Simon, The Jewish Publication Society of America, Philadelphia, 1944, pp. 261-287.
5. *Ibid.*, pp. 174-194.
6. *Essays, Letters, Memoirs*, pp. 71-75.
7. *Selected Essays*, pp. 202-206; 96-100.

AARON DAVID GORDON

8. *A. D. Gordon: Selected Essays*, translated by Frances Burnce, League for Labor Palestine, N. Y., 1938, pp. 4-15.
9. *Ibid.*, pp. 31-38.
10. *Ibid.*, pp. 50-57.
11. *Ibid.*, pp. 94-98.
12. *Ibid.*, pp. 77-82.
13. *Ibid.*, pp. 216-218.
14. *Ibid.*, pp. 284-286.
15. *Ibid.*, pp. 289-295.
16. *Ibid.*, pp. 267-273.

ABRAHAM ISAAC KUK

17. *Banner of Jerusalem*, Jacob Agus, Bloch Publishing Co., New York, 1946, pp. 130-131, 139, 140, translated by Agus from *Zikkaron*, 1945 and from Kuk's *Orot Ha-Kodesh* and *Ha-Tarbut Ha-Yisraelit*.
18. *Ibid.*, pp. 167-190, translated by Agus from Kuk's *Ha-Machs Shavah, Ha-Yisraelit, Zikkaron* and *Orot Ha-Kodesh.*
19. *Ibid.*, pp. 217-220, translated by Agus from Kuk's *Olat R'iyah.*
20. *Ibid.*, pp. 198-199, translated by Agus from Kuk's *Aider Hay'hor* and *Ikvei Hatzon.*

22. *The Zionist Idea*, edited and translated by Arthur Hertzberg, Doubleday and Company and Herzl Press, Garden City, New York, 1959, pp. 419-422.
23. *Ibid.*, pp. 424-426.
24. *Ibid.*, pp. 427-431.

HERMANN COHEN

25. *Jüdische Schriften*, Hermann Cohen, C. A. Schwetsche & Son, Berlin, 1924, Vol. I, translated by Ephraim Fischoff, pp. 87 ff.
26. *Ibid.*, pp. 92-96.
27. *Ibid.*, pp. 96-99.
28. *Religion der Vernunft*, Hermann Cohen, G. Foch, Leipzig, 1919, translated by Ephraim Fischoff, pp. 180-182.
29. *Ibid.*, pp. 251-262.
30. *Jüdische Schriften*, Vol. I, pp. 310-316.
31. *Jüdische Schriften*, Vol. II, pp. 153 ff.
32. *Ibid.*, pp. 136-141.
33. *Ibid.*, pp. 150-152.
34. *Religion der Vernunft*, pp. 530-533.

LEO BAECK

35. *Essence of Judaism*, Leo Baeck, Schocken Books, New York, 1948, pp. 84-88.
36. *Ibid.*, pp. 96-99.
37. *Ibid.*, pp. 104-105, 145-146.
38. *Ibid.*, pp. 184-185.
39. *Ibid.*, pp. 263-265.
40. *Judaism and Christianity*, translated with an introduction by Walter Kaufman, The Jewish Publication Society of America, Philadelphia, 1958, pp. 171-184.
41. *Ibid.*, pp. 189-196.

FRANZ ROSENZWEIG

42. *Franz Rosenzweig: His Life and Thought*, presented by Nahum N. Glatzer, a Schocken Book published with Farrar, Straus and Young, Inc., New York, 1953, pp. 214-221.
43. *Ibid.*, pp. 228-234.
44. *Ibid.*, pp. 266-269.
45. *On Jewish Learning*, edited by Nahum N. Glatzer, Schocken Books, New York, 1955, pp. 77-87.
46. *Franz Rosenzweig: His Life and Thought*, pp. 247-249.
47. *Ibid.*, pp. 271-275.

MARTIN BUBER

48a. *I and Thou*, translated by Ronald Gregor Smith, Charles Scribner's Sons, New York, 1958, second edition, pp. 3-6, 11-12.
48b. *Between Man and Man*, translated by Ronald Gregor Smith, Beacon Press, Boston, 1955, published by Kegan Paul, London, 1947, pp. 19-20.
49. *Eclipse of God: Studies in the Relation between Religion and Philosophy*, Harper and Brothers, New York, 1952, pp. 15-18.
50. *At the Turning*, Farrar, Straus and Young, New York, 1952, pp. 58-62.

51. *Moses*, East and West Library, Oxford, 1946, pp. 13-19.
52. *Israel and Palestine: The History of an Idea*, translated by Stanley Goodman, East and West Library, London, pp. ix-xiv.
53. *Israel and the World: Essay in a Time of Crisis*, Martin Buber, Schocken Books, New York, 1948, pp. 160-163.
54. *Hasidism and Modern Man*, edited and translated by Maurice Friedman, Horizon Press, New York, 1958, pp. 130-176.

KAUFMANN KOHLER

55. From a lecture on "Evolution and Morality" delivered Sunday, December 4, 1887 at Temple Beth El in New York.
56. *Jewish Theology, Systematically and Historically Considered*, The Macmillan Company, 1918, pp. 72-79.
57. *Ibid.*, pp. 146-151.
58. *Ibid.*, pp. 273-277.
59. *The Reform Advocate*, May 6, 1911, pp. 469-473.
60. *Studies, Addresses and Personal Papers*, The Alumni Association of the Hebrew Union College, New York, 1931, pp. 188-191.
61. *Hebrew Union College Monthly*, November 1914. Included in *A Living Faith*, Hebrew Union College Press, Cincinnati, 1948, pp. 139-144.
62. *Central Conference of American Rabbis' Year Book*, Vol. 34, 1925, pp. 222-229.

MORDECAI M. KAPLAN

63. *The Meaning of God in Modern Jewish Religion*, Behrman House, New York, 1937, pp. 2-9.
64. *Questions Jews Ask*, Reconstructionist Press, New York, 1956, pp. 82-85.
65. *The Future of the American Jew*, The Macmillan Company, New York, 1948, pp. 211-230.
66. *Ibid.*, pp. 417-420.
67. *Ibid.*, pp. 442-446.
68. *A New Zionism*, Theodor Herzl Foundation, New York, 1955, pp. 135-140.
69. *The Future of the American Jew*, The Macmillan Company, 1948, pp. 106-122.

Index

CONTEMPORARY JEWISH THOUGHT

Edited by SIMON NOVECK

This work makes available, for the first time under one cover, selections from nine twentieth-century outstanding philosophers.

These selections are brought together from more than thirty different volumes, some of which are no longer in print, and the writings of Hermann Cohen are made available in English for the first time. This book has great value for Jews and non-Jews alike. First, it reveals through their writings, the keenness of mind, erudition and unique approach of each man. More important, these writings indicate where each stands on some of the basic issues in contemporary Judaism.

Second, they provide material for study of the great ideas of Judaism as interpreted by the leading minds of the twentieth century.

Finally, this Reader has inspirational value—many of the selections contained herein are deeply moving and directly relevant to the spiritual perplexities of our time.